THE EXPERIENCE OF GOD

THE EXPERIENCE OF

BEING, CONSCIOUSNESS, BLISS

David Bentley Hart

Yale UNIVERSITY PRESS

New Haven and London

Published with assistance from the Louis Stern Memorial Fund.

Yale University Press books may be purchased in quantity for
educational, business, or promotional use. For information, please
e-mail sales.press@yale.edu (U.S. office) or sales@yaleup.co.uk (U.K. office).

Set in Adobe Garamond type by Integrated Publishing Solutions,
Grand Rapids, Michigan. Printed in the United States of America.

The Library of Congress has cataloged the hardcover edition as follows:
Hart, David Bentley.
The experience of God : being, consciousness, bliss / David Bentley Hart.
pages cm
Includes bibliographical references and index.
ISBN 978-0-300-16684-2 (cloth : alk paper)   1. God.   2. Experience
(Religion)   I. Title.
BL473.H37 2013
211—dc23   2013007118

ISBN 978-0-300-20935-8 (pbk.)

A catalogue record for this book is available from the British Library.

10 9 8 7 6 5 4 3 2

For Richard Shaker
—whose vision of reality often differs
from mine considerably—
in gratitude for forty years of
an indispensable friendship

Contents

Contents

Acknowledgments

I owe my greatest thanks to my wife, Solwyn, and my son, Patrick, for their patience with me and with my sporadic work habits and capriciously shifting schedule during the writing of this book.

I must also thank my farseeing and longsuffering editor at Yale University Press, Jennifer Banks, who endured far more delays in the delivery of a final manuscript than I myself would have tolerated, and did so with a grace of manner I could not even attempt to emulate.

To my indefatigable agent Giles Anderson I owe an immense debt of gratitude.

And, finally, I must sincerely thank Roland W. Hart for his friendship, for allowing me to learn from the wisdom with which he approaches all of life, and for his willingness to listen to me on our numerous long walks together through the woods.

Introduction

This is either an extremely ambitious or an extremely unambitious book. I tend to think it is the latter, but I can imagine how someone might see it quite otherwise. My intention is simply to offer a definition of the word "God," or of its equivalents in other tongues, and to do so in fairly slavish obedience to the classical definitions of the divine found in the theological and philosophical schools of most of the major religious traditions. My reason for wanting to do this is that I have come to the conclusion that, while there has been a great deal of public debate about belief in God in recent years (much of it a little petulant, much of it positively ferocious), the concept of God around which the arguments have run their seemingly interminable courses has remained strangely obscure the whole time. The more scrutiny one accords these debates, moreover, the more evident it becomes that often the contending parties are not even talking about the same thing; and I would go as far as to say that on most occasions none of them is talking about God in any coherent sense at all. It is not obvious to me, therefore, that their differences really amount to a meaningful disagreement, as one cannot really have a disagreement without some prior agreement as to what the basic issue of contention is. Perhaps this is not really all that surprising a situation. The fiercest disputes are often prompted by misapprehensions, and some of the most appalling battles in history have been fought by mistake. But I am enough of a romantic to believe that, if something is worth being rude about, it is worth understanding as well.

This book, then, will be primarily a kind of lexicographical exercise, not a work of apologetics, though that is a distinction that cannot be perfectly maintained throughout. Honestly, though, my chief purpose is not to advise atheists on what I think they should believe; I want merely to make sure that they have a clear concept of what it is they claim not to believe. In that sense, I should hope the more amiable sort of atheist might take this book as a well-intended gift. I am not even centrally concerned with traditional "proofs" of the reality of God, except insofar as they help to explain how the word "God" functions in the intellectual traditions of the developed religions (by which I mean faiths that include sophisticated and self-critical philosophical and contemplative schools). I shall touch on the essential logic of those proofs where necessary, but shall not devote more attention than necessary to the larger arguments surrounding them. There are many texts that do that already (a few of which are listed at the end of this book), and there is no great need for yet another. By the same token, this will not be a book about theology either, or even about any single religion. The current fashion in belligerent atheism usually involves flinging condemnations around with a kind of gallant extravagance, more or less in the direction of all faiths at once, with little interest in precise aim; I would not want to be any less generous in response.

I know, of course, that there are many persons who object in principle to any fraternization between different religious vocabularies, for various reasons—anxiety for creedal purity, fear that any acknowledgment of commonalities with other faiths might lead souls astray from the "one true path," intellectual scruples regarding the contradictory claims made by different traditions, fear of a colonialist domestication of "the other," a firm conviction that no religion can be true unless all others are clearly false, and so on— but those sorts of concerns leave me icily unmoved. For one thing, all the major theistic traditions claim that humanity as a whole has a knowledge of God, in some form or another, and that a perfect ignorance of God is impossible for any people (as Paul, for example, affirms in the letter to the Romans). For another, one can insist on absolutely inviolable demarcations between religions at every level only at the price of painfully unrefined accounts of what each tradition teaches. Religions ought never to be treated as though each were a single discrete proposition intended to provide a single exclusive answer to a single exhaustive question. It goes without saying that one generally should not try to dissolve disparate creeds into one another, much less into some vague, syncretistic, doctrinally vacuous "spirituality." It should also go without saying, however, that large religious traditions are complex things: sometimes they express themselves in the dream-languages of myth and sacred art, at other times in the solemn circumlocutions of liturgy and praise, at others in the serenity of contemplative prayer— or in ethical or sapiential precepts, or in inflexible dogmas, or in exactingly precise and rigorous philosophical systems. In all of these modes they may be making more or less proximate approaches to some dimension of truth; inevitably, however, they must employ many symbols that cannot fully explain the truth in itself, but can only point toward it. It may be that one faith is truer than any other, or contains that ultimate truth to which all faiths aspire in their various ways; but that still would hardly reduce all other religions to mere falsehood. More to the point, no one really acquainted with the metaphysical and spiritual claims of the major theistic faiths can fail to notice that on a host of fundamental philosophical issues, and especially on the issue of how divine transcendence should be understood, the areas of accord are quite vast.

Certainly the definition of God I offer below is one that, allowing for a number of largely accidental variations, can be found in Judaism, Christianity, Islam, Vedantic and Bhaktic Hinduism, Sikhism, various late antique paganisms, and so forth (it even applies in many respects to various Mahayana formulations of, say, the Buddha Consciousness or the Buddha Nature, or even to the earliest Buddhist conception of the Unconditioned, or to certain aspects of the Tao, though I do not want to upset Western converts to Buddhism or philosophic Taoism by insisting on the point here). There is an old Scholastic distinction between religious treatises written "*de Deo uno*" and those written "*de Deo trino*": between, that is, those that are "about the one God" known to persons of various faiths and philosophies and those that are "about the Trinitarian God" of Christian doctrine. I want to distinguish in a similar way between, on the one hand, metaphysical or philosophical descriptions of God and, on the other, dogmatic or confessional descriptions, and then to confine myself to the former. This may leave some readers disappointed, and some may wish that I had written a book marked either by more philosophical completeness or by more evangelical zeal. But clarity is a precious thing, to the degree it can be achieved, if only because it can spare us the effort of needless boring arguments.

Not that clarity is always welcome, at least not by everyone. A straw man can be a very convenient property, after all. I can see why a plenteously contented, drowsily complacent, temperamentally incurious atheist might find it comforting—even a little luxurious—to imagine that belief in God is no more than belief in some magical invisible friend who lives beyond the clouds, or in some ghostly cosmic mechanic invoked to explain gaps in current scientific knowledge. But I also like to think that the truly reflective atheist would prefer not to win all his or her rhetorical victories against childish caricatures. I suppose the success of the books of the "new atheists"—which are nothing but lurchingly spasmodic assaults on whole armies of straw men—might go some way toward proving the opposite. Certainly, none of them is an impressive or cogent treatise, and I doubt posterity will be particularly kind to any of them once the initial convulsions of celebrity have subsided. But they have definitely sold well. I doubt that one should make much of that, though. The new atheists' texts are manifestoes, buoyantly coarse and intentionally simplistic, meant to fortify true unbelievers in their unbelief; their appeal is broad but certainly not deep; they are supposed to induce a mood, not encourage deep reflection; and at the end of the day they are probably only a passing fad in trade publishing, directed at a new niche market. It is hardly surprising, moreover, that the new atheist vogue should have arisen chiefly in English-speaking countries, where philosophical subtlety is not a virtue very assiduously cultivated in schools or universities. The movement's only real interest is that it is symptomatic of a larger cultural forgetfulness on the part of believers and unbelievers alike. I may occasionally mention the new atheist books below, as providing examples of the sort of confusions that I want to get past, but I do not think they warrant more attention than that. And I would appeal to any thoughtful atheist who might wander this way to accept that I say this with good cause and in good faith. The human longing for God or the transcendent runs very deep—perhaps far too deep to be trusted, but also too deep to treat as mere primitive folly—and it has produced much good and much evil in human history. It lies at the heart of all human culture. All civilizations to this point have grown up around one or another sacred vision of the cosmos, which has provided a spiritual environment and a vital impulse for the arts, philosophy, law, public institutions, cultural revolutions, and so on. Whether there will ever be such a thing as a genuinely secular civilization—not a mere secular society, but a true civilization, entirely founded upon secular principles—is yet to be seen. What is certain is that, to this point, most of the unquestionably sublime achievements of the human intellect and imagination have arisen in worlds shaped by some vision of transcendent truth. Only a thoughtless person can possibly imagine that the vast majority of those responsible for such achievements have all clung pathetically to an understanding of the transcendent as barbarously absurd as the one casually presumed in the current texts of popular unbelief. We really ought to put such things away and discuss these matters like adults.

Finally, just as a proleptic defense against certain objections I think I can anticipate, I want to make a few simple points. The first is that, however idiosyncratic my method may sometimes seem, I shall restrict myself to the most classical definitions of God, those that have the authority of centuries of reflection behind them. This is important to stress for a number of reasons. For one thing, my experience has been that, whenever one begins to describe God in unapologetically metaphysical terms in the context of the current debates, one of the perfunctory accusations that routinely comes floating down from the atheist galleries is that one is only resorting to such cloudy abstractions because religious thought has been backed into a corner by advances in the sciences, which have progressively diminished the area that God has to occupy. Now, the notion that any discovery of empirical science could possibly reduce God's circumstances, so to speak, or have any effect whatsoever on the logical content of the concept of God or of creation is one of the vulgar errors I wish to expose below. But the more important point here is that there is absolutely nothing novel about the language I use in this book; it is a faithful digest of the primary claims made about the nature of God in the traditions I have named above. Far from being some weak, etiolated remnant of the more robust flora of the age of faith, it is the strongest and most comprehensive set of claims about God that it is possible to make. There is no note of desperation or diffidence in this language; it forthrightly and unhesitatingly describes a God who is the infinite fullness of being, omnipotent, omnipresent, and omniscient, from whom all things come and upon whom all things depend for every moment of their existence, without whom nothing at all could exist.

Even when that much is established, however, the more persistent sort of skeptic will often then assert that, be that as it may, it hardly matters what the philosophers and theologians may think, because the "common believer" has only a hazy notion of any of that, and "most people" think of God in a much more primitive way. On the one hand, this is an entirely irrelevant argument. It is always true, for any shared body of knowledge, conviction, or belief, that the principles and logic of the whole "system" are most fully known only to a few individuals who have gone to the trouble to study them. As a rule, for instance, most persons have only a vague, metaphorical, and largely pictorial understanding of the findings of the sciences; they may know a little *about* particle physics or palaeontology or molecular biology, but they do not really understand any of it, and even what little they know they accept on the authority of others. That would hardly make it intellectually respectable for, say, a young earth creationist to reject the evolution of species or the vast antiquity of the earth based solely on the crude, indistinct, popular misconceptions that "most people" have about such matters. And much the same is true in every sphere of thought—philosophical, political, economic, aesthetic, religious, or what have you. An honest and honorable critic of any idea will always seek out and try to understand the strongest possible formulations of that idea, as well as the most persuasive arguments in its favor, before attempting its refutation. On the other hand, however, I have to note that in this case the skeptic's complaint is not really true anyway, or at least not nearly as true as he or she imagines. Certainly the average believer may have very little knowledge of the history of metaphysics or the technical language of philosophy, and might not be able to formulate propositions regarding the logic of divine transcendence with the practiced ease of some saturnine old Jesuit in some Midwestern Catholic college's philosophy faculty or of some frail but strangely effervescent Vedantist sadhu lecturing his disciples by the banks of the Ganges in Benares. Nevertheless, if one asks that average believer certain questions about what he or she understands God to be, the answers will often be in principle perfectly concordant with the more arcane formulae of the metaphysicians: that God is Spirit, incorporeal, not an object located somewhere in space, not subject to the limitations of time, not a product of cosmic nature, not simply some craftsman who creates by manipulating materials external to himself, not composed of parts, but rather residing in all things while remaining perfectly one, present to us in the depths of our own beings . . . (and so forth). As a practical reality, the God of faith and the God of the philosophers are in many crucial respects recognizably one and the same.

The last point I want to make here is that this book is to a great degree a rather personal approach to the question of God. I do not mean that it is subjective or confessional; rather, I mean that it takes the structure of personal experience—not mine particularly, but anyone's—not only as an authentic way of approaching the mystery of the divine but as powerful evidence of the reality of God. In a sense, the perspective from which I write might vaguely be described as "Platonic." I start from the conviction that many of the most important things we know are things we know before we can speak them; indeed, we know them—though with very little in the way of concepts to make them intelligible to us—even as children, and see them with the greatest immediacy when we look at them with the eyes of innocence. But, as they are hard to say, and as they are often so immediate to us that we cannot stand back from them objectively, we tend to put them out of mind as we grow older, and make ourselves oblivious to them, and try to silence the voice of knowledge that speaks within our own experiences of the world. Wisdom is the recovery of innocence at the far end of experience; it is the ability to see again what most of us have forgotten how to see, but now fortified by the ability to translate some of that vision into words, however inadequate. There is a point, that is to say, where reason and revelation are one and the same. I know that, in putting the matter thus, I risk losing the sympathy of a large number of readers—both rationalists and fideists, both the skeptical and the devout—but I hope my meaning will become clear in what follows. God is not only the ultimate reality that the intellect and the will seek but is also the primordial reality with which all of us are always engaged in every moment of existence and consciousness, apart from which we have no experience of anything whatsoever. Or, to borrow the language of Augustine, God is not only *superior summo meo*—beyond my utmost heights—but also *interior intimo meo*—more inward to me than my inmost depths. Only when one understands what such a claim means does one know what the word "God" really means, and whether it is reasonable to think that there is a reality to which that word refers and in which we should believe.

PART ONE

God, Gods, and the World

A man who is asleep and deeply dreaming still usually has some awareness of the real world around him, and often this awareness shapes his dream. This means in turn that, while he sleeps, his dream is the only form in which he can know and interpret the world that he inhabits. He hears a wind chime ringing somewhere outside his open window, but in his dream it is transformed into the tolling of a bell in a high tower on a distant hill. A breeze enters at the window and passes over him, but to him it is the wind blowing through the valley in which he stands as he gazes upward toward that tower. The wind also causes the leaves of a tree below his window to rustle softly, but to him it is the sound of reeds stirring along the banks of a stream nearby, as a golden snake slips silently into the flowing water. The first pale light of morning reaches him from the window, but to him it is the last pale light of evening, before the night entirely descends over the valley. He hears the voice of someone who loves him trying to rouse him gently from his sleep, because it is time for him to awake, but he hears it as the mysterious and vaguely menacing voice of a stranger, coming from far away, and from some place he cannot see.

CHAPTER ONE

"God" Is Not a Proper Name

I

An absolutely convinced atheist, it often seems to me, is simply someone who has failed to notice something very obvious—or, rather, failed to notice a great many very obvious things. This is not any sort of accusation or reproach. Something can be incandescently obvious but still utterly unintelligible to us if we lack the conceptual grammar required to interpret it; and this, far from being a culpable deficiency, is usually only a matter of historical or personal circumstance. One age can see things that other ages cannot simply because it has the imaginative resources to understand what it is looking at; one person's education or cultural formation may have enabled him or her to recognize meaning where others will find only random disorder. If a man raised in a culture without any written language, for instance, or anything analogous, were to happen upon an abandoned city built by a vanished civilization that long ago copiously recorded its history, literature, philosophy, and music in indelible ink on imperishable paper, and stored the whole archive in a great and indestructible library, everything he could ever hope to know about that ancient people would be laid out before him in those books; but it would mean nothing to him. The situation would not be entirely hopeless: sooner or later he or one of his compatriots would probably realize that the letters of that unknown alphabet were more than bland decorative motifs pointlessly preserved in irregular sequences, and would begin to grasp the mysterious principle behind them. Even then, though, real understanding would lie only at the end of a long and excruciatingly laborious process.

This may be a somewhat defective metaphor, however; I am not even entirely sure how I wish it to be taken, or whether it constitutes more of an exaggeration or an understatement. Seen in one way, certainly, contemporary atheist discourse is not separated from the language of the great theistic traditions by anything as vast as the abyss separating that illiterate explorer from the meaning of those texts. If it were, things might be much simpler. Unfortunately, one of the more insidious aspects of today's public debates over belief and unbelief is that they are often sustained by the illusion that both sides are using the same words in the same way; since there are no immediately obvious linguistic barriers to overcome, each side understands the other just well enough to be deceived into thinking that both are working within the same conceptual frame. There are times when that illiterate explorer's blank stare of incomprehension, accompanied by a long tentative silence, would be dearly welcome. Seen in another way, however, the separation may actually be a great deal more radical than my metaphor suggests. After all, once the illiterate culture has solved the enigma of those texts and penetrated their fascinating veils of symbols, it might find a people much like its own on the other

side, with many of the same beliefs and intuitions and expectations of the universe. I sometimes wonder, however, whether in
the case of modern atheism and theistic tradition what is at issue
is the difference between two entirely incommensurable worlds,
or at least two entirely incommensurable ways of understanding
the world. It may be that what the atheist lacks the conceptual
means to interpret may be nothing as elementary as a foreign language or an alien medium of communication, but rather the very
experience of existence itself.

In the end, though, I doubt that the problem is really as extreme as all that. I retain a belief, however naive, in a sort of universal grammar of human nature, which makes it possible to overcome any cultural or conceptual misunderstanding; and, without
discounting the immense power of culture to shape and color our
encounter with the one world that we all together inhabit, I also
believe there are certain common forms of experience so fundamental to human rationality that, without them, we could not
think or speak at all. They make all other experiences possible,
from the most quotidian to the most extraordinary; they underlie
and animate all the great ventures of the human intellect: art, science, philosophy, and so forth. Starting from that most primordial level, reciprocal understanding is always in principle possible,
assuming there is enough good will on both sides. All I want to do
in the pages that follow is to attempt to explain, as lucidly as I can,
how traditional understandings of God illuminate and are illuminated by those experiences.

That may seem a somewhat minimalist project, I know, but
the conviction behind it is not; in fact, it could scarcely be more
"maximal." Just to make clear what my peculiar prejudices are, I

acknowledge up front that I do not regard true philosophical atheism as an intellectually valid or even cogent position; in fact, I see it as a fundamentally irrational view of reality, which can be sustained only by a tragic absence of curiosity or a fervently resolute will to believe the absurd. More simply, I am convinced that the case for belief in God is inductively so much stronger than the case for unbelief that true philosophical atheism must be regarded as a superstition, often nurtured by an infantile wish to live in a world proportionate to one's own hopes or conceptual limitations. Having said this, though, I have to qualify it, because it is a much more limited assertion than it at first appears to be. I do not mean that there is anything intellectually contemptible in being formally "godless"—that is, in rejecting all religious dogmas and in refusing to believe in the God those dogmas describe. One might very well conclude, for instance, that the world contains far too much misery for the pious idea of a good, loving, and just God to be taken very seriously, and that any alleged creator of a universe in which children suffer and die hardly deserves our devotion. It is an affective—not a strictly logical—position to hold, but it is an intelligible one, with a certain sublime moral purity to it; I myself find it deeply compelling; and it is entirely up to each person to judge whether he or she finds any particular religion's answer to the "problem of evil" either adequate or credible. I also do not mean that there is any deep logical inconsistency in an attitude of agnostic aloofness from all theologies and spiritual practices; one either finds them plausible or one does not. When I say that atheism is a kind of obliviousness to the obvious, I mean that *if* one understands what the actual philosophical definition of "God" is in most of the great religious traditions, and *if* consequently one understands what is logically entailed in denying that there is any God so defined, *then* one cannot reject the reality of God *tout court* without embracing an ultimate absurdity.

This, it seems to me, ought to be an essentially inoffensive assertion. The only fully consistent alternative to belief in God, properly understood, is some version of "materialism" or "physicalism" or (to use the term most widely preferred at present) "naturalism"; and naturalism—the doctrine that there is nothing apart from the physical order, and certainly nothing supernatural—is an incorrigibly incoherent concept, and one that is ultimately indistinguishable from pure magical thinking. The very notion of nature as a closed system entirely sufficient to itself is plainly one that cannot be verified, deductively or empirically, from within the system of nature. It is a metaphysical (which is to say "extranatural") conclusion regarding the whole of reality, which neither reason nor experience legitimately warrants. It cannot even define itself within the boundaries of its own terms, because the total sufficiency of "natural" explanations is not an identifiable natural phenomenon but only an arbitrary judgment. Naturalism, therefore, can never be anything more than a guiding prejudice, an established principle only in the sense that it must be indefensibly presumed for the sake of some larger view of reality; it functions as a purely formal rule that, like the restriction of the king in chess to moves of one square only, permits the game to be played one way rather than another. If, moreover, naturalism is correct (however implausible that is), and if consciousness is then an essentially material phenomenon, then there is no reason to believe that our minds, having evolved purely through natural selection, could possibly be capable of knowing what is or is not true about reality as a whole. Our brains may necessarily have equipped us to recognize certain sorts of physical objects around us and enabled us to react to them; but, beyond that, we can assume only that nature will have selected just those behaviors in us most conducive to our survival, along with whatever structures of thought and belief might be essentially or accidentally associated with them, and there is no reason to suppose that such structures—even those that provide us with our notions of what constitutes a sound rational argument—have access to any abstract "truth" about the totality of things. This yields the delightful paradox that, if naturalism is true as a picture of reality, it is necessarily false as a philosophical precept; for no one's belief in the truth of naturalism could correspond to reality except through a shocking coincidence (or, better, a miracle). A still more important consideration, however, is that naturalism, alone among all considered philosophical attempts to describe the shape of reality, is radically insufficient in its explanatory range. The one thing of which it can give no account, and which its most fundamental principles make it entirely impossible to explain at all, is nature's very existence. For existence is most definitely not a natural phenomenon; it is logically prior to any physical cause whatsoever; and anyone who imagines that it is susceptible of a natural explanation simply has no grasp of what the question of existence really is. In fact, it is impossible to say how, in the terms naturalism allows, nature could exist at all.

These are all matters for later, however. All I want to say here is that none of this makes atheism untenable in any final sense. It may be perfectly "rational" to embrace absurdity; for, if the universe does not depend upon any transcendent source, then there is no reason to accord the deliverances of reason any particular authority in the first place, because what we think of as rationality is just the accidental residue of physical processes: good for helping us to acquire food, power, or sex but probably not very reliable in the realm of ideas. In a sense, then, I am assuming the truth of a perfectly circular argument: it makes sense to believe in God if one believes in the real power of reason, because one is justified in believing in reason if one believes in God. Or, to phrase the matter in a less recursive form, it makes sense to believe in both reason and God, and it may make a kind of nonsensical sense to believe in neither, but it is ultimately contradictory to believe in one but not the other. An honest and self-aware atheism, therefore, should proudly recognize itself as the quintessential expression of heroic irrationalism: a purely and ecstatically absurd venture of faith, a triumphant trust in the absurdity of all things. But most of us already know this anyway. If there is no God, then of course the universe is ultimately absurd, in the very precise sense that it is irreducible to any more comprehensive "equation." It is glorious, terrible, beautiful, horrifying—all of that—but in the end it is also quite, quite meaningless. The secret of a happy life then is either not to notice or not to let it bother one overly much. A few blithe spirits even know how to rejoice at the thought.

II

There have been atheists in every age, of course, but much of modern Western atheism is something quite novel in human history: not mere personal unbelief, and not merely the eccentric doctrine of one or another small philosophical sect, but a conscious ideological, social, and philosophical project, with a broad popular constituency—a cause, a dogma, a metaphysics, a system of values. Many modern atheists object to that description, of course, but only because they are deceiving themselves. When it first arose, however, like any new creed, modern atheism had to win its converts from other adherences; and so its earliest apostles were persons who had for the most part been formed by a culture absolutely soaked in the language, images, ideas, and sentiments of belief. All of them had at least some understanding not only of the nature of religious claims but of the pathos of faith. No matter how much the new convert may have hated his or her native religion, a complete ignorance of its guiding ideas or of its affects and motives was all but impossible. And this remained the case until only fairly recently. Now, however, we have arrived at an odd juncture in our cultural history. There has sprung up a whole generation of confident, even strident atheist proselytizers who appear to know almost nothing about the religious beliefs they abominate, apart from a few vague and gauzily impressionistic daubs or aquarelle washes, and who seem to have no real sense of what the experience of faith is like or of what its rationales might be. For the most part, they seem not even to know that they do not know. It is common now for atheist polemicists (A. C. Grayling is a particularly dazzling example here) to throw off extraordinarily sure and contemptuous pronouncements about the beliefs or motivations or intellectual habits of Christians or of religious persons in general, only to end up demonstrating an almost fantastic ignorance not only of remarkably elementary religious tenets, but of the most rudimentary psychology of belief. And, in general, what is most astonishing about the recent new atheist bestsellers has not been the patent flimsiness of their arguments—as I have noted, they are not aimed at an audience likely to notice or to care—but the sheer lack of intellectual curiosity they betray.

This is not a very terrible indictment, I suppose. No one is obliged in the abstract to be curious about religious claims. Still, though, if one is going to go to all the trouble of writing a book about the deficiencies of religious ideas, one should probably also go to the trouble of first learning what those ideas are. The major religions do, after all, boast some very sophisticated and subtle philosophical and spiritual traditions, and the best way for the enterprising infidel to avoid recapitulating arguments that have been soundly defeated in the past is to make some effort to understand those traditions. The physicist Victor Stenger, for instance, wrote a book not long ago with the subtitle *How Science Shows That God Does Not Exist.* Had he only inquired, any decently trained philosopher with a knowledge of the history of metaphysics, ontology, and modal logic could have warned him of the catastrophic category error in that phrase—suggesting as it does a fundamental misunderstanding not only of the word "God" but of the word "science" as well—but apparently he did not inquire, and as a consequence the book he wrote turned out to be just a long non sequitur based on a conceptual confusion and a logical mistake. Or consider Richard Dawkins: he devoted several pages of *The God Delusion* to a discussion of the "Five Ways" of Thomas Aquinas but never thought to avail himself of the services of some scholar of ancient and mediaeval thought who might have explained them to him, perhaps while strolling beside the somberly gliding Thames on some long, lustrous Oxford afternoon. As a result, he not only mistook the Five Ways for Thomas's comprehensive statement on why we should believe in God, which they most definitely are not, but ended up completely misrepresenting the logic of every single one of them, and at the most basic levels: Not knowing the scholastic distinction between primary and secondary causality, for instance, he imagined that Thomas's talk of a "first cause" referred to the initial temporal causal agency in a continuous temporal series of discrete causes. He thought that Thomas's logic requires the universe to have had a temporal beginning, which Thomas explicitly and repeatedly made clear is not the case. He anachronistically mistook Thomas's argument from universal natural teleology for an argument from apparent "Intelligent Design" in nature. He thought that Thomas's proof from universal "motion" concerned only physical movement in space, "local motion," rather than the ontological movement from potency to act. He mistook Thomas's argument from degrees of transcendental perfection for an argument from degrees of quantitative magnitude, which by definition have no perfect sum. (Admittedly, those last two are a bit difficult for modern persons, but he might have asked all the same.) As for Dawkins's own attempt at an argument against the likelihood of God's existence, it is so crude and embarrassingly confused as to be germane to nothing at all, perhaps not even to itself.[1]

Now, none of this is to say that, had either man taken the time to understand the ideas against which he imagined he was contending, he would not have rejected them all the same. The Five Ways, if properly understood, are far richer and more interesting than Dawkins grasps, but they are certainly not irresistibly persuasive (nor are they intended to be). While it is usually imprudent for any scholar to stray too intrepidly outside the boundaries of his or her expertise, at least without a trained guide, there is no reason why a scientist committed to some form of philosophical naturalism, who is as willing to learn as to pontificate, should not enter the debate. Not that, at the moment, there is any real public debate about belief in God worth speaking of. There is scarcely even a public conversation in any meaningful sense. At present, the best we seem able to manage is a war of assertions and recriminations, and for the most part each side is merely talking past the other. And the new atheists have yet to make a contribution of any weight whatsoever. If one could conclusively show that the philosophical claims the major religions make about the nature and reality of God were fundamentally incoherent or demonstrably false, that would be a significant achievement; but if one is content merely to devise images of God that are self-evidently nonsensical, and then proceed triumphantly to demonstrate just how infuriatingly nonsensical they are, one is not going to accomplish anything interesting. For the sake of harmony, I for one am more than willing to acknowledge that the God described by the new atheists definitely does not exist; but, to be perfectly honest, that is an altogether painless concession to make.

Would that I could, however, lay the blame for many of these misunderstandings entirely to the charge of the atheists. I cannot, sadly. Late modernity in the West has been marked, as no other period ever has, by the triumph of ideological extremism. The twentieth century gave birth to fundamentalism in religion, but also in politics, social theory, economics, and countless other spheres of abstract conjecture and personal commitment. Radical materialisms bred mass murder, radical political movements and radical religious fideisms bred terrorism; never before had abstract ideas proved to be such lethal things. What the cause or causes of this peculiarly modern pathology might be is a fascinating but tangential question here. Whatever the case, the results have spanned the full spectrum, from the unspeakably tragic to the ineffably banal. It is true that a great deal of the rhetoric of the new atheism is often just the confessional rote of materialist fundamentalism (which, like all fundamentalisms, imagines that in fact it represents the side of reason and truth); but it is also true that the new atheism has sprung up in a garden of contending fundamentalisms. There would not be so many slapdash popular atheist manifestoes, in all likelihood, if there were not so many soft and inviting targets out there to provoke them: young earth creationists who believe that the two contradictory cosmogonic myths of the early chapters of Genesis are actually a single documentary account of an event that occurred a little over six millennia ago, and that there really was a Noah who built a giant ark to rescue a compendious menagerie from a universal deluge, or Hindu nationalists who insist that Rama's Bridge was actually built by Hanuman's monkeys, and so forth. Here, certainly, the new atheism has opponents against which it is well matched.

It should be noted, though, just out of fairness, that the emergence of fundamentalism in the last century was not some sort of retreat to a more original or primitive form of faith. Certainly the rise of the Christian fundamentalist movement was not a recovery of the Christianity of earlier centuries or of the apostolic church. It was a thoroughly modern phenomenon, a strange and somewhat poignantly pathetic attempt on the part of culturally deracinated Christians, raised without the intellectual or imaginative resources of a living religious civilization, to imitate the evidentiary methods of modern empirical science by taking the Bible as some sort of objective and impeccably consistent digest of historical data. It is of course absurd to treat the Bible in that way—though, frankly, no more absurd than thinking that "science shows that God does not exist"—but it is also most definitely *not* the way the Bible was read in the ancient or mediaeval church. The greatest Church Fathers, for instance, took it for granted that the creation narratives of Genesis could not be treated literally, at least not in the sense we give to that word today, but must be read allegorically—which, incidentally, does not mean read as stories with codes to be decrypted but simply read as stories whose value lies in the spiritual truths to which they can be seen as pointing. Origen of Alexandria (185–254), in many ways the father of patristic exegesis, remarked that one would have to be rather simple to imagine that there could have been "days" before the creation of the sun, or that God literally planted an orchard with physical trees whose fruits conferred wisdom or eternal life, or that God liked to amble through his garden in the gloaming, or that Adam could have hidden from him behind a tree; no one could doubt, he said, that these are figural tales, communicating spiritual mysteries, and certainly not historical records. As Gregory of Nyssa (c. 335–c. 396) said, if one does not read scripture in a "philosophical" fashion one will see only myths and contradictions. And it was something of a theme in patristic texts that one must not mistake the Genesis narratives for scientific descriptions of the origin of the world. If nothing else, it would have offended against many Christian philosophers' understanding of divine transcendence to imagine that God really made the world through a succession of cosmic interventions; they assumed that God's creative act is eternal, not temporal, occurring not at a discrete instant in the past, but rather pervading all of time. Basil of Caesarea (330–379) argued that the "beginning" mentioned in the first verse of Genesis ought not to be thought of as a moment of time, as such a moment would itself be something divisible, with a beginning of its own that would then itself have had to have a beginning, and so on ad infinitum; rather, he said, creation should be conceived of as the eternal, indivisible, and immediate bringing into existence of the whole of creation, from its beginning to its end. Many of the Fathers—Origen, John Chrysostom (c. 349–407), Augustine (354–430), for example—took "beginning" as a reference to the eternal "principle" of God's *Logos*. Thus it made perfect sense for Gregory of Nyssa and Augustine to speculate that, while the act of creation is timeless, the world had unfolded progressively in time, out of its own intrinsic potencies and principles, with nature itself acting as the craftsman. And such was the pattern of "higher" biblical exegesis for centuries thereafter. Certainly anyone searching mediaeval commentaries on the creation narratives of Genesis for signs of fundamentalist literalism will be largely disappointed. There is a good reason why, among Darwin's contemporaries, even as orthodox a Christian thinker as John Henry Newman (1801–1890)—who was, among other things, a great patristics scholar—could find nothing in the science of evolution contrary to or problematic for the doctrine of creation.[2]

Not that we need to exaggerate the sophistication of Christians or of religious persons in general down the centuries, or imagine that they could foresee future advances in cosmology, geology, or genetics. Intelligence, education, curiosity are always variable properties, and the average person as a rule has only a vague interest in what the remote origins of the world may have been, or where the demarcation between legend and history lies. Moreover, no ancient thinker, however brilliant, had access to modern knowledge regarding the age of the earth or the phylogeny of species. What we can say, however, at least with regard to Western culture, is that it was not until the modern period (and, really, not until the late modern period) that a significant minority of believers became convinced that the truth of their faith depended upon an absolutely literal—an absolutely "factual"—interpretation of scripture, and felt compelled to stake everything on so ludicrous a wager. Now the Bible came to be seen as what it obviously is not: a collection of "inerrant" oracles and historical reports, each true in the same way as every other, each subject to only one level of interpretation, and all perfectly in agreement with one another. As I say, this was largely the result of a cultural impoverishment, but it also followed from the triumph of a distinctly modern concept of what constitutes reliable knowledge; it was the strange misapplication of the rigorous but quite limited methods of the modern empirical sciences to questions properly belonging to the realms of logic and of spiritual experience. I think it fair to say that the early fundamentalist movement opposed itself to Darwinism not simply because the latter seemed to contradict the biblical story, and not even simply out of dismay at the rise of the eugenics movement or of other forms of "social Darwinism" (though that was definitely one of the issues involved); rather, many genuinely believed that there was some sort of logical conflict between the idea that God had created the world and the idea that terrestrial life had evolved over time. This was and is a view held, of course, by any number of atheists as well. In either case, however, it is a bizarre belief. After all, one assumes that fundamentalist Christians and fundamentalist materialists alike are aware that Christians believe God is the creator of every person; but presumably none of them would be so foolish as to imagine that this means each person is not also the product of a spermatozoon and ovum; surely they grasp that here God's act of creation is understood as the whole event of nature and existence, not as a distinct causal agency that in some way rivals the natural process of conception. Somehow, though, even in the minds of some Christians, God has come to be understood not as the truly transcendent source and end of all contingent reality, who creates through "donating" being to a natural order that is complete in itself, but only as a kind of supreme mechanical cause located somewhere within the continuum of nature. Which is only to say that, here at the far end of modernity, the concept of God is often just as obscure to those who want to believe as to those who want not to. Ours is in many ways a particularly unsubtle age.

III

There are two senses in which the word "God" or "god" can properly be used. Most modern languages generally distinguish between the two usages as I have done here, by writing only one of them with an uppercase first letter, as though it were a proper name—which it is not. Most of us understand that "God" (or its equivalent) means the one God who is the source of all things, whereas "god" (or its equivalent) indicates one or another of a plurality of divine beings who inhabit the cosmos and reign over its various regions. This is not, however, merely a distinction in numbering, between monotheism and polytheism, as though the issue were merely that of determining how many "divine entities" one happens to think there are. It is a distinction, instead, between two entirely different kinds of reality, belonging to two entirely disparate conceptual orders. In fact, the very division between monotheism and polytheism is in many cases a confusion of categories. Several of the religious cultures that we sometimes inaccurately characterize as "polytheistic" have traditionally insisted upon an absolute differentiation between the one transcendent Godhead from whom all being flows and the various "divine" beings who indwell and govern the heavens and the earth. Only the one God, says Swami Prabhavananda, speaking more or less for the whole of developed Vedantic and Bhaktic Hinduism, is "the uncreated": "gods, though supernatural, belong . . . among the creatures. Like the Christian angels, they are much nearer to man than to God."[3] Conversely, many creeds we correctly speak of as "monotheistic" embrace the very same distinction. The *Adi Granth* of the Sikhs, for instance, describes the One God as the creator of Brahma, Vishnu, and Shiva.[4] In truth, Prabhavananda's comparison of the gods of India to Christianity's angels is more apt than many modern Christians may realize. Late Hellenistic pagan thought often tended to draw a clear demarcation between the one transcendent God (or, in Greek, *ho theos,* God with the definite article) and any particular or local god (any mere "inarticular" *theos*) who might superintend this or that people or nation or aspect of the natural world; at the same time, late Hellenistic Jews and Christians recognized a multitude of angelic "powers" and "principalities," some obedient to the one transcendent God and some in rebellion, who governed the elements of nature and the peoples of the earth. To any impartial observer at the time, coming from some altogether different culture, the theological cosmos of a great deal of pagan "polytheism" would have seemed all but indistinguishable from that of a great deal of Jewish or Christian "monotheism."

To speak of "God" properly, then—to use the word in a sense consonant with the teachings of orthodox Judaism, Christianity, Islam, Sikhism, Hinduism, Baháʾí, a great deal of antique paganism, and so forth—is to speak of the one infinite source of all that is: eternal, omniscient, omnipotent, omnipresent, uncreated, uncaused, perfectly transcendent of all things and for that very reason absolutely immanent to all things. God so understood is not something posed over against the universe, in addition to it, nor is he the universe itself. He is not a "being," at least not in the way that a tree, a shoemaker, or a god is a being; he is not one more object in the inventory of things that are, or any sort of discrete object at all. Rather, all things that exist receive their being continuously from him, who is the infinite wellspring of all that is, *in whom* (to use the language of the Christian scriptures) all things live and move and have their being. In one sense he is "beyond being," if by "being" one means the totality of discrete, finite things. In another sense he is "being itself," in that he is the inexhaustible source of all reality, the absolute upon which the contingent is always utterly dependent, the unity and simplicity that underlies and sustains the diversity of finite and composite things. Infinite being, infinite consciousness, infinite bliss, from whom we are, by whom we know and are known, and in whom we find our only true consummation. All the great theistic traditions agree that God, understood in this proper sense, is essentially beyond finite comprehension; hence, much of the language used of him is negative in form and has been reached only by a logical process of abstraction from those qualities of finite reality that make it insufficient to account for its own existence. All agree as well, however, that he can genuinely be known: that is, reasoned toward, intimately encountered, directly experienced with a fullness surpassing mere conceptual comprehension.

By contrast, when we speak of "gods" we are talking not of transcendent reality at all, but only of a higher or more powerful or more splendid dimension of immanent reality. Any gods who might be out there do not transcend nature but belong to it. Their theogonies can be recounted—how some rose out of the primal night, how some were born of other, more titanic progenitors, how others sprang up from an intermingling of divine and elemental forces, and so on—and according to many mythologies most of them will finally meet their ends. They exist in space and time, each of them is a distinct being rather than "being itself," and it is they who are dependent upon the universe for their existence rather than the reverse. Of such gods there may be an endless diversity, while of God there can be only one. Or, better, God is not *merely* one, in the way that a finite object might be merely singular or unique, but is oneness as such, the one act of being and unity by which any finite thing exists and by which all things exist together. He is one in the sense that being itself is one, the infinite is one, the source of everything is one. Thus a plurality of gods could not constitute an alternative to or contradiction of the unity of God; they still would not belong to the same ontological frame of reference as he.

Obviously, then, it is God in the former—the transcendent—

sense in whom it is ultimately meaningful to believe or not to believe. The possibility of gods or spirits or angels or demons, and so on, is a subordinate matter, a question not of metaphysics but only of the taxonomy of nature (terrestrial, celestial, and chthonic). To be an atheist in the best modern sense, however, and so to be a truly intellectually and emotionally fulfilled naturalist in philosophy, one must genuinely succeed in not believing in *God*, with all the logical consequences such disbelief entails. It is not enough simply to remain indifferent to the whole question of God, moreover, because thus understood it is a question ineradicably present in the very mystery of existence, or of knowledge, or of truth, goodness, and beauty. It is also the question that philosophical naturalism is supposed to have answered exhaustively in the negative, without any troubling explanatory lacunae, and therefore the question that any aspiring philosophical naturalist must understand before he or she can be an atheist in any intellectually significant way. And the best way to begin is to get a secure grasp on how radically, both conceptually and logically, belief in God differs from belief in the gods. This ought not to be all that difficult a matter; in Western philosophical tradition, for instance, it is a distinction that goes back at least as far as Xenophanes (c. 570–c. 475 BC). Yet the most pervasive error one encounters in contemporary arguments about belief in God—especially, but not exclusively, on the atheist side—is the habit of conceiving of God simply as some very large object or agency within the universe, or perhaps alongside the universe, a being among other beings, who differs from all other beings in magnitude, power, and duration, but not ontologically, and who is related to the world more or less as a craftsman is related to an artifact.

At a trivial level, one sees the confusion in some of the more shopworn witticisms of popular atheism: "I believe neither in God nor in the fairies at the bottom of my garden," for instance, or "All people are atheists in regard to Zeus, Wotan, and most other gods; I simply disbelieve in one god more." Once, in an age long since vanished in the mists of legend, those might even have been amusing remarks, eliciting sincere rather than merely liturgical laughter; but, even so, all they have ever demonstrated is a deplorable ignorance of elementary conceptual categories. If one truly imagines these are all comparable kinds of intellectual conviction then one is clearly confused about what is at issue. Beliefs regarding fairies are beliefs about a certain kind of object that may or may not exist within the world, and such beliefs have much the same sort of intentional shape and rational content as beliefs regarding one's neighbors over the hill or whether there are such things as black swans. Beliefs regarding God concern the source and ground and end of all reality, the unity and existence of every particular thing and of the totality of all things, the ground of the possibility of anything at all. Fairies and gods, if they exist, occupy something of the same conceptual space as organic cells, photons, and the force of gravity, and so the sciences might perhaps have something to say about them, if a proper medium for investigating them could be found. We can, if nothing else, disabuse ourselves of belief in certain gods by simple empirical methods; we know now, for example, that the sun is not a god named Tonatiuh, at least not one who must be nourished daily on human blood lest he cease to shine, because we have withheld his meals for centuries now without calamity. God, by contrast, is the infinite actuality that makes it possible for either photons or (possibly) fairies to exist, and so can be "investigated" only, on the one hand, by acts of logical deduction and induction and conjecture or, on the other, by contemplative or sacramental or spiritual experiences. Belief or disbelief in fairies or gods could never be validated by philosophical arguments made from first principles; the existence or nonexistence of Zeus is not a matter that can be intelligibly discussed in the categories of modal logic or metaphysics, any more than the existence of tree frogs could be; if he is there at all, one must go on an expedition to find him, or at least find out his address. The question of God, by contrast, is one that can and must be pursued in terms of the absolute and the contingent, the necessary and the fortuitous, potency and act, possibility and impossibility, being and nonbeing, transcendence and immanence. Evidence for or against the existence of Thor or King Oberon would consist only in local facts, not universal truths of reason; it would be entirely empirical, episodic, psychological, personal, and hence elusive. Evidence for or against the reality of God, if it is there, saturates every moment of the experience of existence, every employment of reason, every act of consciousness, every encounter with the world around us.

Now, manifestly, one should not judge an intellectual movement by its jokes (even if one suspects that there is little more to it than its jokes). But exactly the same confusion shows itself in the arguments that many contemporary atheists make in earnest: For instance, "If God made the world, then who made God?" Or the famous dilemma drawn, in badly garbled form, from Plato's *Euthyphro,* "Does God command a thing because it is good, or is it good because God commands it?" I address both questions below (in my third and fifth chapters, respectively), so I shall not do so here. I shall, however, note that not only do these questions not pose deep quandaries for believers or insuperable difficulties for a coherent concept of God; they are not even relevant to the issue. And, until one really understands why this is so, one has not yet begun to talk about God at all. One is talking merely about some very distinguished and influential gentleman or lady named "God," or about some discrete object that can be situated within a class of objects called "gods" (even if it should turn out that there happens to be only one occupant of that class).

As it happens, the god with whom most modern popular atheism usually concerns itself is one we might call a "demiurge" (*dēmiourgos*): a Greek term that originally meant a kind of public technician or artisan but that came to mean a particular kind of divine "world-maker" or cosmic craftsman. In Plato's *Timaeus,* the demiurge is a benevolent intermediary between the realm of eternal forms and the realm of mutability; he looks to the ideal universe—the eternal paradigm of the cosmos—and then fashions lower reality in as close a conformity to the higher as the intractable resources of material nature allow. He is, therefore, not the source of the existence of all things but rather only the Intelligent Designer and causal agent of the world of space and time, working upon materials that lie outside and below him, under the guidance of divine principles that lie outside and above him. He is an immensely wise and powerful being, but he is also finite and dependent upon a larger reality of which he is only a part. Later Platonism interpreted the demiurge in a variety of ways, and in various schools of Gnosticism in late antiquity he reappeared as an incompetent or malevolent cosmic despot, either ignorant or jealous of the true God beyond this cosmos; but none of that is important here. Suffice it to say that the demiurge is a maker, but not a creator in the theological sense: he is an imposer of order, but not the infinite ocean of being that gives existence to all reality ex nihilo. And he is a god who made the universe "back then," at some specific point in time, as a discrete event within the course of cosmic events, rather than the God whose creative act is an eternal gift of being to the whole of space and time, sustaining all things in existence in every moment. It is certainly the demiurge about whom Stenger and Dawkins write; neither has actually ever written a word about God. And the same is true of all the other new atheists as far as I can tell.

To be fair to all sides, however, I should also point out that the demiurge has had some fairly vociferous champions over the past few centuries, and at the moment seems to be enjoying a small resurgence in popularity. His first great modern revival came in the Deism of the seventeenth and eighteenth centuries, a movement whose adherents were impatient with the metaphysical "obscurities" and doctrinal "absurdities" of traditional religion, and who preferred to think of God as some very powerful spiritual individual who designed and fabricated the universe at the beginning of things, much as a watchmaker might design and fabricate a watch and then set it running. In David Hume's *Dialogues Concerning Natural Religion* this is the view of God advanced by Cleanthes and then elegantly dismantled by Philo (the traditional metaphysical and theological view of God is represented by Demea, though not very well, and against him Philo marshals an altogether different—and much weaker—set of arguments). And, while Deism had more or less died out before Darwin's day, the argument from cosmic or biological design, which was its chief philosophical support, has never entirely lost its charm for some. The recent Intelligent Design movement represents the demiurge's boldest adventure in some considerable time. I know that it is fashionable to heap abuse upon this movement, and that is not my intention here. After all, if one looks at the extraordinary complexity of nature and then interprets it as a sign of superhuman intelligence, one is doing something perfectly defensible; even some atheists have done as much (the brilliant and eccentric Fred Hoyle being a notable example). Moreover, if one already believes in God, it makes perfect sense to see, say, the ever more extraordinary discoveries of molecular biology, or the problem of protein folding, or the incredible statistical improbabilities of a whole host of cosmological conditions (and so on) as bearing witness to something miraculous and profoundly rational in the order of nature, and to ascribe these wonders to God. But, however compelling the evidence may seem, one really ought not to reverse the order of discovery here and attempt to deduce or define God from the supposed evidence of design in nature. As either a scientific or a philosophical project, Intelligent Design theory is a deeply problematic undertaking; and, from a theological or metaphysical perspective, it is a massive distraction.

To begin with, much of the early literature of this movement concerned instances of supposedly "irreducible complexity" in the biological world, and from these developed an argument for some sort of intelligent agency at work in the process of evolution. That would, of course, be a fascinating discovery if it could be shown to be true; but I do not see how in principle one ever could conclusively demonstrate such a thing. It could never be more than an argument from probability, because one cannot prove that any organism, however intricate, could not have been produced by *some* unguided phylogenic history. Probability is a powerful thing, of course, but notoriously difficult to measure in the realm of biology's complex systems of interdependence, or over intervals of time as vast as distinct geological epochs. And it would be quite embarrassing to propose this or that organism or part of an organism as a specimen of an irreducibly complex biological mechanism, only for it to emerge later that many of its components had been found in a more primitive form in some other biological mechanism, serving another purpose. Even if all this were not so, however, seen in the light of traditional theology the argument from irreducible complexity looks irredeemably defective, because it depends on the existence of causal discontinuities in the order of nature, "gaps" where natural causality proves inadequate. But all the classical theological arguments regarding the order of the world assume just the opposite: that God's creative power can be seen in the rational coherence of nature as a perfect whole; that the universe was not simply the factitious product of a supreme intellect but the unfolding of an omnipresent divine wisdom or logos. For Thomas Aquinas, for instance, God creates the order of nature by infusing the things of the universe with the wonderful power of moving of themselves toward determinate ends; he uses the analogy of a shipwright able to endow timbers with the power to develop into a ship without external intervention. According to the classical arguments, universal rational order—not just this or that particular instance of complexity—is what speaks of the divine mind: a cosmic harmony as resplendently evident in the simplicity of a raindrop as in the molecular labyrinths of a living cell. After all, there may be innumerable finite causes of complexity, but a good argument can be made that only a single infinite cause can account for perfect, universal, intelligible, mathematically describable order. If, however, one could really show that there were interruptions in that order, places where the adventitious intrusions of an organizing hand were needed to correct this or that part of the process, that might well suggest some deficiency in the fabric of creation. It might suggest that the universe was the work of a very powerful, but also somewhat limited, designer. It certainly would not show that the universe is the creature of an omnipotent wisdom, or an immediate manifestation of the God who is the being of all things. Frankly, the total absence of a single instance of irreducible complexity would be a far more forceful argument in favor of *God's* rational action in creation.[5]

As for theistic claims drawn from the astonishing array of improbable cosmological conditions that hold our universe together, including the cosmological constant itself, or from the mathematical razor's edge upon which all of it is so exquisitely balanced, these rest upon a number of deeply evocative arguments, and those who dismiss them casually are probably guilty of a certain intellectual dishonesty. Certainly all of the cosmos's exquisitely fine calibrations and consonances and exactitudes should speak powerfully to anyone who believes in a transcendent creator, and they might even have the power to make a reflective unbeliever curious about supernatural explanations. But, in the end, such arguments also remain only probabilistic, and anyone predisposed to explain them away will find plentiful ways of doing so: perhaps the extravagant hypothesis that there are vastly many universes generated by quantum fluctuations, of the sort Stephen Hawking has recently said does away with any role for God in the origin of the universe, or perhaps the even more extravagant hypothesis that every possible universe must be actual (the former hypothesis reduces the odds considerably, and the latter does away with odds altogether). But in a sense none of this really matters, because ultimately none of these arguments has much to do with God in the first place.

This is obvious if one considers the terms in which they are couched. Hawking's dismissal of God as an otiose explanatory hypothesis, for instance, is a splendid example of a false conclusion drawn from a confused question. He clearly thinks that talk of God's creation of the universe concerns some event that occurred at some particular point in the past, prosecuted by some being who appears to occupy the shadowy juncture between a larger quantum landscape and the specific conditions of our current cosmic order; by "God," that is to say, he means only a demiurge, coming after the law of gravity but before the present universe, whose job was to nail together all the boards and firmly mortar all the bricks of our current cosmic edifice. So Hawking naturally concludes that such a being would be unnecessary if there were some prior set of laws—just out there, so to speak, happily floating along on the wave-functions of the quantum vacuum—that would permit the spontaneous generation of any and all universes. It never crosses his mind that the question of creation might concern the very possibility of existence as such, not only of this universe but of all the laws and physical conditions that produced it, or that the concept of God might concern a reality not temporally prior to this or that world, but logically and necessarily prior to all worlds, all physical laws, all quantum events, and even all possibilities of laws and events. From the perspective of classical metaphysics, Hawking misses the whole point of talk of creation: God would be just as necessary even if all that existed were a collection of physical laws and quantum states, from which no ordered universe had ever arisen; for neither those laws nor those states could exist of themselves. But—and here is the crucial issue—those who argue for the existence of God principally from some feature or other of apparent cosmic design are guilty of the same conceptual confusion; they make a claim like Hawking's seem solvent, or at least relevant, because they themselves have not advanced beyond the demiurgic picture of God. By giving the name "God" to whatever as yet unknown agent or property or quality might account for this or that particular appearance of design, they have produced a picture of God that it is conceivable the sciences could some day genuinely make obsolete, because it really is a kind of rival explanation to the explanations the sciences seek. This has never been true of the God described in the great traditional metaphysical systems. The true philosophical question of God has always been posed at a far simpler but far more primordial and comprehensive level; it concerns existence as such: the logical possibility of the universe, not its mere physical probability. God, properly conceived, is not a force or cause within nature, and certainly not a kind of supreme natural explanation.[6]

Anyway, at this point I shall largely leave the new atheists, fundamentalists of every adherence, and Intelligent Design theorists all to their own devices, and perhaps to one another, and wish them all well, and hope that they do not waste too much time chasing after one another in circles. If I mention them below, it will be only to make a point in passing. From here onward, it is God—not gods, not the demiurge—of whom I wish to speak.

V

The terms in which I have chosen to speak of God, as the title page of this volume announces, are "being," "consciousness," and "bliss." This is a traditional ternion that I have borrowed from Indian tradition: in Sanskrit, the terms are *sat, chit,* and *ananda,* which are often fused into the single substantive *satchidananda* (there are alternative spellings). The word *sat* is often rendered as "truth," admittedly, rather than as "being," and for certain schools of Indian thought this has come to be its primary connotation. But it is in fact the present participle of the verb *as,* "to be," and has come to mean "truth" chiefly in the sense of "essential truth" or "reality"; it more or less encompasses the meanings of, in Greek, both *on* and *ousia* or, in Latin, both *ens* and *essentia,* and its privative form, *asat,* can mean both "nonbeing" and "falsehood." In any event, the three terms taken together constitute a particularly venerable Indian definition of the Godhead, with roots that reach back into the metaphysics of the *Upanishads,* and I have chosen to use them for a number of reasons.[7]

The first is that, as a set, they provide a particularly elegant summary of many of the most ancient metaphysical definitions of the divine nature found in a number of traditions. One of the special appeals such language has for anyone familiar with the history of Christian theology, for instance, is how hauntingly close it comes to certain classical formulations of the trinitarian nature of the divine. Gregory of Nyssa, for example, describes the divine life as an eternal act of knowledge and love, in which the God who is infinite being is also an infinite act of consciousness, knowing himself as the infinitely good, and so is also an infinite love, at once desiring all and receiving all in himself. "The life of that transcendent nature is love," he writes, "in that the beautiful is entirely lovable to those who know it (and the divine does know it), and so this knowledge becomes love, because the object of recognition is in its nature beautiful." Augustine describes the divine Son as the perfect and eternal image of the Father, God's self-knowledge as infinite beauty, and hence "that ineffable conjunction of the Father and his image is never without fruition, without love, without rejoicing"; moreover, "that love, delight, felicity or beatitude" is "the Holy Spirit, not begotten, but of the begetter and begotten alike the very sweetness, filling all creatures, according to their capacities, with his bountiful superabundance and excessiveness": thus, "in that Trinity is the highest origin of all things, and the most perfect beauty, and the most blessed delight." Other examples drawn from the Church Fathers, mystics, and divines could be multiplied at great length. Many Christians in India, moreover—like the Benedictine monk Henri le Saux (1910–1973), also known as Abhishiktananda, or like Brahmabandhab Upadhyay (1861–1907), the author of the great Trinitarian hymn *Vande Satchidananda*—have used these ancient Sanskrit words to describe their own understandings of God. And one finds analogous descriptions of the divine in all of the major theistic traditions. The great Sufi thinker Ibn Arabi (1165–1240), for instance, plays upon the common etymological root of the words *wujud* (being), *wijdan* (consciousness), and *wajd* (bliss) in order to describe the mystical knowledge of God as absolute Reality.[8]

My second reason for adopting these terms, however, is that they are ideal descriptions not only of how various traditions understand the nature of God, but also of how the reality of God can, according to those traditions, be experienced and known by us. For to say that God is being, consciousness, and bliss is also to say that he is the one reality in which all our existence, knowledge, and love subsist, from which they come and to which they go, and that therefore he is somehow present in even our simplest experience of the world, and is approachable by way of a contemplative and moral refinement of that experience. That is to say, these three words are not only a metaphysical explanation of God, but also a phenomenological explanation of the human encounter with God. Here before us, or so a great many traditions claim, in certain of our most immediate and primal experiences, lies our first knowledge of the mystery of God, as well as a kind of ubiquitous natural evidence of the supernatural. Whether that evidence is real or only an illusion generated by deep and desperate yearnings is of course open to argument; but what is certain is that it is here that one should look if one cares to know what, historically speaking, talk of God means.

And my final reason for using precisely these three words is that, so it seems to me, they perfectly designate those regions of human experience that cannot really be accounted for within the framework of philosophical naturalism without considerable contortions of reasoning and valiant revisions of common sense. They name essential and perennial mysteries that, no matter how we may try to reduce them to purely natural phenomena, resolutely resist our efforts to do so, and continue to point beyond themselves to what is "more than nature." In the case of "being," this should be fairly obvious. As I have said above, and will say again at greater length, there simply cannot be a natural explanation of existence as such; it is an absolute logical impossibility. The most a materialist account of existence can do is pretend that there is no real problem to be solved (though only a tragically inert mind could really dismiss the question of existence as uninteresting, unanswerable, or unintelligible). As for "consciousness" and "bliss," it may not be as immediately apparent that these words point toward anything quite so irreducibly mysterious; but each in its way delineates an aspect of reality that constantly eludes the narrative or explanatory powers of materialist thought, and—at the very least—*suggests* that the idea of "pure" or "self-sufficient" physical nature is an illusion. To state the matter more tersely and (for the moment) somewhat more enigmatically, these are the three "supernatural" forms of the natural. For us, they are the prior conditions that must be in place before anything called nature can be experienced at all, and as such they precede and exceed the mechanisms of natural causality. They are, to adopt the mediaeval term, transcendental. At least, so I shall argue. And I shall also argue that these three mysteries are absolutely fundamental to what we are and know and desire, at even the most ordinary and familiar of levels, and yet they irresistibly raise the question of the transcendent for us when we are truly attentive to them. This is why, whether there is a God or not, for truly rationally reflective persons—persons, that is, who allow themselves neither to lapse into brutish indifference to everything other than practical concerns nor to fall under the sway of some inflexible materialist ideology—the question of God never ceases to pose itself anew, and the longing to know about God never wholly abates.

CHAPTER TWO

Pictures of the World

I

If philosophy had the power to establish incontrovertible truths, immune to doubt, and if philosophers were as a rule wholly disinterested practitioners of their art, then it might be possible to speak of progress in philosophy. In fact, however, the philosophical tendencies and presuppositions of any age are, to a very great degree, determined by the prevailing cultural mood or by the ideological premises generally approved of by the educated classes. As often as not, the history of philosophy has been a history of prejudices masquerading as principles, and so merely a history of fashion. It is as possible today to be an intellectually scrupulous Platonist as it was more than two thousand years ago; it is simply not in vogue. Over the last century, Anglo-American philosophy has for the most part adopted and refined the methods of "analytic" reasoning, often guided by the assumption that this is a form of thinking more easily purged of unexamined inherited presuppositions than is the "continental" tradition. This is an illusion. Analytic method is dependent upon a number of tacit assumptions that cannot be verified in their turn by analysis: regarding the relation between language and reality, or the relation between language and thought, or the relation between thought and reality's disclosure of itself, or the nature of probability and possibility, or the sorts of claims that can be certified as "meaningful," and so on. In the end, analytic philosophy is no purer and no more rigorous than any other style of philosophizing. At times, in fact, it functions as an excellent vehicle for avoiding thinking intelligently at all; and certainly no philosophical method is more apt to hide its own most arbitrary metaphysical dogmas, most egregious crudities, and most obvious flaws from itself, and no other is so likely to mistake a descent into oversimplification for an advance in clarity. As always, the rules determine the game, and the game determines the rules. More to the point, inasmuch as the educated class is usually, at any given phase in history, also the most thoroughly indoctrinated, and therefore the most intellectually pliable and quiescent, professional philosophers are as likely as their colleagues in the sciences and humanities (and far more likely than the average person) to accept a reigning consensus uncritically, even credulously, and to adjust their thinking about everything accordingly. Happily, their philosophical training often aids them in doing so with a degree of ingenuity that protects them from the sharper pangs of conscience.

If all of this seems a counsel of despair in regard to reason's power to illuminate reality, it is not. "Philosophy" and "reason" are not synonyms. If rational thought is a possibility at all—that is, if there is some real correspondence between mind and world, rather than just a fortuitous and functional liaison forged by evolution—then there are many philosophical questions that the reasoning mind may address fruitfully, and the philosopher who is attentive to those questions, and who discusses them without instinctively resorting to some canon of philosophical dogma, is engaged in an intrinsically worthwhile pursuit. All I mean to urge here is that one should never be too naive regarding the quality of the current philosophical culture, or imagine that the most recent thinking is in any meaningful sense more advanced or more authoritative than that of a century or a millennium or two millennia ago. There are certain perennial problems to which all interesting philosophy returns again and again; but there are no such things as logical discoveries that consign any of the older answers to obsolescence. Certain classical answers to those problems endure and recur, sometimes because they remain far more powerful than the answers (or evasions) produced by later schools of thought. And, conversely, weaker answers often enjoy greater favor than their rivals simply because they are in keeping with the prejudices of the age. I think it fair to say that a majority of academic philosophers these days tends toward either a strict or a qualified materialist or physicalist view of reality (though many might not use those terms), and there may be something of a popular impression out there that such a position rests upon a particularly sound rational foundation. But, in fact, materialism is among the most problematic of philosophical standpoints, the most impoverished in its explanatory range, and among the most willful and (for want of a better word) magical in its logic, even if it has been in fashion for a couple of centuries or more. And, of course, fashions change. Three or four decades ago, a comfortable and complacent atheism was the nearly universal consensus of philosophical faculties throughout the developed world, but over the past generation or so there has been a resurgence of extremely sophisticated forms of theistic philosophy in the academic realm, including a remarkable revival of many traditional theistic arguments. Many of the better and more reflective atheist philosophers openly acknowledge that their position is largely an ideological commitment, not simply the inevitable conclusion of conscientious reasoning, and that the other side has formidable arguments of its own.[1]

To my mind, however, the truly interesting question about modern philosophical reflection on God or on the nature of existence is not what the relative preponderance of this or that academic faction may be at any given moment, but what assumptions persons on all sides tend to share, and how those assumptions have been shaped by the larger currents of cultural history. As much as movements in philosophy can affect the course of social and political history (and, sadly, they often have), the philosophy of any given time and place is often only a mirror of the larger culture's predominant picture of the world, the model of reality that most persons are in the habit of presupposing before they begin thinking about much of anything, and the average trained philosopher is often engaged in nothing more significant than an attempt to provide a formal account and rationalization of that picture as he or she understands it. Modern philosophy took shape in an age in which the understanding both of nature and of reason had changed radically from what it had been in antiquity or the High Middle Ages. In some respects, though not the most important, this change had been a matter of a revision of cosmic geography and of the physics of moving bodies: the shift from geocentrism to heliocentrism, the gradual disappearance of the planetary spheres and their replacement by the vacuum of space, the discovery of inertia, the recognition of elliptical orbits, and so forth. In other respects, however, it was a revision of the methods used to explore nature and of the metaphysical principles that those methods seemed to imply. In the former case, the change was brought about in part by real discoveries about the physical order; in the latter, it was brought about by a combination of practical and ideological concerns. Within a relatively short time, however, it became almost impossible for most persons properly to distinguish the genuine advances in scientific knowledge from accidental alterations of preconceptions. The new picture of the world came into being as a unified whole, in which—as is always the case—truth and error, established knowledge and baseless prejudice, were inseparably intermingled.

II

Most persons with any basic knowledge of cultural history probably have some sense of the architecture of the antique, mediaeval, and early modern universe, described in an "incomplete" form by Aristotle (384–322 BC) and given its most enduring finishing touches by Ptolemy (AD c. 90–c. 168). The earth stood immovably at the center of the system of interlocking heavens: immutable transparent spheres, each save one of them immediately encompassed by another larger than itself, in a regular succession upward and outward; each of the first seven spheres contained a "planet" (in order, the moon, Mercury, Venus, the sun, Mars, Jupiter, and Saturn), the next beyond those was the *stellatum,* or region of the fixed stars, and the next beyond that the mysterious *primum mobile,* or "first movable" heaven. Beyond that, however, lay the "realm" of the Unmoved Mover, understood either as a changeless spiritual intellect not directly involved in lower things, a pure "thought thinking thought," or as God the active creator of the universe. As for how a "place" beyond the heavens was to be conceived, there was some ambiguity. Aristotle thought of whatever reality lay beyond the stars as pure form and pure actuality, existing in neither any kind of space nor any kind of time (for space and time exist only where there is some unrealized potential for movement or change, some deficit of actuality, and for him the Prime Mover was absolutely actual and complete); but he also, in his *Physics,* could speak of the Unmoved Mover as somehow located outside or at the circumference of the heavens. For Christian thinkers, the ambiguity was of a different kind, but just as real: for them, beyond the primum mobile lay the infinite and infinitely beautiful luminosity of the empyrean, God's own heaven; but, at the same time, they did not believe that God was located in any particular place, since he is transcendent of space and time and so is fully and immediately present in each place and at each moment. In any event, for pagans and Christians alike, the Unmoved Mover was the cause of the ceaseless rotations of the heavens not because it or he exerted some kind of external prompting force upon them, but because it or he acted as an irresistible force of attraction. The primum mobile was moved by its love for the Unmoved Mover, its natural desire for and inclination toward the highest excellence, and "sought" to imitate the changeless perfection of the divine in the best way a changing thing can: a continuous and unalterable rotation. So the First Moved of the heavens coursed around the entire circuit of the lower heavens once each day, east to west, with such ardent force that it caused the lower spheres—which would have hastened to follow it if they could—to fall back and rotate, much more sluggishly, in the opposite direction, west to east.[2]

This cosmos was at once a scientific and a metaphysical conjecture, but also an object of great imaginative beauty, full of heights and depths and intricacies, splendor and sublimity and delicacy; its picture of the everlasting dance of the stars, moved by a primordial power of love that draws all things toward the divine, could scarcely have been more graceful in its poetry. It was full of light, in fact: in this scheme, there was no natural darkness in the heavens because the incandescence of the empyrean pervaded all the spheres; night existed only here below, a feeble conical shadow cast out by the Earth into the endless oceans of celestial radiance. This was not a picture of reality that simply went unchallenged down the centuries; there were scientists in late antiquity and the Middle Ages, Christian and Muslim, who occasionally called it into question, in whole or part. But, broadly speaking, it seemed to "save the appearances" of things better than any other available model. It did not, however, hold quite the emotional significance that modern persons often think it did. It is a careless commonplace, for instance, to say that resistance to Copernicanism in the early modern period was inspired by some desperate attachment to geocentrism prompted by the self-aggrandizing conviction that humanity occupies the center of all reality. This is simply wrong. It is true that, having little grasp of the principle of inertia and unable for the most part to believe in the possibility of a true vacuum, ancient and mediaeval persons naturally assumed that any movement of the Earth itself would cause obvious displacements of terrestrial objects and trajectories, and that it must therefore be stable and the heavens must revolve around it; but this does not mean they saw the earth as enjoying some sort of exalted status among the spheres—quite the opposite, really. In the old model, it was much more the case that the earth and its inhabitants were placed at the lowest and most defective level of reality. Here below, all was mutability: generation, decay, death, and ceaseless change. Below the sphere of the moon the four cardinal elements were in constant flux, the atmosphere was a turbulence of contending winds, corruption was everywhere. There above, by contrast, lay the region of the incorruptible fifth element, the aether, and of the unchanging heavens, and of an immaculate and lovely heavenly light of which we here on earth perceive only faint, diluted, and inconstant traces. Hence Dante's famous "inverted" image of the cosmos in the twenty-eighth canto of the *Paradiso,* in which the poet, granted a temporary glimpse of creation's spiritual form, sees God's burning light as the center of all things, with the primum mobile revolving around it as the smallest, swiftest, and inmost sphere and with all the other spheres radiating out in "reverse" order and proportion from there, all of them filled with their differing orders of angels, and with our world at the farthest remove from the center of that eternal heavenly dance. To many, what was most startling about the new cosmology was not that humanity had been expelled from the heart of reality, but that change and disorder had been introduced into the beautiful harmonies above.

The disappearance of the geocentric model of the universe, however, as disorienting as it may have been, was not really the most radical change in perspective produced in the early modern period. The larger revision of reality occurred at a much subtler level. For the philosophers and scientists of premodern times, stretching back to the beginning of philosophical and scientific thought in the West, no absolute division could be drawn between physical and metaphysical explanations of the cosmos, or at least between material and "spiritual" causes. The universe was shaped and sustained by an intricate interweaving of immanent and transcendent agencies and powers. It was the effect of an inseparable union of what Daniel Dennett likes to call "cranes" and "sky-hooks": that is, both causes that rise up from below, so to speak, and causes that descend from above. The principal way in which late antique and mediaeval thinkers understood the order of nature was in terms of Aristotle's four categories of causation: the material, formal, efficient, and final. The first of these is simply the underlying matter from which any given thing is formed—say, the marble upon which a sculptor works or the glass from which a bottle is made—the lowest and most ubiquitous level of which is "prime matter," the substrate of all physical things, so absolutely indeterminate as to be nothing in itself but pure potentiality, with no actuality independent of the forms that give it substance and shape. The formal cause is what makes a particular substance the kind of thing it is—say, a statue or a bottle—along with all the attributes proper to that kind of substance, such as cold, static solidity and representational form, or such as fragility, translucency, and fluid capacity. The efficient cause is the fashioning or prompting agency that brings form and matter together in a single substance—say, the sculptor or glassblower, along with the instruments of his craft. And the final cause is the ultimate aim or purpose or effect of a thing, the use for which it is intended or the good that it serves or the consequence to which it is innately (even if unconsciously) directed, which in a sense *draws* efficient causality toward itself—say, commemoration of a great event or evocation of aesthetic delight, or the storage and transport of wine or whisky. Perhaps, however, I ought not to choose only human artifacts for my examples, since in the classical view all finite things are produced by the workings of these four kinds of causality: elephants, mountains, and stars no less than statues or bottles. And then, beyond all these four, at least in the Christian period, there was yet another kind of causality, not always explicitly delineated from the others as it should have been but far more exorbitantly different from them than they were from one another. This we might call the "ontological" cause, which alone has the power not only to make, but to create from nothing: that infinite source of being that donates existence to every contingent thing, and to the universe as a whole, without which nothing—not even the barest possibilities of things—could exist.

We are not much in the habit today, of course, of thinking of "form" or "finality" as causes at all, especially not outside the realm of human fabrication. As a rule, we think of physical realities as caused exclusively by other physical realities, operating as prior and external forces and simply transferring energy from themselves to their effects. We may grant that, where a rational agent is involved, purposes and plans also may act as causes in an analogous or metaphorical sense; but nature we tend to see as a mindless physical process, matter in motion, from which form and purpose emerge accidentally, as consequences rather than causes. This is in large part because the intellectual world in which we have been reared is one whose master discourses—its sciences, philosophies, and ideologies—evolved in the aftermath of the displacement of the "Aristotelian" world by the "mechanical philosophy," as well as by the more inductive and empirical scientific method that began to take shape in late scholastic thought and that achieved a kind of coherent synthesis in the early modern period, in the work of Francis Bacon (1561–1626) and others (though, in fact, Bacon was not quite as thoroughgoing a mechanist as he is reputed to have been). The older view of reality allowed the physical cosmos and all its parts to be approached as organic structures that could be interpreted purposively and formally because nearly everyone assumed that merely material processes could not, of themselves, generate or vivify the ordered world of nature; more "spiritual"— or, at any rate, immaterial—causes had to be invoked to explain how the potencies of matter could be made actual and integrated into the coherent wholes of which nature is constituted. The problem with this assumption, though, at least in the eyes of those who argued for the "new instrument" of modern empirical method, was not so much logical as practical. Final and formal causes, even where they may be presumed, cannot really be investigated very well and can all too easily be invoked as explanations without sufficient empirical evidence. Better then, perhaps, to approach nature as a collection of mechanisms, the principle of whose order is not some mystical indwelling form or innate teleology but the purely functional arrangement of its distinct parts and actions. Rather than starting one's investigations from the ends to which one imagines nature is directed, better to start from the most elementary material facts, inductively, experimentally, and to advance from those only by cautious and cumulative steps. Thus, to speak in Aristotelian terms, the mechanical philosophy bracketed formal and final causes out of consideration altogether and confined scientific inquiry to material and efficient causes. In the process it radically reconceived material and efficient causality, depicting matter "in itself" no longer as mere potentiality requiring the imposition of some higher form to become something actual, but rather as some kind of substantial and efficient agency in its own right that merely needed to be arranged into working mechanical order by some kind of efficient ordering power (most early modern scientists were quite content to imagine this power as the divine designer of nature).

Needless to say, a very great part of the marvelous power and fecundity of modern science can be attributed to the ascetic regime that this new empiricism imposed upon scientific thought. The scrupulous refusal of all metaphysical conjecture, or of any recourse to "higher" causes whatsoever, required of scientists a far more laborious attentiveness to details, a more precise inventory of facts, a more relentless application of experiment, classification, and observation. It is not true, strictly speaking, that the rapid and constant progress of scientific understanding and achievement in the modern age has been the result solely of simple, unadorned empirical research, but very little of it would have come about apart from the revision of scientific thinking that the new empirical approach demanded. This makes it all the more poignantly sad that, as was probably inevitable, the new anti-metaphysical method soon hypertrophied into a metaphysics of its own. Over the course of a very short time, relatively speaking (a few generations at most), the heuristic metaphor of a purely mechanical cosmos became a kind of ontology, a picture of reality as such. The reasons for this were many—scientific, social, ideological, even theological—but the result was fairly uniform: Western persons quickly acquired the habit of seeing the universe not simply as something that can be investigated according to a mechanistic paradigm, but as in fact a machine. They came to see nature not as a reality guided and unified from within by higher or more spiritual causes like formality and finality, but as something merely factitiously assembled and arranged from without by some combination of efficient forces, and perhaps by one supreme external efficient cause—a divine designer and maker, a demiurge, the god of the machine, whom even many pious Christians began to think of as God.

It is difficult to exaggerate how profound a conceptual shift this constituted for the culture—intellectual and, in time, popular—of the West. By comparison, the abandonment of the Aristotelian and Ptolemaic cosmology required only a small adjustment of thinking, and that at a very clear and conscious level. But the loss of the larger sense of an integral unity of metaphysical and physical causes, and of a spiritual rationality wholly pervading and sustaining the universe—a loss that occurred at a subtler, more tacit, more unconscious level—opened an imaginative chasm between the premodern and modern worlds. Human beings now in a sense inhabited a universe different from that inhabited by their ancestors. In the older model, the whole cosmos—its splendor, its magnificent order, its ever vaster profundities—had been a kind of theophany, a manifestation of the transcendent God within the very depths and heights of creation. All of reality participated in those transcendental perfections that had their infinite consummation in God and that came to utterance in us, in our rational contemplation and coherent articulation and artistic celebration of the beauty and grandeur of existence. The human wakefulness to the mystery of being was thus also already an openness to the divine, because the world was an image of and participation in the God who is the wellspring of all being. Again, and emphatically, this was a vision of creation's rational order immeasurably remote from the Deist's or Intelligent Design theorist's notion of the world as a wonderful machine, designed and fabricated by a particularly enterprising superhuman intellect. To see the cosmos as wholly pervaded, unified, and sustained by a divine intellectual power, at once transcendent and immanent (logos or nous or, casting a glance eastward, dharma or tao), reaching down to the barest possibilities of things and rising up to the highest actuality, is not at all to see the cosmos merely as an artifact, constructed from disparate parts by some kind of very resourceful mind but itself mindless and mechanical, with even its beauty and mystery reduced to only so many arbitrary decorative effects. In the former case, one sees creation as a reflection of God's nature, open to transcendence from within; in the latter case, one sees the world as a reflection only of divine power, and as closed in upon itself.

According to the model that replaced the old metaphysical cosmology, in fact, at least in its still reflexively deistic form, there is no proper communion between mind and matter at all. The mindless machinery of nature is a composite of unrelated parts, in which the unified power of intellect has no proper or necessary place. Even the human mind inhabits the universe only as a kind of tenant or resident alien and not as an integral participant in the greater spiritual order of all things, able to interpret physical reality through a natural intellectual sympathy with and aptitude for it. In mediaeval philosophy it had been a standard precept that the human intellect can know an external object for two related reasons: first, because the intellect and that object both, according to their distinct modes of activity, participate in a single shared rational form (the form, for instance, that is embodied and made particular in a certain pale yellow rose languidly nodding over the rim of its porcelain vase, but that is also present in my thoughts as something at once conceptually understood and sensually intuited in the moment in which I encounter that rose); and, second, because the intellect and that object both together flow from and are embraced within the one infinite source of intelligibility and being that creates all things. Thus to know anything is already, however faintly and imperfectly, to know the act of God, both within each thing and within the self: a single act, known in the consonance and unity of two distinct instances or poles, one "objective" and one "subjective," but ultimately inseparable. By contrast, René Descartes (1596–1650)—the philosopher most typically invoked as emblematic of the transition from premodern to modern philosophical method—is often said to have envisaged the human soul as (in Gilbert Ryle's phrase) a "ghost in the machine." Whether or not this is entirely fair, it is certainly true that Descartes thought of all organisms, including the human body, as mechanisms, and he certainly thought of the soul as an immaterial "occupant" of the body (although he allowed, in some inadequately explicated way, for interactions between these two radically disparate kinds of substance, and even for their collaboration in a third kind of substance). According to the earlier model, one could know of God in knowing finite things, simply through one's innate openness to and dependence upon the logos that shines forth in all things, and on account of the indissoluble, altogether nuptial unity of consciousness and being. According to the Cartesian model, however, in which the soul merely indwells and surveys a mechanical reality with which it has no natural continuity and to which it is related only extrinsically, nothing of the sort is possible. This is largely why, for Descartes, the first "natural" knowledge of God is merely a kind of logical, largely featureless deduction of God's "existence," drawn chiefly from the presence in the individual mind of certain abstract ideas, such as the concept of the infinite, which the external world is impotent to have implanted there. All of this was perfectly consistent with the new mechanical view of nature, and all of it set both the soul and God quite apart from the cosmic machine: the one haunting it from within, the other commanding it from without.

As I have said, the dissolution of the geocentric cosmos, with its shimmering meridians and radiant crystal vaults and imperishable splendors, may have been an imaginative bereavement for Western humanity, but it was a loss easily compensated for by the magnificence of the new picture of the heavens. Far more significant in the long run was the disappearance of this older, metaphysically richer, immeasurably more mysterious, and far more spiritually inviting understanding of transcendent reality. In the age of the mechanical philosophy, in which all of nature could be viewed as a boundless collection of brute events, God soon came to be seen as merely the largest brute event of all. Thus in the modern period the argument between theism and atheism largely became no more than a tension between two different effectively atheist visions of existence. As a struggle between those who believed in this god of the machine and those who did not, it was a struggle waged for possession of an already godless universe. The rise and fall of Deism was an episode not so much within religious or metaphysical thinking as within the history of modern cosmology; apart from a few of its ethical appurtenances, the entire movement was chiefly an exercise in defective physics. The god of Deist thought was not the fullness

of being, of whom the world was a wholly dependent manifestation, but was merely part of a larger reality that included both
himself and his handiwork; and he was related to that handiwork
only extrinsically, as one object to another. The cosmos did not
live and move and have its being in him; he lived and moved and
had his being in it, as a discrete entity among other entities, a
separate and definite thing, a mere paltry Supreme Being. And,
inasmuch as his role was only that of the first efficient cause within
a continuous series of efficient causes, it required only the development of physical and cosmological theories that had no obvious
need of "that hypothesis" (as Laplace put it) to conjure him away.

It was the arrival of Darwinian theory, needless to say, that
initiated the final phase of this process, and that transformed an
implicit cultural *fait accompli* into an explicit conceptual *fait établi*.
In the ancient or mediaeval worlds, the idea of the evolution of
species would not necessarily have posed a very great intellectual
challenge for the educated classes, at least not on religious grounds.
Aristotelian orthodoxy maintained the fixity of species, true, but
one often finds a remarkably undogmatical approach to the questions of natural history in classical, patristic, and mediaeval sources,
and (as I have noted) no dominantly great interest in a literalist
reading of the creation narratives of scripture. It would not have
been drastically difficult for philosophers or theologians to come
to see such evolution as the natural unfolding of the rational principles of creation into forms primordially enfolded within the indwelling rational order of things. In the wake of the triumph of
the mechanical philosophy, however, when nature's "rationality"
had come to be understood only as a matter of mechanical design
engineered from without, the Darwinian proposal of natural se-

lection suggested the possibility that nature might instead be the product of wholly indeterminate—wholly mindless—forces. This was indeed, as Daniel Dennett has said, a dangerous idea to many minds; once enunciated, the concept of generative and cumulative indeterminate selection could perhaps come to be seen as an explanation for everything. Today, in fact, some physicists even wonder whether our universe and its physical laws might not in some sense be the product of such selection, played out among an unimaginably immense variety of universes. Who knows? Whatever the case, however, it seemed a dangerous idea only because of the metaphysical epoch in which it was first proposed. In a different age it would have threatened merely to modify the prevailing picture of how "higher" causes work upon material nature, but it would not have been mistaken for a rival metaphysics. Nor should it ever have been. Natural selection obviously cannot by itself account for the existence of the universe, or for the lawfulness of nature, because—to sound again one of this book's persistent motifs—the question of being cannot be answered by a theory that applies only to physical realities, and because even natural selection must be bound to an ensemble of physical laws to which it could not itself have given rise. By the latter half of the nineteenth century, however, very few persons remembered how to ask either the question of being or the question of nature's lawfulness properly; both had been largely lost sight of, even by most philosophers and theologians, somewhere behind the imposing and seemingly urgent question of cosmic design. Ontology had been displaced by cosmology, and cosmology had been reduced to a matter of mechanics. In an age in which God had come to be thought of merely as the architect and technician of an intrinsically mindless natural order, the thought that the appearance of design in nature might actually be only the residue of a long and varied history of fortuitous attritions and mutations seemed to imply that an adventitious designer had no necessary part to play in the grand scheme of things. There was simply no longer any need for this ghost beyond the machine.

III

Today the sciences are not bound to the mechanical philosophy as far as theoretical and practical methods are concerned; they never were, really, at least not beyond a certain point. Even so, the mechanical philosophy's great metaphysical master narrative—its governing picture of nature as an aggregate of mechanistic functions and systems, accidentally arranged out of inherently lifeless and purposeless elements—remains the frame within which we now organize our expectations of science and, consequently, of reality. And, since the days of Galileo or Bacon, Western intellectual culture's commitment to the mechanistic view of things has become ever more ardent. We are far more unremitting than the first modern empiricists in our efforts to exorcise our ghosts. As early as 1748, Julien Offray de la Mettrie (1709–1751) argued against Descartes's dualism of mind and body, claiming instead that human beings are nothing but machines, and that ratiocinative consciousness is nothing but one mechanical function among many; but his was an eccentric view at best. Today it is casually assumed by (I suspect) a pretty healthy majority of cognitive scientists that the conscious mind really is nothing but a mechanical material function of the brain. Even among philosophers of mind who are aware of the formidable logical difficulties entailed in such a position, a majority—not quite as preponderant, perhaps, but appreciable— presumes some version of a materialist view of consciousness. It has become common in some circles to speak of the brain as a kind of computer and of thought as merely a kind of programmed system of calculation—which is nonsense, as it happens (but that can wait till later). Even many philosophers of mind who recognize that they are not obliged to choose between this sort of mechanistic "computationalism" and an equally mechanistic Cartesian dualism tend to think that only one or another kind of materialist position can truly be credible. Having ruled all "sky-hooks" out of consideration in advance, they have left no room in their thinking for the possibility that the experience of consciousness might best be explained in terms of an integral unity of "higher" and "lower" causalities. This is simply the current *status quaestionis.*

It is, moreover, symptomatic of a kind of consensus not just in the sciences but also in culture at large. In fact, the mechanistic view of consciousness remains a philosophical and scientific premise *only* because it is now an established cultural bias, a story we have been telling ourselves for centuries, without any real warrant from either reason or science. The materialist metaphysics that emerged from the mechanical philosophy has endured and prevailed not because it is a necessary support of scientific research, or because the sciences somehow corroborate its tenets, but simply because it determines in advance which problems of interpretation we can all safely avoid confronting. As a purely practical matter, physical science has never been able to proceed very far without some reference to form or finality. Both may be excluded from consideration as objectively real causal agencies, for ideological reasons, but both still retain an indispensable interpretive power for making sense of the objects of scientific analysis. In the end, pure induction is a fantasy. The human mind could never arrive at an understanding of reality simply by sorting through its collections of bare sense impressions of particulars, trying to arrange them into intelligible and reiterative patterns. It must begin the work of interpretation at even the most elementary of levels, by attempting to impose some kind of purposive meaning upon each datum. Even if form and purpose have in principle been conceptually demoted to the rank of posterior effects, produced by the unguided interactions of material forces and "selected" by purely material conditions, in practice the scientist must frequently proceed *as if* forms and ends were causes. Evolutionary biologists, for instance, often try to explain an evolutionary adaptation by "reverse engineering" it from whatever purposes it serves in the present, trying all the while to discern what other purposes its earlier forms might have served in very different settings. Indeed, as many biologists guilelessly concede, the best approach to understanding an organism is often to treat it as though it were an intentional system, oriented toward specific purposes and ends, even if the researcher happens to be personally committed to the purely metaphysical presupposition that such purposes and ends are nothing more than useful metaphors (which would seem to make their hermeneutical efficacy something of an enchanting, perhaps positively magical coincidence).

More broadly speaking, there is scarcely a field in the higher sciences today that does not make use of the concept of "information," however it may subordinate the "form" in that term to the purely physical realm. And information is notoriously difficult to separate logically into that which is caused and that which causes, or into real and merely apparent purposes. In fact, it is positively impossible to do so from the perspective of modern scientific method, because that method precludes "emergent" properties in the hard sense—properties, that is, that are in any sense discontinuous from the properties of the prior causes from which they arise. Anything, in principle, should be reducible, by a series of "geometrical" steps, to the physical attributes of its ingredients. Information can be combined in new configurations, perhaps, but it cannot be conjured into being as something magically supervenient upon that process. And this conceptual inseparability of causative and resultant information holds good no less in the realm of modern physics than in that of chemistry or biology. It is worth considering, for example, at least as a thought experiment, whether either the metaphysical remains of mechanistic thinking or something more like the Aristotelian understanding of the relation between form and matter—or between actuality and potentiality—provides us with a self-evidently more coherent way of portraying to ourselves the relation between the incommensurable worlds of phenomenal objects and of quantum events. It is certainly not the science involved, in any event, that demands that we prefer one model to the other. Quantum reality rarely invites us to think in classically mechanistic categories, but it offers no very spirited resistance to any analogies we might care to draw between quantum indeterminacy and the indeterminate "prime matter" of the older metaphysics (just such an analogy was proposed by Heisenberg, in fact).

This point—mild, agnostic, unambitious assertion that it is—

needs to be emphasized here. One of the deep prejudices that the age of mechanism instilled in our culture, and that infects our religious and materialist fundamentalisms alike, is a version of the so-called genetic fallacy: to wit, the mistake of thinking that to have described a thing's material history or physical origins is to have explained that thing exhaustively. We tend to presume that if one can discover the temporally prior physical causes of some object—the world, an organism, a behavior, a religion, a mental event, an experience, or anything else—one has thereby eliminated all other possible causal explanations of that object. But this is a principle that is true only if materialism is true, and materialism is true only if this principle is true, and logical circles should not set the rules for our thinking. In the older metaphysics it was impossible for one kind of causality to exclude another, not simply because each occupied a unique logical space but because all forms of causality were seen as thoroughly and integrally complementary to one another. To identify the material and the efficient causes of a thing could never be proof of the absence or logical superfluity of formal and final causes; and, even today, no advance in the sciences obliges us to think otherwise. Whether, for example, the appearance of purpose in nature is the result of a long process of attrition and selection, or whether that long process is itself the result of the imperatives of a greater purpose, is not a matter that can be adjudicated empirically. Logically, in fact, both could be true, inasmuch as distinct levels of causality can be at once qualitatively different from, but necessarily integrated with, one another. In fact, it may very well be the case that both *must* be true, as otherwise the order and intelligibility of physical reality would be impossible. After all, the sciences can shed no light upon the origin of the lawfulness that informs material nature, since they must presume that lawfulness as the prior condition of all physical theories. Material aetiology and formal teleology are separable theoretically, perhaps, but not empirically, and the privilege we accord the former as our index of what is truly real follows not from any discovery of reason or of the sciences, but only from a decision we have collectively made. Even if we should ever succeed at tracing back the entire physical narrative of reality to its origin from "matter" (using that word in the broadest sense, as an alternative to all things "spiritual") and to a set of immutable physical laws (like the law of gravity) describable by mathematics, we shall still not have dispensed with form or finality. What, after all, are laws, and why can mathematics describe them at all?

We should then, at any rate, ignore the oft-repeated claim that the successes of the modern sciences have somehow proved the nonexistence or conceptual emptiness of "higher" forms of causality. We can grant the truth of the weaker claim that much of modern science has demonstrated that a marvelously vast inventory of discoveries becomes possible when one views nature according to a more or less mechanistic calculus of its physical parts and processes, without any commitment to the reality of other kinds of causality; but we should also note that it is essentially tautologous. If we look exclusively for material and efficient processes, then indeed we find them, precisely where everyone, of nearly any metaphysical persuasion, expects them to be found. All this shows is that we can coherently describe physical events in mechanical terms, at least for certain limited practical purposes; it certainly does not prove that they cannot also be described otherwise with as much or more accuracy. To paraphrase Heisenberg, the sorts of answers that nature provides are determined by the sorts of questions we pose of her. To bracket form and finality out of one's investigations as far as reason allows is a matter of method, but to deny their reality altogether is a matter of metaphysics. If common sense tells us that *real* causality is limited solely to material motion and the transfer of energy, that is because a great deal of common sense is a cultural artifact produced by an ideological heritage—and nothing more.[3]

Above all, we should not let ourselves forget precisely what method is and what it is not. A method, at least in the sciences, is a systematic set of limitations and constraints voluntarily assumed by a researcher in order to concentrate his or her investigations upon a strictly defined aspect of or approach to a clearly delineated object. As such, it allows one to see further and more perspicuously in one particular instance and in one particular way, but only because one has first consented to confine oneself to a narrow portion of the visible spectrum, so to speak. Moreover, while a given method may grant one a glimpse of truths that would remain otherwise obscure, that method is not itself a truth. This is crucial to understand. A method, considered in itself, may even in some ultimate sense be "false" as an explanation of things and yet still be probative as an instrument of investigation; some things are more easily seen through a red filter, but to go through life wearing rose-colored spectacles is not to see things as they truly are. When one forgets the distinction between method and truth, one becomes foolishly prone to respond to any question that cannot be answered from the vantage of one's particular methodological perch by dismissing it as nonsensical, or by issuing a promissory note guaranteeing a solution to the problem at some juncture in the remote future, or by simply distorting the question into one that looks like the kind one really can answer after all. Whenever modern scientific method is corrupted in this fashion the results are especially unfortunate. In such cases, an admirably severe discipline of interpretive and theoretical restraint has been transformed into its perfect and irrepressibly wanton opposite: what began as a principled refusal of metaphysical speculation, for the sake of specific empirical inquiries, has now been mistaken for a comprehensive knowledge of the metaphysical shape of reality; the art of humble questioning has been mistaken for the sure possession of ultimate conclusions.

This makes a mockery of real science, and its consequences are invariably ridiculous. Quite a few otherwise intelligent men and women take it as an established principle that we can know as true only what can be verified by empirical methods of experimentation and observation. This is, for one thing, a notoriously self-refuting claim, inasmuch as it cannot itself be demonstrated to be true by any application of empirical method. More to the point, though, it is transparent nonsense: most of the things we know to be true, often quite indubitably, do not fall within the realm of what can be tested by empirical methods; they are by their nature episodic, experiential, local, personal, intuitive, or purely logical. The sciences concern certain facts as organized by certain theories, and certain theories as constrained by certain facts; they accumulate evidence and enucleate hypotheses within very strictly limited paradigms; but they do not provide proofs of where reality begins or ends, or of what the dimensions of truth are. They cannot even establish their own working premises—the real existence of the phenomenal world, the power of the human intellect accurately to reflect that reality, the perfect lawfulness of nature, its interpretability, its mathematical regularity, and so forth—and should not seek to do so, but should confine themselves to the truths to which their methods give them access. They should also recognize what the boundaries of the scientific rescript are. There are, in fact, truths of reason that are far surer than even the most amply supported findings of empirical science because such truths are not, as those findings must always be, susceptible of later theoretical revision; and then there are truths of mathematics that are subject to proof in the most proper sense and so are more irrefutable still. And there is no one single discourse of truth as such, no single path to the knowledge of reality, no single method that can exhaustively define what knowledge is, no useful answers whose range has not been limited in advance by the kind of questions that prompted them. The failure to realize this can lead only to delusions of the kind expressed in, for example, G. G. Simpson's self-parodying assertion that all attempts to define the meaning of life or the nature of humanity made before 1859 are now entirely worthless, or in Peter Atkins's ebulliently absurd claims that modern science can "deal with every aspect of existence" and that it has in fact "never encountered a barrier." Not only do sentiments of this sort verge upon the deranged, they are nothing less than violent assaults upon the true dignity of science (which lies entirely in its severely self-limiting rigor).[4]

One of the most disagreeable present consequences of this failure to understand what method is, and hence what the limits of any method must be, is our current fashion in respectable pseudoscience. Every scientific epoch has been hospitable to charlatanry and hermetic nonsense, admittedly; but these days our shared faith

in the limitless power of scientific method has become so pervasive and irrational that, as a culture, we have become shamefully
tolerant of all those lush efflorescences of wild conjecture that grow
up continuously at the margins of the hard sciences and thrive on
a stolen credibility. This is especially true at the fertile purlieus
of Darwinian theory, which enjoys the unfortunate distinction of
being the school of scientific thought most regularly invoked to
justify spurious theories about practically everything. Evolutionary
biology, properly speaking, concerns the development of physical
organisms by way of replication, random mutation, and natural
selection, and nothing else. The further the tropes of Darwinian
theory drift from this very precise field of inquiry, the more willfully speculative, metaphysically unmoored, and empirically useless they become. Yet texts purporting to provide Darwinian explanations of phenomena it has no demonstrable power to describe
pour in ceaseless torrents from the presses and the inexhaustible
wellsprings of the Internet. There are now even whole academic
disciplines, like evolutionary psychology, that promote themselves
as forms of science but that are little more than morasses of metaphor. (Evolutionary psychologists often become quite indignant
when one says this, but a "science" that can explain *every* possible
form of human behavior and organization, however universal or
idiosyncratic, and no matter how contradictory of other behaviors, as *some* kind of practical evolutionary adaptation of the modular brain, clearly has nothing to offer but fabulous narratives—
Just So Stories, as it were—disguised as scientific propositions.) As
for the even more daringly speculative application of Darwinian
language to spheres entirely beyond the physiological, like economics, politics, ethics, social organization, religion, aesthetics, and

73

so on, it may seem a plausible practice at first glance, and it is quite in keeping with our cultural intuition that evolutionary imperatives somehow lie at the origin of everything (an intuition, incidentally, impossible to prove, either as a premise or as a conclusion), but it is a purely analogical, not empirical, approach to things: pictorial, not analytic. It produces only theories that are neither true nor false, entertainingly novel metaphors, some more winsome folklore to add to the charming mythopoeia of materialism; and there is no way in which it could ever do any more than this. As soon as one moves from the realm of physiological processes to that of human consciousness and culture, one has taken leave of the world where evolutionary language can be tested or controlled. There are no longer any physical interactions and replications to be measured, and no discrete units of selection that can be identified (assuming one is not so gullible as to take the logically incoherent and empirically vacuous concept of "memes" seriously). Even if one believes that human consciousness and culture are the results solely of evolutionary forces, one still cannot prove that they function only in a Darwinian fashion, and any attempt to do so soon dissolves into a rosy mist of picturesque similes.

No doubt it says something about the extraordinarily high esteem in which the sciences are held today, after so many remarkable advances over so sustained a period, that there is scarcely a field of inquiry in the academic world that would not like a share in their glamor. It also goes some way toward explaining the propensity of some in the sciences to imagine that their disciplines endow them with a sort of miraculous aptitude for making significant pronouncements in fields in which they actually have received no tutelage. It is perfectly understandable, for example, but also painfully embarrassing, when Stephen Hawking and Leonard Mlodinow casually and pompously declare that philosophy is dead (as they recently have). They might even conceivably be right, but they certainly would not be competent to know if they are (as the fairly elementary philosophical errors in their book show). Every bit as silly are the pronouncements of, say, Richard Feynman or Steven Weinberg regarding the apparent "meaninglessness" of the universe revealed by modern physics (as if any purely physical inventory of reality could possibly have anything to tell us about the meaning of things). High accomplishment in one field—even genius in that field—does not necessarily translate into so much as the barest competence in any other. There is no such thing, at least among finite minds, as intelligence at large: no mind not constrained by its own special proficiencies and formation, no privileged vantage that allows any of us a comprehensive insight into the essence of all things, no expertise or wealth of experience that endows any of us with the wisdom or power to judge what we do not have the training or perhaps the temperament to under-stand. To imagine otherwise is a delusion, no less in the case of a physicist than in the case of a barber—more so, perhaps, as the barber, not having been indoctrinated with any very peremptory professional dogmas regarding the nature of reality, would no doubt be far easier to disabuse of his confidence in the limitless capacities of tonsorial method.

The whole power, beauty, and (for want of a better word) piety of the sciences lie in that fruitful narrowness of focus that I men-tioned above, that austere abdication of metaphysical pretensions that permits them their potentially interminable inductive and theoretical odyssey through the physical order. It is the purity of this vocation to the particular that is the special glory of science. This means that the sciences are, by their very nature, commendably fragmentary and, in regard to many real and important questions about existence, utterly inconsequential. Not only can they not provide knowledge of everything; they cannot provide complete knowledge of anything. They can yield only knowledge of certain aspects of things as seen from one very powerful but inflexibly constricted perspective. If they attempt to go beyond their methodological commissions, they cease to be sciences and immediately become fatuous occultisms. The glory of human reason, however, is its power to exceed any particular frame of reference or any single perspective, to employ an incalculable range of intellectual faculties, and to remain open to the whole horizon of being's potentially infinite intelligibility. A wise and reflective person will not forget this. A microscope may conduct the eye into the mysteries of a single cell, but it will not alert one to a collapsing roof overhead; happily we have more senses than one. We may even possess spiritual senses, however much we are discouraged from trusting in them at present. A scientist, as a reasoning person, has as much call as anyone else to ponder the deepest questions of existence, but should also recognize the threshold at which science itself falls silent—for the simple reason that its silence at that point is the only assurance of its intellectual and moral integrity.

IV

My purpose in saying all of this is to make a simple but necessary point. One of the more persistent and inexcusable rhetorical conceits that corrupt the current popular debates over belief in God is the claim that they constitute an argument between faith and reason or between religion and science. They constitute, in fact, only a contest between different pictures of the world: theism and naturalism (this seems the most satisfactory and comprehensive term, at any rate), each of which involves a number of basic metaphysical convictions; and the latter is by far the less rationally defensible of the two. Naturalism is a picture of the whole of reality that cannot, according to its own intrinsic premises, address the being of the whole; it is a metaphysics of the rejection of metaphysics, a transcendental certainty of the impossibility of transcendental truth, and so requires an act of pure credence logically immune to any verification (after all, if there is a God he can presumably reveal himself to seeking minds, but if there is not then there can be no "natural" confirmation of the fact). Thus naturalism must forever remain a pure assertion, a pure conviction, a confession of blind assurance in an inaccessible *beyond;* and that beyond, more paradoxically still, is the beyond of no beyond. And naturalism's claim that, by confining itself to purely material explanations for all things, it adheres to the only sure path of verifiable knowledge is nothing but a feat of sublimely circular thinking: physics explains everything, which we know because anything physics cannot explain does not exist, which we know because whatever exists must be explicable by physics, which we know because physics explains everything. There is something here of the mystical.

The picture of the world with which naturalism presents us, we should also recall, is not the phenomenal world we all experience but rather an intuition of its hidden principles, a supposition regarding its secret essence. It is not the case that, as we sometimes lazily assume, materialism is a natural default position for our thinking because we have direct knowledge only of the material order. There are, for one thing, inherent logical difficulties in the materialist position that make it anything but a natural picture of the world, as I have noted and will note again. There are, as well, innumerably many things we know (take the truths of mathematics, for instance) that are not material realities in any meaningful sense. More to the point, though, we have no actual direct experience of the material world as such at all, at least not as pure materialism depicts it. Our primordial experience of reality is an immediate perception of phenomena—appearances, that is—which come to us not directly through our senses, but through sensations as interpreted by thought, under the aspect of organizing eidetic patterns. We do not encounter the material substrate of things, but only the intelligible forms of things, situated within an interdependent universe of intelligible forms, everywhere governed by purposes: organic, artificial, moral, aesthetic, social, and so forth. We know, also, that those forms are not simple structural aggregates of elementary physical realities, as if atoms were fixed components stacked one upon another like bricks until they added up to stable physical edifices; the forms remain constant, while atomic and subatomic reality is in perpetual flux and eludes that sort of local composition altogether. Phenomenal forms and the quantum realm upon which they are superimposed do not constitute a simple, unilinear, mechanical continuum. And even in the purely physiological realm, we have no direct knowledge of *unguided* material forces simply spontaneously producing the complex order that constitutes our world. A mere agitation of molecules, for instance, does not simply "amount to" a game of chess, even though every physical structure and activity involved in that game may be in one sense reducible without remainder to molecules and electrical impulses and so on; it is not the total ensemble of those material forces that adds up to the chess game, but only that ensemble as organized to an end by higher forms of causality. Viewed from another and equally valid perspective, when one looks at that chess game one sees an immense and dynamic range of physical potentialities and actualities assumed into a complex unity by the imposition of rational form. One sees a variety of causalities, from below and from above, perfectly integrated and inseparable, and none obviously sufficient in itself to account for the whole.

I should be clear here: this is a point of logic, and not a proposition regarding what we should conclude from the evidence produced by the sciences. Scientific truth, after all, may very well be counterintuitive, and is not bound to conform to the experiences of phenomenal consciousness. I am saying only that the interpretation of the evidence produced by science can never really yield a proof of materialism, or even a coherent way of thinking in materialist terms. Science and philosophy are both reductive arts, and necessarily so; both attempt, as an indispensable part of each of their journeys toward understanding, to reduce reality to its simplest constituents and most elementary functions (physical or logical). This, however, can yield a complete account of the whole of reality only if, once the total reduction of nature has been accomplished (which, incidentally, is certainly impossible), there follows a rational reconstruction of nature that can lead back seamlessly from reality's barest constituents to the phenomenal world from which the process of reduction first departed, and do so without any prospective, guiding reference to that world as a final cause. If this is not possible, all that remains of naturalism is an irrational creed, sustained by a catechetical commitment to an insidious "nothing but" or "only": as in, "You are *nothing but* your genes" or "Reality is *only* molecules, atoms, and subatomic particles in motion."

I am not, incidentally, suggesting that there is any clear break in the continuity between these different levels of causality, from the subatomic to the atomic to the molecular to the organic to the social (or what have you). With my sympathy for classical metaphysics, I certainly want to assume the perfect rational integrity of nature. What the principles of order are, however, that arrange those causal levels into a unified phenomenal event cannot be reductively identified by attempting to reassemble that event—with its whole complex web of the essential and the accidental, the fortuitous and the intentional—from its discrete physical parts. This is not a matter of mere practical limits, as if the only problem were that we simply do not have a sufficiently comprehensive view of the physical events involved; it is not the case that, as the Marquis de Laplace (1749–1827) fantasized, we could reconstruct the entire past of the universe and predict its entire future if only we knew the precise disposition of all particles in the universe at any given instant. There is also the more fundamental problem of the conceptual inseparability of different causal descriptions. It lies beyond the range of any physical logic, as I have said, to distinguish absolutely between information as caused and information as causing. Hence, for example, the somewhat poignant limitations of those computer programs devised to demonstrate the fertility of Darwinian "algorithms" by showing how complex organization can develop out of random variation and cumulative selection: whether of the crude sort, like Richard Dawkins's program for generating the phrase "Methinks it is like a weasel" (which had a target phrase written into it as well as a protocol for the prospective retention of useful variations, and so operated in a far more Aristotelian than Darwinian fashion), or more sophisticated programs for generating the patterns of spider webs (which still must start from some concept of what a web is for). Since all such programs begin with a set of already highly informed objects and functions, like replication of virtual DNA, and some general prior purpose for directing the progress of cumulative selection, and since they must (not to state the obvious) be programmed by a programmer, all they really show is that, where a great deal of information is involved in some process, highly informed consequences follow. Such programs have their use, certainly, if they can demonstrate how stochastic variations within replicating organisms might be selected by environmental conditions, but they most certainly do not prove anything about the adequacy of a materialist view of reality. Even if one could conceivably prove, as is occasionally suggested these days, that cosmic information is somehow ceaselessly generated out of quantum states, this still would not have decided the issue of causality in favor of the naturalist position. As a brilliant physicist friend of mine often and somewhat tiresomely likes to insist, "chaos" could not produce laws unless it were already governed by laws.

In the end, one is of course perfectly free to believe in the, so to speak, "just-there-ness" of the quantum order and of the physical laws governing it. I tend to see this as bordering upon a belief in magic, but that may be mere prejudice. What is absolutely certain is that the naturalist view of things is, as I have said, just a picture of the world, not a truth about the world that we can know, nor even a conviction that rests upon a secure rational foundation. The picture that naturalism gives us, at least at present, is twofold. On the one hand, the cosmos of space and time is a purely mechanistic reality that, if we are to be perfectly consistent, we must see as utterly deterministic: that is to say, to work a small variation on Laplace's fantasy, if we could know the entire history of the physical events that compose the universe, from that first inflationary instant to the present, including the course of every particle, we would know also the ineluctable necessity of everything that led to and follows from the present; even what we take to be free acts of the will would be revealed as the inevitable results of physical forces reaching all the way back to the beginning of all things. On the other hand, this deterministic machine floats upon a quantum flux of ceaseless spontaneity and infinite indeterminacy. Together, these two orders close reality within a dialectical totality—a perfect union of destiny and chance, absolute determinism and pure fortuity—hermetically sealed against all transcendence. And yet, once again, the picture is radically incomplete, not only because it is unlikely that the classical Newtonian universe and the universe of quantum theory can be fitted together so seamlessly, but because neither level of reality explains the existence of the other, or of itself. And, also once again, nothing we know obliges us to find this picture more convincing than one in which higher causes (among which we might, for instance, include free will) operate upon lower, or in which all physical reality is open to a transcendent order that reveals itself in the very existence of nature.

In any event, I do not wish to take this line of argument any further for now. I am not so much interested in arguing for the superior rationality of one picture of the world or the other as in simply drawing a clear distinction between any picture of the world and rationality as such. For reasons that will become clear below, I happen to believe in those higher causes that naturalist orthodoxy boldly claims have been rendered incredible by the advances of science; and I happen also to believe that their exclusion by naturalism leads to absurdities or, at the very least, irresoluble problems. I suppose that if I had to give a kind of portmanteau name to the view of things I find most convincing, it would be the "metaphysics of eminence"—borrowing the scholastic notion that lower reality is always "more eminently" or "virtually" contained in higher realities, while the higher is participated in and expressed by the lower. Or perhaps one could simply call this the metaphysics of the transcendental, which includes such (by current standards) incredible beliefs as: beautiful things are caused by, among other things, transcendent beauty. Whatever one calls it, however, and however dependent it is on the clearly inadequate spatial metaphors of the above and the below, it is a vision of reality in which the higher is not the epiphenomenal and largely illusory residue of the lower—down there where reality is really real, as it were—but a causal order in its own right, comprising the forms and ends and rational harmonies that shape and guide and explain the world. Then, beyond all those forms of causality, comprehending, transcending, pervading, underlying, and creating them, is that which is highest and most eminent of all, the boundless source of all reality, the infinity of being, consciousness, and bliss that is God.

As I have said, it is not my aim to prove the truth of this vision of things so much as to describe it. This book is not an exhortation to faith, though it does implicitly contain an invitation to seek. I cannot, however, avoid explaining why I find this vision more intellectually persuasive than its naturalist alternative, as metaphysical description devoid of some explanation of philosophical rationale is a practical impossibility, and so some degree of philosophical argument is inevitable; but I shall try to confine such argument to the meagerest essentials, relegate as much of it as I can to my notes (where the overly curious can look if they care to), and leave it to my bibliographical postscript to direct readers to fuller treatments of the issues involved. My aim truly is to achieve clarity in order to avert misunderstanding wherever possible. I should also admit here, however, that I proceed in this way because, as I have begun to grow somewhat older than I really want to be, I have also begun to vest less faith in certain forms of argument, or at least in their power to persuade the unwilling, and more in certain sorts of experience—certain ways of encountering reality, to phrase the matter with infuriating vagueness. My chief desire is to show that what is most mysterious and most exalted is also that which, strangely enough, turns out to be most ordinary and nearest to hand, and that what is most glorious in its transcendence is also that which is humblest in its wonderful immediacy, and that we know far more than we are usually aware of knowing, in large part because we labor to forget what is laid out before us in every moment, and because we spend so much of our lives wandering in dreams, in a deep but fitful sleep.

PART TWO

Being, Consciousness, Bliss

The sleeper, as he ascends from his dream toward the morning's light, may momentarily drift back again more deeply into the illusory world—or half-illusory world—from which he is trying to emerge. He continues to hear his name called but still lingers at the boundary between sleep and waking consciousness. For a time, the figures of his dream retain a certain ghostly clarity, even as they have begun to melt away before the realities they symbolize, as though the dream were reluctant to release him. In a few moments, however, his eyes open and the fantasy entirely fades: the tower vanishes amid the soft ringing of wind chimes, the windblown valley dissolves beneath the billowing of white cotton curtains stirred by the breeze, the murmur of the reeds along the river's bank becomes the rustling of the leaves below the sill, and the voice that seemed so strange and faintly dreadful is all at once familiar and inviting. In the more vivid light of the waking world, he knows he has returned to a reality far richer and more coherent than the one he has left behind.

Having, however, passed through distinct levels of awareness in his ascent from the twilight in that valley to the radiance of this morning, he might momentarily wonder whether even now he is entirely awake, or whether there remains a still greater wakefulness, and a still fuller light, to which he might yet rise.

CHAPTER THREE

Being (*Sat*)

I

The beginning of all philosophy, according to both Plato and Aristotle, lies in the experience of wonder. One might go further and say that the beginning of all serious thought—all reflection upon the world that is not merely calculative or appetitive—begins in a moment of unsettling or delighted surprise. Not, that is, a simple twinge of curiosity or bafflement regarding some fact out there not yet in one's possession: if anything, it is the sudden awareness that no mere fact can possibly be an adequate explanation of the mystery in which one finds oneself immersed at every moment. It is the astonishing recollection of something one has forgotten only because it is always present: a primordial agitation of the mind and will, an abiding amazement that lies just below the surface of conscious thought and that only in very rare instants breaks through into ordinary awareness. It may be that when we are small children, before we have learned how to forget the obvious, we know this wonder in a more constant, innocent, and luminous way, because we are still trustingly open to the sheer inexplicable givenness of the world. In the dawn of life we sense with a perfect immediacy, which we have no capacity or inclination to translate into any objective concept, how miraculous it is that—as Angelus Silesius (1624–1677) says—"Die Rose ist ohne warum, sie blühet, weil sie blühet": "The rose is without 'why'; it blooms because it blooms." As we age, however, we lose our sense of the intimate otherness of things; we allow habit to displace awe, inevitability to banish delight; we grow into adulthood and put away childish things. Thereafter, there are only fleeting instants scattered throughout our lives when all at once, our defenses momentarily relaxed, we find ourselves brought to a pause by a sudden unanticipated sense of the utter uncanniness of the reality we inhabit, the startling fortuity and strangeness of everything familiar: how odd it is, and how unfathomable, that anything at all exists; how disconcerting that the world and one's consciousness of it are simply there, joined in a single ineffable event. When it comes, it is a moment of alienation from the ordinary perhaps, but not one of disaffection or loss; as long as the experience lasts, in fact, it has a certain quality of mystifying happiness about it, the exhilarating feeling that one is at the border of some tremendous and beautiful discovery. One realizes that everything about the world that seems so unexceptional and drearily predictable is in fact charged with an immense and imponderable mystery. In that instant one is aware, even if the precise formulation eludes one, that everything one knows exists in an irreducibly gratuitous way: "what it is" has no logical connection with the reality "that it is"; nothing within experience has any "right" to be, any power to give itself existence, any apparent "why." The world is unable to provide any account of its own actuality, and yet there it is all the same. In that instant one recalls that one's every encounter with the world has always been an encounter with an enigma that no merely physical explanation can resolve.

One cannot dwell indefinitely in that moment, of course, any more than one can remain a child forever. For one thing, there is an almost paralyzing fullness to the experience, a kind of surfeit of immediacy that is at the same time an absolute remoteness from practical things. For another, there is nothing to hold on to in the experience, because the source of one's amazement is not some particular object among the objects of the world but simply the pure eventuality of the world as such. The question of why anything at all exists is one that already exceeds its occasion, already goes beyond the reality of all particular things, and attempts to lay hold, however uncertainly, of the transcendent conditions of that reality. Sooner or later, therefore, one simply must let the apprehension slip away, just so that one can get on with the business of life. One has to revert to one's habitual obliviousness to the mystery, to a "single-mindedness" that can once again close the chasm that has briefly opened between "what" and the "that" of reality, or one will not be able to start moving forward again. At times, the memory of the experience may even need to be forcibly suppressed with ingenious or (at least) convenient rationalizations. One may, for instance, dismiss this fleeting shock of "ontological surprise" as a transient neurological aberration, a momentary phantom doubling of reality in the mind producing the false impression of some kind of dichotomy between the world and its own existence—rather as one might decide to interpret an episode of déjà vu as nothing more than the brain processing a single perception twice in indiscernibly quick succession, thus creating a kind of mental echo that feels like a trace of memory. If it is one's sordid fate to be an academic philosopher, one might even try to convince oneself that the question of existence is an inept or false query generated by the seductions of imprecise grammar, or one might simply adopt the analytic philosopher's classic gesture of flinging one's hands haplessly in the air and proclaiming that one simply finds the question entirely unintelligible. All of this, however, is an abdication of the responsibility to think. This rare and fleeting experience of being's strangeness within its very familiarity is not a transitory confusion or trivial psychological mood but a genuine if tantalizingly brief glimpse into an inexhaustibly profound truth about reality. It is the recognition, simply said, of the world's absolute contingency. The world need not be thus. It need not be at all. If, moreover, one takes the time to reflect upon this contingency carefully enough, one will come to realize that it is an ontological, not merely an aetiological, mystery; the question of existence is not one concerning the physical origins of things, or of how one physical state may have been produced by a prior physical state, or of physical persistence across time, or of the physical constituents of the universe, but one of simple logical or conceptual possibility: How is it that any reality so obviously fortuitous— so lacking in any mark of inherent necessity or explanatory self-sufficiency—can exist at all?

The American philosopher Richard Taylor once illustrated this mystery, famously and fetchingly, with the image of a man out for a stroll in the forest unaccountably coming upon a very large translucent sphere. Naturally, he would immediately be taken aback by the sheer strangeness of the thing, and would wonder how it should happen to be there. More to the point, he would certainly never be able to believe that it just happened to be there without any cause, or without any possibility of further explanation; the very idea would be absurd. But, adds Taylor, what that man has not noticed is that he might ask the same question equally well about any other thing in the woods too, a rock or a tree no less than this outlandish sphere, and fails to do so only because it rarely occurs to us to interrogate the ontological pedigrees of the things to which we are accustomed. What would provoke our curiosity about the sphere would be that it was so obviously out of place; but, as far as existence is concerned, everything is in a sense out of place. As Taylor goes on to say, the question would be no less intelligible or pertinent if we were to imagine the sphere either as expanded to the size of the universe or as contracted to the size of a grain of sand, either as existing from everlasting to everlasting or as existing for only a few seconds. It is the sheer unexpected "thereness" of the thing, devoid of any transparent rationale for the fact, that prompts our desire to understand it in terms not simply of its nature, but of its very existence.[1]

The mystery of being becomes deeper, however, and even somewhat urgent, when one reflects not only upon the seeming inexplicability of existence as such, but also upon the nature of the things that have existence. The physical order confronts us at every moment not simply with its ontological fortuity but also with the intrinsic ontological poverty of all things physical—their necessary and total reliance for their existence, in every instant, upon realities outside themselves. Everything available to the senses or representable to the mind is entirely subject to *annicha* (to use the Buddhist term): impermanence, mutability, transience. All physical things are composite, which is to say reducible to an ever greater variety of distinct parts, and so are essentially inconstant and prone to dissolution. All things are subject to time, moreover: they possess no complete identity in themselves, but are always in the process of becoming something else, and hence also in the process of becoming nothing at all. There is a pure fragility and necessary incompleteness to any finite thing; nothing has its actuality entirely in itself, fully enjoyed in some impregnable present instant, but must always receive itself from beyond itself, and then only by losing itself at the same time. Nothing within the cosmos contains the ground of its own being. To use an old terminology, every finite thing is the union of an essence (its "what it is") with a unique existence (its "that it is"), each of which is utterly impotent to explain the other, or to explain itself for that matter, and neither of which can ever be wholly or permanently possessed by anything. One knows of oneself, for instance, that every instant of one's existence is only a partial realization of what one is, achieved by surrendering the past to the future in the vanishing and infinitesimal interval of the present. Both one's essence and one's existence come from elsewhere—from the past and the future, from the surrounding universe and whatever it may depend upon, in a chain of causal dependencies reaching backward and forward and upward and downward—and one receives them both not as possessions secured within some absolute state of being but as evanescent gifts only briefly grasped within the ontological indigence of becoming. Everything that one is is a dynamic and perilously contingent synthesis of identity and change, wavering between existence and nonexistence. To employ another very old formula, one's "potential" is always being reduced or collapsed into the finitely "actual" (always foreclosing forever all other possibilities for one's existence), and only in this way can one be liberated into the living uncertainty of the future. Thus one lives and moves and has one's being only at the sufferance of an endless number of enabling conditions, and becomes what one will be only by taking leave of what one has been. Simply said, one is contingent through and through, partaking of being rather than generating it out of some source within oneself; and the same is true of the whole intricate web of interdependencies that constitutes nature.

There are various directions in which reflection on the contingency of things can carry one's thoughts. One can follow, at least in principle, the chain of anything's dependency back through ever deepening layers of causality, both physical and chronological—descending toward the subatomic, retreating toward the initial singularity—and still ultimately arrive at only the most elementary contingencies of all, no closer to an explanation of existence than one was before setting out. Alternatively, if one prefers metaphysical logic to the multiplication of genetic enigmas, one can forgo this phantasmagoric regress toward primordial causes altogether and choose instead to gaze out over the seas of mutability and dependency in search of that distant stable shore that, untouched by becoming, prevents everything from flowing away into an original or final nothingness. Or one may attempt to turn one's thoughts from the world's multiplicity and toward that mysterious unity that quietly persists amid the spectacle of incessant change: that oneness that is everywhere and nowhere, at once in the world and in one's consciousness of it, holding all things together as a coherent totality while also preserving each separate thing in its particularity, and each part of each thing, and each part of that part, and so on ad infinitum. In seeking to understand the world in any of these ways, however, one may be tempted to try to reduce the essential mystery of existence to something one can contain in a simple concept, like a mechanical or physical cause, or a trivial predicate, or something else that one can easily grasp and thereafter ignore. Thinkers in all the great religious traditions have repeatedly warned that it is far easier to think about beings than about being as such, and that we therefore always risk losing sight of the mystery of being behind the concepts we impose upon it. Having briefly awakened to a truth that precedes and exceeds the totality of discrete things, we may end up all the more oblivious to it for having tried to master it.

Even so, one must try to understand, even if only now and then. Reason is restless before this question. And any profound reflection upon the contingency of things must involve the question of God, which—whether or not one believes it can be answered— must be posed again and again in the course of any life that is truly rational.

II

Whether or not the question of God can be answered satisfactorily, however, or even formulated satisfactorily, these reflections should at least make it clear, once again, that it is entirely different in kind from any merely local or psychological or cultic question regarding "gods" or "a god." The gods are enfolded within nature and enter human thought as the most exalted expressions of its power; they emerge from the magnificent energy of the physical order. God, however, is first glimpsed within nature's still greater powerlessness—its transitoriness and contingency and explanatory poverty. He is known or imagined or hoped for as that reality that lies beyond the awful shadow of potential nothingness that falls across all finite things, the gods included. The gods are beings among other beings, the most splendid beings of all, but are still dependent upon some prior reality that constitutes the imperturbable foundation of their existence. God, however, is beyond all mere finite beings, and is himself that ultimate ground upon which any foundations must rest. Thus the *Mundaka Upanishad* speaks of Brahma, the first-born among the gods, coming forth from Brahman, the eternal Godhead who is the source of all being, and then teaching the other gods about Brahman. The gods could not exist apart from nature; nature could not exist apart from God.[2]

It should be no less clear, moreover, that philosophical naturalism could never serve as a complete, coherent, or even provisionally plausible picture of reality as a whole. The limits of nature's powers are the same whether they are personified as deities or not. It is at the very point where physical reality becomes questionable, and reason finds it has to venture beyond the limits of nature if it is to make sense of nature, that naturalism demands reason turn back, resigned to pure absurdity, and rest content with a non-answer that closes off every avenue to the goal the mind necessarily seeks. The question of existence is real, comprehensible, and unavoidable, and yet it lies beyond the power of naturalism to answer it, or even to ask it. An old and particularly sound metaphysical maxim says that between existence and nonexistence there is an infinite qualitative difference. It is a difference that no merely quantitative calculation of processes or forces or laws can ever overcome. Physical reality cannot account for its own existence for the simple reason that nature—the physical—is that which by definition already exists; existence, even taken as a simple brute fact to which no metaphysical theory is attached, lies logically beyond the system of causes that nature comprises; it is, quite literally, "hyperphysical," or, shifting into Latin, *super naturam.* This means not only that at some point nature requires or admits of a supernatural explanation (which it does), but also that at no point is anything purely, self-sufficiently natural in the first place. This is a logical and ontological claim, but a phenomenological, epistemological, and experiential one as well. We have, in fact, no direct access to nature as such; we can approach nature only across the interval of the supernatural. Only through our immediate encounter with the being of a thing are we permitted our wholly mediated experience of that thing as a natural object; we are able to ask *what* it is only in first knowing *that* it is; and so in knowing nature we have always already gone beyond its intrinsic limits. No one lives in a "naturalistic" reality, and the very notion of nature as a perfectly self-enclosed continuum is a figment of the imagination. It is the supernatural of which we have direct certainty, and only in consequence of that can the reality of nature be assumed, not as an absolutely incontrovertible fact but simply as far and away the likeliest supposition.

Herein lies the annoyingly persistent logical error of those physicists (like Alexander Vilenkin, Victor Stenger, or Lawrence Krauss) who claim that physics has now discovered how the universe can have spontaneously arisen from "nothingness," without divine assistance. It does not really matter whether the theoretical models they propose may one day prove to be correct. Without

exception, what they are actually talking about is merely the formation of our universe by way of a transition from one physical
state to another, one manner of existence to another, but certainly
not the spontaneous arising of existence from nonexistence (which
is logically impossible). They often produce perfectly delightful
books on the subject, I hasten to add, considered simply as tours
of the latest developments in speculative cosmology; but as interventions in philosophical debates those books are quite simply
irrelevant. As a matter of purely intellectual interest, it would be
wonderful some day to know whether the universe was generated
out of quantum fluctuation, belongs either to an infinite "ekpy-
rotic" succession of universes caused by colliding branes or to a
"conformally cyclic" succession of bounded aeons, is the result of
inflationary quantum tunneling out of a much smaller universe,
arose locally out of a multiverse in either limited constant or eternal chaotic inflation, or what have you. As a matter strictly of
ontology, however, none of these theories is of any consequence,
because no purely physical cosmology has any bearing whatsoever
upon the question of existence (though one or two such cosmolo-
gies might point in its direction). Again, the "distance" between
being and nonbeing is qualitatively infinite, and so it is immaterial here how small, simple, vacuous, or impalpably indeterminate
a physical state or event is: it is still infinitely removed from nonbeing and infinitely incapable of having created itself out of nothing. That the physical reality we know is the result of other physical realities has more or less been the assumption of most human
cultures throughout history; but that, unfortunately, casts no light
whatsoever on why it is that physical reality, being intrinsically
contingent, should exist at all.

To be clear here: not only has physics not yet arrived at an answer to this question, it never can. All physical events—all physical causes, all physical constituents of reality—are embraced within the history of nature, which is to say the history of what already has existence. The question of existence, however, concerns the very possibility of such a history, and the expectation that the sciences could possibly have anything to say on the matter is an example of what might be called the "pleonastic fallacy": that is, the belief that an absolute qualitative difference can be overcome by a successive accumulation of extremely small and entirely relative quantitative steps. This is arguably the besetting mistake of all naturalist thinking, as it happens, in practically every sphere. In this context, the assumption at work is that if one could only reduce one's picture of the original physical conditions of reality to the barest imaginable elements—say, the "quantum foam" and a handful of laws like the law of gravity, which all looks rather nothing-ish (relatively speaking)—then one will have succeeded in getting as near to nothing as makes no difference. In fact, one will be starting no nearer to nonbeing than if one were to begin with an infinitely realized multiverse: the difference from nonbeing remains infinite in either case. All quantum states are states within an existing quantum system, and all the laws governing that system merely describe its regularities and constraints. Any quantum fluctuation therein that produces, say, a universe is a new state within that system, but not a sudden emergence of reality from nonbeing. Cosmology simply cannot become ontology. The only intellectually consistent course for the metaphysical naturalist is to say that physical reality "just is" and then to leave off there, accepting that this "just is" remains a truth entirely in excess of all physical properties and causes: the single ineradicable "super-natural" fact within which all natural facts are forever contained, but about which we ought not to let ourselves think too much.

III

Probably the best way to grasp what the metaphysical content of the word "God" is in the intellectual traditions of the great theistic faiths, and to see why that word occupies a logical space that no other kind of causal explanation can intrude upon, is to consider the basic shape of all the classical philosophical attempts to deduce the reality of God from the fact of cosmic contingency. Reduced to their simplest, all such arguments begin from some form of what is usually called the principle of causality, which might properly be formulated as: All things that do not possess the cause of their existence in themselves must be brought into existence by something outside themselves. Or, more tersely, the contingent is always contingent on something *else*. This is not a difficult or rationally problematic proposition. The complications lie in its application. Before all else, however, one must define what real contingency is. It is, first, simply the condition of being conditional: that is, the condition of depending upon anything external or prior or circumambient in order to exist and to persist in being. It is also mutability, the capacity to change over time, to move constantly from potential to actual states, and to abandon one actual state in favor of another. It is also the condition of being extended in both space and time, and thus of being incapable of perfect "self-possession" in some absolute here and now. It is the capacity and the tendency both to come into and pass out of being. It is the condition of being composite, made up of and dependent upon logically prior parts, and therefore capable of division and dissolution. It is also, in consequence, the state of possessing limits and boundaries, external and internal, and so of achieving identity through excluding—and thus, inevitably, depending upon—other realities; it is, in short, finitude. This last applies, incidentally, even to the universe as a whole, at least insofar as it is a physical reality (there may be some metaphysical truth of the universe beyond its physical composition, but that is another matter): even a universe physically infinite in both size and duration would still be metaphysically finite, in that it must be complex, admit of processes and changes, be extended, and so on. And most important of all, perhaps, contingency is a logical designation: it is the condition of any essence logically distinct from its own existence—which is to say, the failure of a thing's proper description to provide any intrinsic rationale for that thing's existence.

The conclusion upon which religious metaphysicians East and West have generally agreed is that it cannot possibly be the case that there are *only* contingent realities. If, beyond the scintillating, shifting, intermingling, coalescing, and dissolving spectacle of finitude, there is no reality that is independent, changeless, and logically self-explanatory, then nothing at all could ever come into or be sustained in existence; on the logical "other side" of all contingent things lies nothingness, and nothing can arise from nothing. As Sarvepalli Radhakrishnan writes, in his magisterial exposition of the metaphysics of the *Upanishads,* "Either we must postulate a first cause, in which case causality ceases to be a universal maxim, or we have an endless regress"; this, he says, is a "puzzle" that is resolved only by the further postulation of the "self-existent Brahman" who is "independent of time, space, and cause."[3] Here, I should note, Radhakrishnan is using the word "cause" to mean "contingent cause" or (in Western scholastic terms) "secondary cause" (see below), but otherwise he is merely stating a logical intuition expressed in some form or another in the metaphysical traditions of all the major theistic creeds. It can be found with equal ease in the thought of a Muslim like Ibn Sina (c. 980–1037), of a Vishishtadvaita Hindu like Ramanuja (tenth to eleventh century), of a Christian like Thomas Aquinas (1225–1274), or of any of a vast number of other thinkers. It is simply the intuition that a reality based entirely upon possibility, not "upheld in being" by the creative power of any self-subsistent source of actuality, could not exist at all. Reason seems to dictate that there cannot be an endless regress of purely contingent causes of existence; each cause in that chain would have to be enabled by some logically prior cause, which would itself have to be enabled by another prior cause, and so on, and if this regress were infinite it would never be reducible back to an actual beginning; the sequence, reaching back as it must into an infinite abyss of unrealized possibilities, would never actually begin. Such an infinite regress would therefore be equivalent to nonexistence. On the other hand, neither could this chain of prior causes be traced back simply to some first finite thing, as nothing intrinsically contingent can come into being without a prior cause; the first cause could not be some limited thing that just magically happens to be there. So a finite regress of dependent causes would also be equivalent to nonexistence. At some point, then, at the source of all sources and origin of all origins, the contingent must rest upon the absolute.

One will not understand this line of reasoning properly, however, unless one recognizes that it is not concerned with the question of the temporal origins of the universe; it would make no difference for the argument whatsoever if it should turn out that the universe has existed forever and will go on existing eternally, without beginning or end, or that it belongs to some beginningless and endless succession of universes. The aforementioned Ramanuja, for instance, had no concept of an absolute beginning to the universe, and he was quite unambiguous in asserting that creation ought to be thought of not as some event occurring in time, but as the logical dependency of the world (in all its recurring cycles) upon God. Ibn Sina (or Avicenna, to give his Latin name) believed that the cosmos was eternal, rather eccentrically for a Muslim perhaps, but still argued that all contingent realities must ultimately depend on one uncaused cause that has "necessary being of itself" (*wajib al-wujud bi-dhatihi*). Thomas, on the other hand, happened to believe as a matter of faith that the created order did have a first moment, but he explicitly stated that there is no independent philosophical warrant for assuming the cosmos has not always existed, and strictly distinguished the question of cosmic beginnings from the question of creation. Whenever he spoke of the "first cause" of beings he was referring to an ontological, not a chronological, priority; and it was solely with this sort of causal priority that he was concerned in, for instance, the first three of his Five Ways (even the third, which is often mistaken—due partly to its almost telegraphic terseness—for an argument regarding how the universe started).[4]

If all of this seems somewhat obscure—how, that is, the putative beginning of the universe differs logically from the creation of
the universe out of nothing, or why the affirmation of one has no
logical relevance to an affirmation of the other—it might be worthwhile to invoke an old Western scholastic distinction between
those causal relations that are "accidental" (*per accidens*) and those
that are "essential" or "intrinsic" (*per se*). The former are principally physical relations (in the broadest sense): transitions of energy, movements of mass, acts of generation or destruction, and so
on. In an extended series of such relations, the consequences of a
particular thing can continue indefinitely after that thing has dis-
appeared, because all causes in the series are ontologically extrinsic
to their effects. The classic example is that of the causal relation
between a man and his grandson: by the time the latter is sired the
former may have been dead for decades; the first act of begetting
was not the *direct* cause of the second. The relation is one of ante-
cedent physical history, not of immediate ontological dependency,
and so the *being* of the grandson does not directly depend upon
the *being* of his grandfather. An example on a grander scale might
be Roger Penrose's postulate of an infinite sequence of universes
that always meet at conformal past and future boundaries: even
this beginningless and endless cosmogonic cycle would add up
to only a causal sequence per accidens. So it may be logically
conceivable that an infinite "horizontal" chain of accidental causes
could exist (I happen to believe, incidentally, that there are insuperable logical problems with such a notion, but they are not relevant here). But even if this kind of eternal chain of events and
substances really were to exist, it would remain the case that, inasmuch as none of the links in that chain could be the source of its

own existence, this entire series of causes and effects would be a contingent reality and would still have to be sustained in being by a "vertical"—a per se or ontological—causality; and this second kind of causal chain most definitely cannot have an infinite number of links. The ultimate source of *existence* cannot be some item or event that has long since passed away or concluded, like a venerable ancestor or even the Big Bang itself—either of which is just another contingent physical entity or occurrence—but must be a constant wellspring of being, at work even now. The metaphor for this sort of ontological dependency that all the great religious traditions seem to share is that of the relation of a candle's or lamp's flame to the light it casts out into a room at night: should the flame be extinguished, in that very instant the room would fall dark. More recent philosophers have sometimes used the image of an electric current that, if shut off at the source, ceases along all power lines at once. Whatever simile takes one's fancy, the cause of being is not some mechanical first instance of physical eventuality that, having discharged its part, may depart the stage; rather, it is the unconditional reality underlying all conditioned things in every instant.

Why is this so? Why must a thing be dependent on any continuously real source of being in order to persist? Why can it not, once it has been caused to exist by something else, just continue on from its physical origin with a kind of existential inertia until it exhausts itself, without any need for some eternal "absolute" to certify it in its contingent existence? Again, though, these questions arise from a confusion between two different orders of cause. When thinking about the cause of some particular thing's *being*— as opposed to thinking about its physical origin—we must do so with an eye to the absolutely conditional nature of that thing. If one considers the terms of one's own existence, for instance, one sees that there is no sense in which one is ever self-existent; one is dependent on an incalculable number of ever greater and ever smaller finite conditions, some of which are temporal, and some of which definitely are not, and all of which are themselves dependent on yet further conditions. One is composed of parts, and those parts of smaller parts, and so on down to the subatomic level, which itself is a realm of contingently subsistent realities that flicker in and out of actuality, that have no ontological ground in themselves, and that are all embraced within a quantum field that contains no more of an essential rationale for its own existence than does any other physical reality. One also belongs to a wider world, upon all of whose physical systems one is also dependent in every moment, while that world is itself dependent upon an immense range of greater physical realities, and upon abstract mathematical and logical laws, and upon the whole contingent history of our quite unnecessary universe. And one is most immediately dependent on the utterly fortuitous and always dynamically incomplete union of essence and existence that one is. In short, all finite things are always, in the present, being sustained in existence by conditions that they cannot have supplied for themselves, and that together compose a universe that, as a *physical* reality, lacks the obviously supernatural power necessary to exist on its own. Nowhere in any of that is a source of existence as such. It is this entire order of ubiquitous conditionality—this entire ensemble of dependent realities—that the classical arguments say cannot be reducible either to an infinite regress of contingent causes or to a first contingent cause. There must then be some truly *un-*

conditioned reality (which, by definition, cannot be temporal or spatial or in any sense finite) upon which all else depends; otherwise nothing could exist at all. And it is this unconditioned and eternally sustaining source of being that classical metaphysics, East and West, identifies as God.[5]

Two other traditional scholastic distinctions might be of some additional help here: that between a *causa in esse* and a *causa in fieri;* and that between the one *causa prima* and the many *causae secundae.* An essential cause or cause "in being" (in esse) is that donation of being, or continuous influx of actuality, that gives existence to what cannot exist of itself, while a cause "in becoming" (in fieri) is an accidental or limited substance or force or event, which can influence other things of the same kind but which does not have the source of its being in itself. The highest causa in esse, therefore, is the "prime cause" of reality, pouring forth its infinite actuality in the finite vessels of individual essences, while "secondary causes" are created and limited realities, with the power to affect and be affected, but lacking the power to create from nothing. The metaphysical concept of creation concerns only the former kind of causality. As Thomas Aquinas rightly points out, therefore, creation from nothingness cannot be some event that occurs at a given moment within time. Neither can it constitute a transition from one state of reality to another, since nothingness is not some kind of substance in which a change can take place. It is wholly an act of prime or essential causation, the eternal gift of *esse* or *sat* or *wujud* (or what have you) to a reality that has no ground of being in itself. And God, therefore, is the creator of all things not as the first temporal agent in cosmic history (which would make him not the prime cause of creation but only the initial secondary cause within it), but as the eternal reality in which "all things live, and move, and have their being," present in all things as the actuality of all actualities, transcendent of all things as the changeless source from which all actuality flows. It is only when one properly understands this distinction that one can also understand what the contingency of created things might tell us about who and what God is.

IV

One of the more provocatively counterintuitive ways of expressing the difference between God and every contingent reality is to say that God, as the source of all being, is, properly speaking, not himself *a* being—or, if one prefer, not a being among other beings. Nicholas of Cusa (1401–1464), for instance, spoke of God as the *non aliud:* the "not other" or "not something else." For the Neoplatonist Plotinus (c. 204–270), the divine is that which is no particular thing, or even "no-thing." The same is true for Christians such as John Scotus Eriugena (c. 815–c. 877) or Meister Eckhart (c. 1260–c. 1327). Angelus Silesius, precisely in order to affirm that God is the omnipotent creator of all things, described God as *"ein lauter Nichts"*—"a pure nothingness"—and even (a touch of neologistic panache here) *"ein Übernichts."* If this all sounds either perilously blasphemous or preciously paradoxical, this is because language of this sort is meant to give us pause, or even offense, in order to remind us as forcefully as possible that, as the great Muslim philosopher Mulla Sadra (c. 1572–1640) insisted, God is not to be found within the realm of beings, for he is the being of all realms. Or, as the Anglican E. L. Mascall put it, God is not "just one item, albeit the supreme one, in a class of beings" but is rather "the source from which their being is derived." Thus God does not "exist" in the sense that some finite object like a tree, an individual mind, or perhaps a god exists, but is himself the very power of unconditioned being from and in which anything that does exist has its dependent and imparted being. This is not to say, however, that God is somehow the totality of all beings (which would still be a finite, bounded, composite, and contingent reality). It is to say rather that he is the indivisible and always transcendent actuality out of which all things receive their immanent actuality in every possible respect. To quote Radhakrishnan again, this time commenting on the thought of the great Advaita Vedantist Adi Shankara (eighth century), to think of God in our categories of existence "would be to reduce God to the level of the finite, making him simply a unit in the indefinite multiplicity of objects, distinct from them all, even as they are distinct from each other, or merging him in the totality of existence in a pantheism which will be practically indistinguishable from atheism."[6]

Now, of course, words like "being" and "existence" are not univocal terms, each having only one fixed meaning irrespective of context. The precise sense in which God is *not* a being, or indeed the sense in which he could even be said not to "exist," is as some discrete object, essentially distinct from all others, "standing forth" (which is what "exist" means, etymologically speaking) from being as such. *A* being of that kind—one to which the indefinite article properly attaches—possesses a certain determinate number of attributes, a certain quantity of potentialities, a certain degree of actuality, and so on, and is at once both intrinsically composite and extrinsically enumerable: that is, every particular being is made up of a collection of parts and is also itself a discrete item within the sum total of existing things. All of this is precisely what classical metaphysical theism says God is not. He is instead the infinite to which nothing can add and from which nothing can subtract, and he himself is not some object in addition to other objects. He is the source and fullness of all being, the actuality in which all finite things live, move, and have their being, or in which all things hold together; and so he is also the reality that is present in all things as the very act of their existence. God, in short, is not a being but is at once "beyond being" (in the sense that he transcends the totality of existing things) and also absolute "Being itself" (in the sense that he is the source and ground of all things). As Sufi tradition says, God is *al-Haqq,* Reality as such, underlying everything. All finite things are limited expressions, graciously imparted, of that actuality that he possesses in infinite abundance. And, simply said, this way of thinking about God is—or so the classical traditions claim—the inevitable result of any genuinely coherent attempt to prescind from the conditions of dependent finitude to a rational definition of the divine.

Another venerable way of formulating the difference of God's being from ours is to say that, whereas our being is wholly contingent, his is "necessary." That, at any rate, is the traditional Western term, though the same idea is found in principle in all the major theistic traditions. In the simplest sense, what this means is that God's nature is such that he quite simply cannot *not* be; his being does not admit of the possibility of nonbeing, as ours must, but transcends that distinction between potentiality and actuality that grants us our finite identities. He is not just something actual, but actuality itself, the uncaused source and ground by which finite actuality and finite potentiality alike are created and sustained (for, without him, nothing is even possible). In one sense, reason arrives at this notion of divine necessity as a kind of purely negative deduction about God, at the end of a progressive logical elimination of everything that makes finite reality contingent in its very essence: conditionality, composition, mutability, boundaries and contrasts and exclusions, and so on. Nothing in the realm of physical existence is beyond the possibility of nonexistence, and no order of magnitude alters this fact; even an infinity of universes would amount only, ontologically speaking, to an infinity of *unnecessary* contingencies, an infinite reiteration of the mystery of existence. In another, more crucial sense, however, talk of God's ontological necessity also has a positive rational content. It serves as a reminder not only of everything that the divine nature is not, but also of the kind of reality that the divine nature is; otherwise it would be no more than an assertion at which one arrives when reason can go no further, with no more force than a sigh of pious ignorance. If nothing else, ontological necessity cannot be merely some natural property that God happens to possess, in the way that I might happen to possess blue eyes or you a deep attraction to persons with blue eyes, or in the way a sage might possess wisdom or a dancer athletic grace. Necessity cannot simply be an attribute possessed by *a* being; it is, rather, a unique logical designation of what God is, or even *who* God is; it is, so to speak, one of his proper names: "I am that I am."

I shall pursue that claim a little further in just a moment. First, however, I should note that there are a number of atheist thinkers who are quite willing to grant the dialectical force of the general

argument leading from the contingency of finite things to a necessary first cause, but who believe it is possible to see the universe
itself as such a first cause, without any further postulate of a God.
It may be the case that the universe is the totality of all physical
realities, they contend, and yet perhaps not the case that the universe is subject as a whole to the contingency intrinsic to its con-
stituent parts. True, the universe cannot create itself from nothing,
as that is logically impossible, and it may be that every single particle in the cosmos is a contingent reality; but the whole may be
far greater than its parts, and very different in nature, and so perhaps the universe might itself be the necessary reality that grounds
all dependent realities, the absolute upon which the contingent
rests. In fact, is not the notion that a totality must possess the same
attributes as its parts what some philosophers call the "composi-
tional fallacy"? The problem with this line of reasoning, however,
is that it covertly violates the boundaries of naturalistic thinking
and so defeats itself. We can certainly concede that a whole is often
far more than the sum of its parts, and as a rule differs from them
in kind. An arboretum constructed from bricks and mortar, tiles
and timber, glass and frames is an arboretum, not a brick or a tile
or a pane of glass. But, that granted, the degree of difference between any whole and its parts still has a certain metaphysical limit.
If one were operating within the context of a philosophy that allowed for those "higher causes" of which I spoke above, then of
course one could presume that, say, the formal cause of the arboretum is in a very radical way different in nature from the materials
it organizes. Even then, though, the material edifice informed by
that higher cause could not differ in essential nature from its physical parts. However much of an advance in formal sophistication

the arboretum is over the brick, it has still been constructed from perishable physical objects and so is itself a perishable physical object; bricks cannot be combined, however ingenious the architect, into an indestructible and immaterial building. No reality entirely composed of contingent ingredients can fail to be a contingent reality, conditional upon what composes it. And, as I mentioned above, modern scientific doctrine is generally in agreement on the broader principle here: there are no such things in nature as "emergent" wholes that cannot be mathematically reduced to the properties of their parts. So, as long as the universe is taken to be a physical reality (which, one assumes, an atheist would insist it must be), it is a composite of its parts and certainly cannot add up to a metaphysical reality that possesses a power of self-subsistence wholly unprecedented in nature.

Perhaps, however—and this line of argument has its champions —it is not as a physical composite but as the physical expression of certain immutable mathematical truths that the universe necessarily exists. Its necessity need not have emerged from its constituents; rather, those constituents may have been created and arranged by a set of laws and formulae so elementary and powerful that they can spontaneously confer existence upon physical reality. At some higher level, then, the universe as a whole may well be necessary, even though at the material level it comprises only contingent things. The cost of such an argument seems, however, rather exorbitant for the committed naturalist. Physical laws, after all, are usually regarded as abstractions that do no more than describe a reality that already exists, and abstract mathematical concepts are usually regarded as rather existentially inert. The moment one ascribes to mathematical functions and laws a rational and ontological power to create, one is talking no longer about nature (in the naturalist sense) at all, but about a metaphysical force capable of generating the physical out of the intellectual: an ideal reality transcendent of and yet able to produce all the material properties of the cosmos, a realm of pure paradigms that is also a creative actuality, an eternal reality that is at once the rational structure of the universe and the power giving it existence. In short, one is talking about the mind of God. I, for one, happen to find that kind of vaguely Pythagorean approach to divine reality extremely appealing, for various reasons; but I sincerely doubt that a truly severe and sinewy atheist, jaws firmly set and eyes fiercely agleam, could really derive much joy from an idealist mysticism of that sort, or happily adopt the strategy of avoiding the word "God" only by periphrastically substituting the word "universe." In the end, ontological necessity is not a property that can intelligibly attach to any nature other than God's. If one wishes to view the physical universe as the ultimate reality—whether one imagines it as having no beginning or as having a beginning without cause—then one must also accept that it is still an entirely contingent reality, one which somehow just happens to be there: an "absolute contingency," to use an unavoidable oxymoron. It may be an absurd picture of things—certainly there seems to be no argument against it more potent than its own perfectly self-evident incoherence—but it seems to me to be an absurdity that one can quite blamelessly embrace so long as one is willing to grasp the nettle and accept that this just-there-ness is logically indistinguishable from magic. Everyone needs a little magic in life now and then.

V

What, then, is necessity in the proper sense—the "necessity" that I claim is one of God's proper names? What does it entail? I am tempted to say that this is a rather simple matter, and certainly there is nearly universal assent among the traditions on what it is in God's nature that distinguishes him from those things whose existence is contingent: God is not composite and so is indissoluble, he is infinite and unconditioned and so is not dependent on anything else, he is eternal and so does not come into being, he is the source of his own being and hence in him there is no division between what he is and that he is, and so on. And, as I have said, these affirmations arise chiefly from a sort of deductive negation of all the obvious conditions of finitude; one can see what it is about, for instance, a tree that makes it contingent, and thus one can see how these same features must be absent from the uncaused cause on which things like trees depend. Alas, simple matters often become devilishly complex when the basic assumptions of the world around them change. The very idea that there could be such a thing as "necessary being" seems a difficult one for many modern Anglophone philosophers who, fettered as they are to certain analytic presuppositions, think of necessity as only a logical property of certain propositions, such as mathematical axioms; and, frankly, many theistic analytic philosophers who feel they have to justify the idea in terms amenable to those presuppositions often create the greatest confusions of all.

I should step back before completing that thought, however, and point out that philosophers often distinguish between the claim that something is "metaphysically necessary" and the claim that something is "logically necessary." The former would describe only something that, if it happens to exist at all, also possesses the quite wondrous attribute of being eternal and incapable of dissolution. Aristotle, for instance, considered the cosmos to be necessary in this sense, since he believed it to be without an origin and incapable of coming to an end. Necessity of this sort, therefore, is a kind of property inhering in a certain kind of substance, but is in no way an explanation of the existence of that substance. To say that something is metaphysically necessary is to say only that it is physically unoriginated and indestructible; but this still tells us nothing of why that thing exists at all. In the case of God, therefore, it would clearly not be enough to say that he possesses only metaphysical necessity. As the formidable atheist philosopher J. L. Mackie observed, any "being" that just happens to be "necessary" in this sense would be "just there," quite inexplicably endowed with the strange but enviable (or, for that matter, unenviable) state of being incapable of not existing. Its just-there-ness would be no less magical—no less purely "happenstantial," so to speak—than that of the "absolute contingent universe" in which the naturalist believes. So a god conceived as necessary in only this sense would not provide any ultimate solution to the question of existence but would himself be just another existential mystery added to all the others. The regress of ontological causes would still not have reached back to its first term. As the now rather old joke goes, God would be just the ultimate turtle at the base of the tower of turtles on which the world is balanced; but upon what would he then be standing?

The great theistic philosophers have always understood this. Thomas Aquinas and Ibn Sina, for instance, were willing to use the term "necessity" in its Aristotelian acceptation and so to ascribe metaphysical necessity to a number of created things; but they also quite clearly stipulated that such necessity was of only a derivative kind, a "necessity by way of another." God alone, by contrast, has necessity in and of himself. That is, if the word "God" has any meaning at all, it must refer to a reality that is not just metaphysically indestructible but necessary in the fullest and most proper sense; it must refer to a reality that is *logically* necessary and that therefore provides the ultimate explanation of all other realities, without need of being explained in turn. And logical necessity is nothing less than the *analytic*—that is, the a priori—impossibility of something either not existing or being otherwise than it is. It is, in a sense, perfectly convertible with the essence of what it defines, in the way that the necessity of a mathematical equation is convertible with the correct definition of all the parts of that equation. In the case of God, then, a logically correct description of what the word "God" means would necessarily imply that there is no coherent sense in which God could not be. Modern philosophers often express this as the proposition that God must exist in all possible worlds, though that is, to my mind, a badly defective way of putting the matter, for any number of reasons. I would prefer to say that no world is possible apart from God's necessity (as I shall shortly discuss). Whatever the case, though, when talking about the source of all reality, the distinction between metaphysical and logical necessity is merely formal, as each is inseparable from and ultimately convertible with the other: God is really metaphysically necessary only if he is logically necessary, and vice versa. This, however, requires some amplification.

Perhaps the most famous attempt in Christian tradition to

demonstrate the logical necessity of God—which is to say, to demonstrate God's reality in purely a priori terms, based simply on the very concept of God, without recourse to any deductions from empirical experience—is that of Anselm of Canterbury (c. 1033–1109). Known as the "ontological argument" (unfortunately), it has never lacked for defenders, even if the weight of philosophical opinion has generally tilted the scales against it. Descartes and others have defended it in various restated forms, and it has been creatively reappropriated in recent decades by a number of thinkers. It has also been rejected by figures as different as Thomas Aquinas and Immanuel Kant (1724–1804)—although Kant's complaint, while widely celebrated, is more a confusion than a solvent critique. And arguments analogous to Anselm's can be found in other traditions as well; among the figures I have cited above, both Mulla Sadra (explicitly) and Shankara (implicitly) pursued similar lines of reasoning. Stated in the most pristine form Anselm gives it, the argument is that God must be conceived as "id quo maius cogitari nequit"—"that than which it is impossible to think anything greater"—which definition supposedly entails existence, because an existent reality surpasses a merely suppositious one in greatness; thus we must affirm that God exists or accept the contradiction that we can conceive of something yet greater than that reality than which none greater can be conceived. Needless to say, this is not an argument that immediately compels assent. It is not quite as lacking in subtlety as some of its detractors imagine, and it has certainly yielded a remarkably rich array of philosophical meditations over the centuries. But it still seems to make far too extravagant a leap from the realm of the conceptual to that of the real. Thomas Aquinas rejected the argument on the grounds that, while we must affirm the logical necessity of God's being as a strictly rational postulate, it is not a truth at which we can arrive by way of our own conceptual powers. We would have to have a direct knowledge and understanding of the essence of God in order to "see," a priori, the logical impossibility of his not being, and no finite mind is capable of that. For Thomas, therefore, it is a truth we arrive at only indirectly, in some sense negatively, by reasoning to God a posteriori as the prime cause of all finite things, and only then coming to the additional conclusion that the prime cause of all things cannot be causally or logically dependent on anything beyond itself, and so must be intrinsically necessary. I happen to think that Thomas's criticism is ever so slightly off the mark; but, even so, I think it clearly correct that, in almost every form in which it has been stated and restated, Anselm's argument fails as a proof of the existence of some discrete particular being out there called "God." Curiously enough, however, I see this as its one peculiar strength. Read from a different angle, it succeeds (if only implicitly and perhaps only by inadvertence) as a partial but illuminating definition of the word "God," and as a demonstration that God has necessary being precisely *because* he is not some discrete particular being that can be numbered as one among other beings.

That may sound like an attempt at coy paradox, but I think I am saying something fairly straightforward. To make my point plain, however, I should probably say precisely what I think Anselm's argument does not and *cannot* accomplish; and, as it happens, this involves rejecting most current attempts by Christian philosophers to recover that argument in a properly analytic form.

At present, as it happens, those in the academic world who are most sympathetic to Anselm's argument tend to defend it in terms of a particular approach to modal logic (that is, logic concerning possibility and impossibility, contingency and necessity) that yields precisely the sort of result that, to my mind, reduces the whole idea of God's necessity to meaninglessness. The best characterization of this "modal version" of the argument that I can manage is to say that it is an attempt to deduce God's logical necessity from his metaphysical necessity, and to deduce his metaphysical necessity from its mere logical possibility, and to deduce that logical possibility merely from the fact of there being no obvious logical contradiction entailed in it. That is a long and perilous path for any argument to tread. There are, however, some very formidable thinkers who believe that it can be followed safely to its end. The most ingenious proponent of this modal revision of Anselm's argument to date has been the distinguished American philosopher Alvin Plantinga. He argues that God can and should be conceived as "a being" who possesses a property called "maximal greatness," and that such a being, if his existence is logically possible, must exist in some possible world. Or, rather, as Plantinga would prefer to phrase the matter (for reasons that are sound but not important here), there is some possible world in which the property of maximal greatness is instantiated or exemplified. Maximal greatness, however, involves not only "maximal excellence" (all possible virtues, powers, and so on) but also necessary existence (supposedly an indispensable "great-making" property); and since a necessary truth is by definition true in every possible reality, in the way that mathematical truths or other strictly logical truths must be, any being with maximal greatness in one possible world must have necessary existence not only in that world but in all possible worlds, including ours.

Obviously, I am not doing Plantinga's argument much justice in condensing it to a few lines, and he is not a man with whom I am particularly eager to cross modal swords; but this argument seems clearly false to me, not just in form but in principle, and for reasons that I think extremely important here. I do not believe one can deduce logical necessity from mere logical possibility, and especially not by way of that sort of "happenstantial" metaphysical necessity. Even if one grants the legitimacy of using talk of possible worlds as a way of determining what is metaphysically possible—even if, that is, one thinks something must be *really* possible just because it seems to entail no obvious logical *contradiction*— the idea of some particular being who possesses "necessary existence," simply as some kind of attribute among other attributes, is bafflingly obscure, as Mackie realized. How could such a being just be there? Would he not be only contingently or derivatively "necessary," and so *necessary* only because he *happens* to exist, and therefore not necessary in the fullest sense? What, in fact, could necessity mean in such a context? Are we not perhaps conflating metaphysical and logical necessity here, without any clear warrant for doing so? After all, it is true that whatever is logically necessary is by definition necessarily the case in every possible world. Two added to two must yield four in any possible frame of reality. But it is certainly not true that any *being* that might just happen to be metaphysically necessary must also exist in every possible world; and surely it is only the existence of a metaphysically necessary being in some possible world that Plantinga's reasoning establishes, since there is no reason to think that the idea of a discrete being who "exemplifies" logical necessity is coherent or meaningful. This being so, it certainly seems that Plantinga's argument must be reversible: since we are talking only about possible worlds and about maximal greatness only as some property possibly instantiated in one of them, and then only because it is a property that does not *seem* to entail a contradiction, we might just as well say that it is always possible to conceive a world in which maximal greatness is *not* instantiated, which means that there is a possible world in which God does *not* exist, which means that he cannot be logically necessary in all possible worlds and so cannot possess necessary existence in any. Nor can one say, using just this talk of logical possibility, that Plantinga's argument has already somehow precluded the possibility of such a godless world; the reverse seems more likely, since the logical content of the claim that some particular being is necessary is terrifically uncertain. The conceivable possibility of a godless world might then turn out to be, after all, a contradiction inherent in the very notion of maximal greatness.

Anyway, I do not want to become entangled in needless complications on this matter, and so I am quite happy to demote all my doubts regarding Plantinga's argument to the lowly status of mere open questions. In truth, they are scarcely important here, because the chief point I want to make is that this is not really an argument about God at all. At least it clearly does not fit the classical pattern of theism. To put the matter very simply, the great traditions would not speak of God merely as some being who might exist *in* some possible world, if only because that seems to make God's reality conditional on some set of prior logical possibilities, which would appear to exclude real logical necessity from his nature at the outset, as well as to contradict the essential claim that he and he alone is the source of all reality. Rather, they proceed in just the opposite fashion and seek to show that the logical possibility of any world at all is conditional upon the prior logical necessity of God. That is to say, God is not *a* being who *might* and therefore *must* exist, but is absolute Being as such, apart from whom nothing else could exist, as either a possibility or an actuality. In God, logical possibility does not translate into logical necessity; it is instead God's necessity, as the unconditioned source of all things, that makes any world possible in the first place. In the simplest terms, no contingent reality could exist at all if there were not a necessary dimension of reality sustaining it in existence, and that is the dimension to which the word "God" properly points. And here, I think, Anselm's famous phrase—commencing as it does with that chastely noncommittal and obligingly obscure "*id*"—flowers into a significance so simple as to be almost trivially true. That than which it is impossible to conceive anything greater is not a being among other beings, not even the greatest possible of beings, but is instead the fullness of Being itself, the absolute plenitude of reality upon which all else depends; and manifestly it would be meaningless to say that Being lacks being or that Reality is not real.

VI

What then, at last, does it really mean to say that God is "Being" or Reality or the source and ground of all reality? What does it mean to think of him as Sufism's al-Haqq, or Jewish mysticism's

Great Reality or "Root of all roots," or Thomas's *actus essendi subsistens* (subsistent act of being), or Eckhart's *Istigkeit* ("Is-ness"), or so on? Can it mean anything at all, or have all the intellectual traditions of the great faiths, throughout their long histories, and despite the enormous number of very impressive minds that have contributed to them, been mired in sheer nonsense on this matter? Some contemporary philosophers—theist, atheist, and agnostic alike—think that they have been. They are quite mistaken, in fact, but theirs is at least an instructive mistake.

I should probably note here that, in the analytic tradition of Anglo-American philosophy, the issue tends to be complicated on the one hand by the methods and conceptual rules generally preferred by analytic thinkers, and on the other by the lack of historical perspective that those methods and rules often encourage. The analytic tradition is pervaded by the mythology of "pure" philosophical discourse, a propositional logic that somehow floats above the historical and cultural contingency of ideas and words, and that somehow can be applied to every epoch of philosophy without any proper attention to what the language and conceptual schemes of earlier thinkers meant in their own times and places. This is a pernicious error under the best of conditions, but it has worked arguably its greatest mischief in the realm of ontology, often as a result of principles that, truth be told, are almost entirely arbitrary.

For one thing, in analytic circles existence is quite often discussed in terms not of what "being" is, or even of what it means for a thing actually to exist, but merely of the grammar of predication. Gottlob Frege (1848–1925), one of the great gray patriarchs of the analytic tribe, argued that the assertion that something exists cannot, properly speaking, concern some concrete thing or other, as one might vulgarly assume, but can apply only to the general category or categories under which that thing might be classed. It is a statement, that is, only about whether a concept (say, "man" or "woman") has at least one concrete instance out there, and definitely not about some particular object. Frege had noticed a certain untidy logical asymmetry between the way we talk about the existence of things and the way we talk about their nonexistence. If you say that some object does *not* exist, after all, your claim cannot actually be about that object as a concrete reality, because if that thing does not exist then it cannot be a real subject of any predications; if existence language were really about concrete objects, the assertion that "Basilisks do not exist" would be equivalent to the assertion that "Those basilisks that exist do not exist." So, if common usage is to be syntactically *systematic* (which, according to the somewhat occult propensities of analytic thought, means *correct*), it must be that when I claim that, say, the dolphin sitting on my veranda drinking coffee exists, I am not really saying anything about that dolphin, and not merely because we find it unbelievable that a dolphin could do such things (keep your assumptions to yourself), but chiefly because to say the opposite—that he does not exist—would look a bit odd when translated into logical notation. Thus what I must be taken to mean is that, among concrete things, there is at least one something out there that instantiates the concept being-a-dolphin. And I hyphenate those last three words to emphasize that the "being" in question belongs primarily to the conceptual realm of delphinity, and not to the actual dolphin sitting on my veranda (who by now may have finished his coffee). This general logic, moreover, extends to how we conceive of all the attributes possessed by a concrete thing: all properties belong to a realm of conceptual abstractions, and they exist only insofar as they are instantiated or exemplified in at least one concrete thing. Therefore, one may say that, in the particular dolphin in question, the properties of genial personality, superlative good taste, and fondness for coffee are exemplified. Still, strictly speaking, it would not be quite proper to say that it is this genial, urbane, coffee-bibbing cetacean as such that exists.

Now, a casual observer might be tempted to regard all this as no more than an insignificant grammatical quibble, demonstrating only that a perfectly intelligible statement in ordinary language is not necessarily one that can be fitted into a totally consistent system of predicative logic, and so to conclude that syntactical consistency is therefore not always of primary importance in helping us to understand reality. But something like Frege's approach, while it has been qualified and disputed over the years, still exercises a strangely potent stricture on ontological reflection for some philosophers today, even some who want to talk about the dependency of creation upon God. The results have often been unfortunate. For one thing, it has made it very hard for many of those philosophers to make much sense of the ancient and necessary premise, common to all classical theistic philosophies, that the words we use about God, to the extent that we use them correctly, have meanings only remotely analogous to what those same words mean when we use them of created things. When we speak of the goodness or wisdom of God, for instance, we cannot imagine that he is good or wise in the same manner as a finite person, who naturally possesses such attributes in an inconstant and imperfect way; in fact, according to most traditional schools, we really should not think of God as having plural attributes at all, but should rather think of words like "goodness" and "wisdom," when applied to God, only as appropriate ways of naming the single undifferentiated divine reality upon which goodness and wisdom in us are dependent (I shall return to this shortly). And when we speak of God's *being,* we are pointing toward something incomprehensibly greater than and qualitatively different from the being of a finite thing. In post-Fregean analytic terms, however, there is very little room for this sort of analogy, open at one end (so to speak) to a meaning that we can only faintly grasp. In analytic terms, existence is often no more than the instantiation of some concept or other, and so everything that exists must exist in precisely the same sense: as a conceptual possibility that happens to have at least one instance out there somewhere. And, of course, all attributes must exist in the same way as well: as abstract properties exemplified in at least one concrete exemplification. Thus to say that God is good or wise is to say that in him those attributes are "instantiated" in much the same way that they might be instantiated in us (though, of course, we may presume that God exemplifies goodness or wisdom better, more consistently, and more efficaciously than we do).

The most curious aspect of this approach to "existence" language, as should be obvious, is that it has absolutely nothing to do with *real* existence at all. Frege's rules regarding how an assertion of existence should be grammatically assigned are ways of talking about *talking about* existence, rather than ways of talking about existence as such. The possibility of actual existence is just blandly assumed, as though there were no mystery to ponder there at all: to say something "exists" means simply that some concept is instantiated, as opposed to not being instantiated, and nothing more; what causes or allows for this instantiation to be a real concrete event in the first place is not really considered. Seen thus, the difference between existence and nonexistence is not ontological, but merely propositional. But how does that help us? A reasonable person, uncorrupted by analytic modes of discourse, might wonder whether something can be said about what concrete existence actually *is:* How is it that any *thing* exists within a world of other existent things? What allows a concrete thing to subsist at all, despite its obvious contingency? It is only in asking this question (which it would be supremely irrational to ignore or dismiss as unintelligible) that it becomes possible for the philosopher to address the question of God meaningfully. Only if the difference between God and creatures can be contemplated as the difference between absolute *actual* being and contingent *actual* being can the word "God" illuminate the mystery of existence in the way classical theism assumes it does.

Many Anglophone theistic philosophers who deal with these issues today, however, reared as they have been in a post-Fregean intellectual environment, have effectively broken with classical theistic tradition altogether, adopting a style of thinking that the Dominican philosopher Brian Davies calls theistic personalism. I prefer to call it monopolytheism myself (or perhaps "monopoly-theism"), since it seems to me to involve a view of God not conspicuously different from the polytheistic picture of the gods as merely very powerful discrete entities who possess a variety of distinct attributes that lesser entities also possess, if in smaller measure; it differs from polytheism, as far as I can tell, solely in that it posits the existence of only one such being. It is a way of thinking that suggests that God, since he is only a particular instantiation of various concepts and properties, is logically dependent on some more comprehensive reality embracing both him and other beings. For philosophers who think in this way, practically all the traditional metaphysical attempts to understand God as the source of all reality become impenetrable. Almost invariably, moreover, the departure from traditional metaphysical claims is prompted by a vaguely Fregean style of thinking, casually applied even where it has no discernible relevance. To take a particularly important example: There is an ancient metaphysical doctrine that the source of all things—God, that is—must be essentially simple; that is, God cannot possess distinct parts, or even distinct properties, and in himself does not allow even of a distinction between essence and existence. I shall discuss this idea below, very soon. Here I shall only record my conviction that the idea is not open to dispute if one believes that God stands at the end of reason's journey toward the truth of all things; it seems obvious to me that a denial of divine simplicity is tantamount to atheism, and the vast preponderance of metaphysical tradition concurs with that judgment. And yet there are today Christian philosophers of an analytic bent who are quite content to cast the doctrine aside, either in whole or in part. I can think of two very prominent American Protestant philosophers, for instance, both regarded as redoubtable champions of theism against its cultured despisers, who do just that with some regularity. One of them likes to argue that in God there must be a real distinction between his essence and his attributes, because attributes are causally inert abstract properties, and God is clearly not just an abstract property. The other has occasionally argued that God's existence and omnipotence cannot be the same reality, because many things possess existence while not possessing omnipotence.[7]

It would be hard to exaggerate the anachronism in such arguments. Reading them, one might never guess that the metaphysical traditions under discussion concern a concept of being that is perfectly cogent in itself but that differs radically from the concepts with which these philosophers are working. One might also never guess that there are some very compelling reasons for saying that God's being cannot be just another instance of the same sort of being that creatures have. To understand the traditional theistic approach to the matter, one has to step back from Anglo-American philosophy's parochial tendency to treat all ideas as either successful or deficient attempts to comply with the rules of contemporary analytic habit, and adopt instead a certain "hermeneutical" respect for the past—a certain willingness to try to understand earlier philosophical systems in their own terms, that is. Philosophy is a history, not a single method, and the meanings of words like "existence" or "attributes" are not static across the span of that history. Analytic method is only one narrow stream of that history, moreover, even if its practitioners too often imagine that it is actually some kind of propositional science capable of addressing all ideas meaningfully, and it is simply silly to allow currently fashionable doctrines about predicative grammar so to determine how one thinks about the question of being and the question of God that one loses sight of how each illumines or qualifies the other. It is that universal and primordial human experience of simple wonder at the being of things to which all true philosophy is ultimately answerable. In purely philosophical terms, then, it simply does not matter very much if some god named "God" might happen to exist, even if he should prove to be the unsurpassable and unique instantiation of the concept "god," as that fact casts no real light on the enigma of existence as such. Even if this demiurge really existed, he would still be just one more being out there whose own existence would be in need of explanation; one would still have to look past him and his marvelous works in order to contemplate what is truly ultimate: the original source of being upon which he and the world must both be dependent. Confronted by so constrained a concept of God, the village atheist would still be well within his rights to protest that, even if the world comes from God, one still must ask where God comes from.

Actually, the argument of my second Protestant philosopher above provides an almost perfect illustration of the difference between "theistic personalism" (to use the politer term) and classical theism. It is easy to see that the argument rests upon the assumption that all real existence is the same thing, so that whatever is true of existence in the case of God would have to be true of existence in the case of, say, a penguin; thus, if God's existence is also omnipotence, then so must the penguin's be. Now, from the classical perspective, the mistake here lies not in thinking that there must be some likeness between God's being and the being of creatures; God's being is the source of created being, after all, so the latter must reflect the former in some measure. The mistake lies in the failure to recognize that the likeness is one of analogy, not of simple identity. That is to say, the assertion that God's being, uniquely, is infinite, uncaused, and absolute, and therefore metaphysically convertible with his infinite power, does not in any way logically entail that the finite, dependent, and contingent being of the penguin must also be convertible with infinite power. But—

and this is where the analogy between divine and created being casts a certain light on "being" in the abstract—it nevertheless is the case that the penguin's *finite* existence is, in a very real way, convertible with the *finite* power intrinsic to being a penguin.

Perhaps the simplest way to frame the distinction, then, is to say that the great metaphysical traditions tend to think of being (and correctly so) in terms of *power,* and so tend to treat attributes (also correctly so) not just as abstract properties to be instantiated, but as various concrete ways in which that power is expressed or embodied. This is not really a very difficult idea to grasp. Actual being—not the proposition that some concept has at least one instance somewhere, but rather the real actuality of some particular thing among other particular things—is that thing's effective power to act and to be acted upon. When we say, for example, that Socrates really existed, we are saying that he, unlike some purely imaginary Socrates summoned up in the collective hallucinations of Plato, Xenophon, and Aristophanes, really had the power to affect and to be affected: to stand barefoot for hours in the Thracian snow, to perform feats of heroism at Potidaea and Delium, to argue with Xanthippe, to resist the sexual advances of Alcibiades, to consult Diotima, and to lift a cup of hemlock to his lips. Being is actuality, and all real beings share in that actuality in diverse ways and diverse degrees. The lowest level of mere existence, which belongs in common to all finite things, grains of sand no less than men and women, is already the first impartation of this power, this dynamic combination of activity and passivity; and all the capacities severally possessed by finite things are elaborations and expressions of this actuality. In creatures, inasmuch as they are finite, composite, limited, and mutable, the act of being is realized in a plurality of attributes; in human beings, for instance, wisdom and power are distinct from one another, with frequently tragic consequences (though, arguably, the more purely they are expressed by human beings, the more indistinguishable from one another they become). God, however, at least as classically conceived, is that boundless fullness of all actuality in which no such distinctions hold; he is the one infinite source in whom that power is always perfectly realized in its true unity, and from whom that power is poured forth in finite things. We, of course, on account of our limitations, have to think about him under a plurality of concepts, like absolute being, omniscience, omnipotence, perfect beatitude, and so forth; but in himself he transcends all plurality, all limitations, in one perfectly replete act of being.

This, at least, is what is meant by the scholastic designation of God's reality as "more eminent" than ours, or as "supereminent": that in him all that we are is possessed in a higher, fuller, purer, and limitless way, and that he donates everything that we are to us out of his infinite plenitude of being, consciousness, and bliss. It also means that the greater the number of real attributes in which a created thing shares, the fuller its expression of this imparted actuality will be. A stone is capable of affecting and being affected, but an insect has a much greater range of affective powers, and a rational animal has powers immeasurably more various and comprehensive still (most especially creative powers); hence, in the rational creature, being's power unfolds itself more fully, for both good and ill, than in things lacking mind or reason. If one wanted a metaphor for this ontology, one might imagine God's infinite actuality as a pure white light, which contains the full visible spectrum in its simple unity, and then imagine the finite essences of creatures as prisms, which can capture that light only by way of their "faceted" finitude, thus diminishing it and refracting it into multiplicity. It is a deficient metaphor, of course, especially inasmuch as prisms exist apart from light, whereas finite essences are always dependent on the being they receive and, so to speak, modulate. Another, very traditional way of putting the matter is to say that created things exist by subtraction: that is, they are finite and somewhat diffuse expressions of an infinite and indivisible reality, and their individual essences are simply special limits graciously set to the boundless power of being that flows from God, special definite modes in which God condescends to share his infinitely expressive plenitude. Or—one more very venerable metaphor—God is the infinite "ocean of being" while creatures are finite vessels containing existence only in limited measure. Whatever images one prefers, however, one must recall that in creatures the relation of existence and essence is not one between two extrinsic things that are mechanically combined to produce a single substance, but one between the power of infinite actuality and the limits of finite possibility; a thing's essence is its form, its natural potentialities, and that thing's existence as an individual reality is a dynamic combination of realization and privation, strength and weakness. In God, however, as he is infinite actuality and supereminent fullness, there can be no distinction between what he is and that he is; infinite existence is its own essence, infinite essence its own existence. And when we refer the attributes— the powers—we possess back to their supereminent source, we do so only analogously, using them as various names for the single ontological, intellectual, creative reality of the divine nature. One may express this irreducible analogical interval within the words we use of God by stating (as Ibn Sina and Thomas and others do) that in God existence and essence are identical, or (as Mulla Sadra does, using the same words differently) that God is existence but not essence, or in any number of other ways. However one expresses it, though, one is affirming a principle on which, again, all the dominant intellectual traditions of the major theistic faiths are more or less unanimous: the simplicity of God.

VII

No claim, I think it fair to say, has traditionally been seen as more crucial to a logically coherent concept of God than the denial that God is in any way composed of separable parts, aspects, properties, or functions. There may not be perfect agreement across schools and traditions as to what all the ramifications of the idea might be, or how it might be explained in relation to various creeds and theological traditions, but in the main the basic metaphysical premise has rarely been in serious dispute. Nor can it be. If God is to be understood as the unconditioned source of all things, rather than merely some very powerful but still ontologically dependent being, then any denial of divine simplicity is equivalent to a denial of God's reality. This is obvious if one remembers what the argument from creaturely contingency to divine necessity implies. To be the first cause of the whole universal chain of per se causality, God must be wholly unconditioned in every sense. He cannot be composed of and so dependent upon severable constituents, physical or metaphysical, as then he would himself be conditional. This point is rather rigorously argued by, among many others, the great

Jewish philosopher Moses Maimonides (1138–1204). God cannot change over time, moreover, as he would then be dependent upon the relation between some unrealized potentiality within himself and some fuller actuality somehow "beyond" himself into which he may yet evolve; again, he would then be a conditional being. He also must possess no limitations of any kind, intrinsic or extrinsic, that would exclude anything real from him. Nothing that exists can be incompatible with the power of being that he is, as all comes from him, and this means that he must transcend all those limits that alienate and exclude finite realities from one another, but in such a manner that he can embrace those finite realities in a more eminent way without contradiction. Again, a classic image of this simplicity is that of white light, which contains the full chromatic range of the optical spectrum, but in a "more eminent" simplicity. Robert Spitzer likes to use the imagery of physical fields, such as the quantum field that is capable of accommodating both particle and wave functions because it is simpler and more comprehensive than the limits that make particles and waves exclusive of one another, or the electromagnetic field that embraces both protons and electrons, or the presumed unified field that embraces both the electromagnetic field and spacetime. The infinite power of being—the power to be, without any reliance upon some other cause of being, as well as the power to impart being to creatures—must be of infinite capacity, which means infinite simplicity.[8]

One must remember, however, that metaphors are just metaphors, and that the simplicity at issue here is not physical but metaphysical. Among composite things, simplicity is often merely a lower level of apparent mechanical complexity; thus an amoeba is in a sense simpler than a giraffe. Even judgments of that sort, however, are often relative and slightly arbitrary. Considered from a variety of perspectives, one object can be structurally simpler than another in some ways while being more complex in others (at the genetic level, for instance). More importantly, even among physical things one object may have a far greater range of powers than another precisely because it is simpler in structure; a broadax and a guillotine can both perform one very similar unpleasant task, but the former can do innumerable other things as well, not nearly as unpleasant, like cutting down a dead tree or hacking a guillotine to pieces. To speak of God's metaphysical simplicity is to speak of the total absence of any of those limitations or conditions that might inhibit the power of actuality that he is. Thus, while God is infinitely richer in power than, say, a single subatomic particle, he is in a metaphysical sense infinitely simpler; in him, unlike that particle, there is not even any distinction between essence and existence.

The principle of divine simplicity, moreover, carries with it certain inevitable metaphysical implications. One is that God is eternal, not in the sense of possessing limitless duration but in the sense of transcending time altogether. Time is the measure of finitude, of change, of the passage from potentiality to actuality. God, however, being infinite actual being, is necessarily what Sikhism calls the Akhal Purukh, the One beyond time, comprehending all times within his eternal "now"; all things are present to him eternally in a simple act of perfect and immediate knowledge. Another implication is that God is in some sense impassible: that is, being beyond change, he also cannot be affected—or, to be more precise, modified—by anything outside himself. For one thing, as he is the infinite sustaining source of all things, nothing could be "outside" of him in that sense to begin with. This is not, however, to say that he is "unfeeling" in the way some physical object simply lacking affective powers is; it means only that his knowledge or bliss or love does not involve any metaphysical change in him, because it is not based on a privation; it is not a reactive but a wholly creative power, not limited by that difference between active and passive states to which finite beings are subject. God's knowledge of something created is not something separate from his eternal act of creating that thing; so he is not modified by that knowledge in the way that we are necessarily modified when we encounter things outside ourselves.

There are, needless to say, all sorts of philosophical problems that spring up around such claims, though usually these follow from a failure properly to think of God's way of being as truly transcendent of ours, rather than as merely another version of our way of being, but on a much more impressive scale. There are those, for instance, who object to the traditional idea of divine eternity on the grounds that, if every event is simultaneous with God's present moment, then every event would also be simultaneous with every other. Obviously, however, those who reason in this fashion are not really thinking of divine eternity as a timeless fullness of presence but simply as a kind of temporal moment devoid of duration; they are still situating God's eternity *in* time. The traditional claim, by contrast, is not that temporal things are really "simultaneous" with God at all—he has no time to be simultaneous with—but rather that they are present to him in a radically different way. This is hardly a conceptually difficult notion, even from a limited human perspective. The Battle of Salamis and my son's most recent words to me are both in a sense present to me right now, as I am thinking of them as I write these words, but that does not make them really simultaneous with one another chronologically. There are, after all, various modes of presence. And perhaps, in our post-Einsteinian world, in which we are accustomed to thinking of time as one of four ordinary topological axes of a single spatiotemporal continuum, the concept of an eternal perspective on time should cause us less perplexity than it might have caused earlier generations. That two distinct moments should be timelessly present to the transcendent God without therefore being simultaneous with one another is really no more problematic a notion than that two distinct places should be present to him without occupying the same point in space.

In similar veins, some contend that divine simplicity and impassibility would make it impossible for God to be affected by and so aware of any contingent truths, or for him to create freely, or for him to create without absolutely determining the course of all events. Again, though, when one chases the premises in such arguments to ground, one invariably finds some tacit but stubborn anthropomorphism at work: an unreflective tendency to think that God is like a finite psychological subject whose knowledge depends on a conditional cognition of external realities, or whose freedom requires arbitrative deliberation among options somehow outside himself, or whose creative acts must effect changes in him in the way that our actions effect changes in us, or whose gift of existence to creatures is like some kind of finite mechanical causation that produces only determinate mechanical results (and so on). None of this is logically compelling. If God is the infinite and unconditioned source of all things, then his creative intention—

whether he creates only one world, or many, or infinitely many—can be understood as an eternal act that involves no temporal change within him. His freedom, moreover, can be understood as consisting not in some temporal act of decision that overcomes some prior state of indecision, but in the infinite liberty with which he manifests himself in the creation he wills from everlasting. His knowledge of contingent realities need require no passive "discovery" of things formerly outside his ken, but only the knowledge of his own creative and sustaining intentions toward creatures (and, in an infinite spiritual intellect, intentions would involve no moving parts or changing substantial states). And his timeless donation of being to creatures need not be conceived as involving a mechanistic determinism but can be thought of as the creation of a contingent reality containing truly free secondary causes (creation from nothingness, after all, is not a kind of causation like any of which we are capable). In the end, the crucial question is whether any of the relations that finite contingencies have to God's infinite absolute being require alterations in God himself; and the traditional assumption is that God is not like some finite bounded substance that undergoes change as a result of external forces but is the transcendent source of the actuality of all substances and forces, and so he does not receive anything from "outside" himself, for everything is always in him and already realized in his own essence in an immeasurably more eminent way. More simply said, the finite does not add to the infinite but merely expresses the power of the infinite in a limited mode.

I do not want to press this much further, however, or pretend that any religious tradition has ever adopted any single set of answers to the questions that the principle of divine simplicity raises;

and to say how the various traditions deal with them in relation to their particular creedal commitments would carry me far beyond my purposes in this book. I will add only that philosophers often tend to overburden the notion of the simplicity and immutability of God's metaphysical *substance* with questions regarding whether God might have had a somewhat different "personal identity" had he chosen not to create as he did, and whether then his decisions "change" him from what he might otherwise be. After all, the choices we make seem subtly to determine who we are in relation to a world of things outside ourselves; whether our choices actually change us as spiritual substances is a rather difficult question, but they do at least shape our personal histories. Whatever the case, however, and as interesting as that question may be, even after one has stripped away all the anthropomorphic imagery—the imagery, that is, of God deliberating over what to do in the future, in accord with various internal and external limitations, until he vanquishes his uncertainty—it is not very germane at this point. What I want to emphasize here is that, whatever elaborations the different traditions have worked upon the idea of divine simplicity—however ingenious or convoluted, clear or obscure—the elementary metaphysical premise remains constant: that God is not like a physical object, composed of parts and defined by limits, and so is dependent upon nothing and subject to neither *substantial* change nor dissolution. There is an old Aristotelian principle, which seems to me quite obviously true, that in any causal relation change occurs in the effect, not in the cause itself. If, when two finite substances are involved in a causal relation, each undergoes some change, this is because each is limited and lacking in some property the other can supply, and so each functions as both a cause and an effect in that relation. Ice melts upon a burning coal but also cools the coal; and neither can affect the other without being affected in turn. God, however, is not a limited physical substance, standing outside other such substances, and his particular spiritual intentions (acts of will and knowledge, that is) toward finite things involve no physical processes and no modifications of his substance from without. And if those intentions somehow "determine" anything about who God is, it certainly could not be a passive determination in any sense, but an eternal act of self-determination or self-expression. More important, they would certainly add nothing new in the order of real being to God, since the "subtracted" reality of finite things is always already embraced within the infinitely fuller reality of divine being.[9]

Beyond this though, inasmuch as God's simplicity is that of an infinite fullness of power, all the traditions concur that it is a reality a finite mind can reason toward, but not one it can understand. We can affirm that God is one, since the infinite unconditioned source of all reality cannot, obviously, be plural. We can affirm that this oneness underlies and sustains all things in their unity and diversity, and that therefore God is, as Maximus the Confessor (580–662) said, not only utterly simple but simplicity itself, the very simplicity of the simple, indwelling all things as the very source of their being; or that, as Sufi tradition says, God as al-Ahad, the One, is also the transcendent unity of all existence, *wahdat al-wujud.* We can affirm also that, as the *Isha Upanishad* says, God dwells in all as transcending all; or that, as Augustine says, God is at once both nearer than what is inmost to me and beyond what is highest in me. We can say all of this with some confidence merely because we can observe the divine simplicity's plural expressions and effects in contingent things, and from those abstract toward the reality of their unconditioned source. But, in the end, how that simplicity might be "modulated" within itself is strictly unimaginable for us. At that uncrossable intellectual threshold, religions fall back upon inscrutable doctrines, philosophers upon inadequate concepts, and mystics upon silence. "Si comprehendis, non est deus," as Augustine says: If you comprehend it, it is not God.

This is why all the major theistic traditions insist at some point that our language about God consists mostly in conceptual restrictions and fruitful negations. "Cataphatic" (or affirmative) theology must always be chastened and corrected by "apophatic" (or negative) theology. We cannot speak of God in his own nature directly, but only at best analogously, and even then only in such a way that the conceptual content of our analogies consists largely in our knowledge of all the things that God is not. This is the *via negativa* of Christianity, the *lahoot salbi* (negative theology) of Islam, Hinduism's "*neti, neti*" ("not this, not this"). For those who take the extreme line in this regard, such as Moses Maimonides, anything said truly of the divine essence has *only* a negative meaning for us. And for the contemplatives of various traditions, the negation of all those limited concepts that delude us that God is just another being among beings, within our intellectual grasp, is an indispensable discipline of the mind and will. It prepares the mind for a knowledge of God that comes not from categories of analytic reason, but from—as Maximus says—the intimate embrace of union, in which God shares himself immediately as a gift to the created soul.[10]

VIII

Whether, at the last, one finds the argument from cosmic contingency to the reality of God convincing, one must nonetheless grant that it cannot be dismissed merely by saying that, even if there were a God, one would still have to explain where he came from. The claim that there cannot be an infinite regress of *contingent* ontological causes raises a truly difficult challenge to pure materialism; but to imagine that it can be extended to undermine the claim that there must be an *absolute* ontological cause is to fall prey to an obvious category error. God, not being some kind of conditioned thing, is a causal explanation of a logically different kind. The terms "contingent" and "absolute" do in fact mark out clearly distinct modal descriptions. If the concept of God were the concept simply of some demiurge—some conditioned being among other conditioned beings—then it would indeed be a concept requiring the supplement of some further causal explanation. But none of the enduring theistic faiths conceives of God in that way. The God they proclaim is not just some especially resplendent object among all the objects illuminated by the light of being, or any kind of object at all, but is himself the light of being. It makes perfect sense to ask what illuminates an object, but none to ask what illuminates light. It makes perfect sense to wonder why a contingent being exists, but none to wonder why Absolute Being "exists."

In any event, the "Who made God?" riposte to theism has never been favored by the more reflective kind of skeptic. It is the resort of the intellectually lazy. For one thing, it is an approach that already concedes the power of the argument against an infinite explanatory regress, which is definitely not a good first move for the committed unbeliever. Subtler atheists and agnostics these days instead tend to attack the basic presuppositions underlying the argument from contingency. Perhaps not everything is really explicable, they argue; perhaps not everything has a cause. There is an old argument by David Hume (1711–1776) to that effect: we can conceive of some object suddenly appearing in the world without any cause, so perhaps the expectation that there must be a causal explanation for everything is just a prejudice. That, however, is an argument that need detain no one, since it is plainly false, as has been pointed out many times: we may be able to *imagine* such an event, because imagination is boundlessly fecund and essentially lawless, but we certainly cannot *conceive* of it; were an object spontaneously to appear before any of us, reason would immediately demand to know its cause (magic, perhaps?) and would certainly not rest content with the claim that no such cause need exist. Some skeptics more *au fait* with modern physics prefer to point to quantum mechanics and claim that there we find physical events that occur without any prior cause: the sudden decay of a radioactive nucleus, for example, which can be predicted probabilistically but not determinately, or the pair creation of particles by a strong electric field, and so on. This argument is fallacious, however. Even if we take it for granted that the standard Copenhagen interpretation of quantum physics is right, and that there are no deterministic "hidden variables" at work in the quantum realm, and that nothing like, say, David Bohm's proposal of an entirely deterministic quantum theory is really plausible (who can say?), still the example of unpredictable quantum events is irrelevant here. It may perhaps be the case that such events do not occur fully deterministically, as a result of some kind of mechanistic efficient force, but this does not mean that they are uncaused in the full sense. It is only dogmatic materialists who believe that all causality is of the mechanistic sort anyway, because that is their metaphysics, and so quantum indeterminacy should be a far graver trial to their consciences than to those of classical theists. Such indeterminacy certainly does not in any way call the principle of ontological contingency into question. Even the most fervent materialist must at least grant that quantum particles and functions are not causally independent in an ultimate sense; they do not literally emerge from nonexistence. Radioactive decay, for instance, still has to occur within radioactive material, and within a physical realm governed by mathematically describable laws. And whatever occurs within a quantum field or vacuum is dependent upon that field or vacuum (and that vacuum is not, as it happens, nothing). And all physical reality is contingent upon some cause of being as such, since existence is not an intrinsic physical property, and since no physical reality is logically necessary.

Today's more ingenious skeptics, however, do not attempt to search out some sort of specific exception to the universal rule of causality, because they understand that what might count as an exception will always be determined in advance by certain metaphysical prejudices. Rather, they try to argue simply that the very premise that there is in principle an answer to every question regarding the causes of or rationales for things may be false. This is certainly a more promising strategy, if only of an evasive kind; it is not, however, one that can possibly succeed. One problem that bedevils almost all arguments of this sort is that they involve the casual conflation of two closely related but nevertheless distinct principles: the Principle of Causation—whatever does not have the cause of its existence in itself must be caused to exist by something beyond itself—and the Principle of Sufficient Reason—any true proposition must have some sufficient explanation for why it is true (that, at least, is the simplest way of phrasing it). The latter principle in some sense presumes the former, because a proposition about an event or about some object's existence will generally be explicable chiefly by reference to the cause of that event or object. But one must remember that propositions can be true in a number of ways, depending on their form and content, and that propositions are not "caused" to be true, even if they are true because they accurately describe how something has been caused. This is important because many philosophers are willing to grant that the argument from contingency does succeed if in fact the Principle of Sufficient Reason is true, but then claim that the principle is in fact false: not everything can be explained.[11]

This, however, would not constitute a sufficient case against classical theism, even if it were formally correct. The argument from the contingency of beings to absolute being is immune to such doubts, whether the denial of the Principle of Sufficient Reason rests upon sound premises or not. I tend to think that, in some form, the principle is not only true but self-evidently so, and that it lies at the foundation of all rationality as such: practical, philosophical, scientific, or what have you. Certainly no committed scientific rationalist could reject it without thereby striking at the foundations of his or her own beliefs. But, even if I am in error about that, the whole argument from the contingency of creation depends only upon the much simpler Principle of Causality, which concerns the existence of substances, not the explicability of propositions, and that simpler principle remains intact. All physical reality is logically contingent, and the existence of the contingent requires the Absolute as its source. *Why* the Absolute produces the contingent may be inconceivable for us; but *that* the contingent can exist only derivatively, receiving its existence from the Absolute, is a simple deduction of reason. Alternatively, reality is essentially absurd: absolute contingency, unconditional conditionality, an uncaused effect. And the antithesis between the two positions can never be made any less stark than that.

Not that it has not been tried. One rather curious argument that has recently been echoing along certain academic corridors suggests that the whole problem of contingent existence should not be posed as an uncompromising choice between the possibility or impossibility of the universe existing apart from the Absolute, but only as an issue of relative probability. That is to say, one traditional way of posing the problem of cosmic contingency is the rather dizzyingly capacious question: "Why is there something rather than nothing?" Perhaps, however, the question is essentially inept. Peter van Inwagen, Derek Parfit, Adolf Grünbaum, and a few other philosophers have suggested that to ask it is also rashly to assume that nonexistence is a more probable or more "natural" state of things than is existence. But, so the argument goes, among all possible worlds, the "empty world" devoid of all contents and properties is only one out of an infinite number of conceivable alternatives, and so the likelihood of the empty world being instantiated, rather than one of those infinitely many other possible worlds, is practically none at all. There is only one way in which there might be nothing, but an infinite number of ways in which there might be something. So what is the problem, really? This argument, however, is merely a category error, and a fairly familiar one. Once again, the grim chill shadow of a vaguely Fregean logic falls across our path. Note that, as before, the question of being has simply been avoided at this point, not answered; one is supposed merely to assume that there *exists* some realm of possibilities of which—without any explanation of how this might happen or even be possible—one or more will simply be instantiated. What *actual* existence is, or how any concrete reality might come to exist in the first place, has not been addressed at all. Worse, the argument confuses the idea of nonexistence with the idea of an "empty world"; but an empty world, conceived as merely one possible state of reality among others, is not nonexistence, but only a kind of existing thing devoid of qualities (whatever that might mean). The real question of existence must be posed logically prior to all worlds, actual or possible. Even abstract possibilities—even "empty" possibilities—must exist in some kind of reality, and nothing is possible at all apart from some source of actuality. Frankly, one might just as well say there are as many possibilities of nonexistence as there are possible worlds, because none of those worlds has necessary existence, and so none of them is *possible* at all in and of itself. One might even say that there are an infinite number of ways in which nothing *might* exist, but only one way in which anything *can* exist: as the product of an uncaused first cause. In any event, it is simply meaningless to speak of relative probability in this context, when the issue is clearly one of logical possibility. The distance between existence (actuality) and nonexistence (which is neither possibility nor actuality) is infinite, and no calculation of pleonastic probabilities can ever reduce that distance.

IX

Anyway, it is probably time to move on. As I have said, my interest in this book is the classical definition of God, and not proof of his reality, however often the demarcation between those aims may seem to have been erased. This has been a long chapter, as could scarcely be avoided, given the centrality of the metaphysics of being to the traditional understanding of God. I may have said too much; but, then again, I may have said far too little. I have paused before a few philosophical thickets that I would rather have summarily circumvented, had I seen a clear path; but I have not made the sort of effort it would require to clear any of them entirely away. In my defense, I can plead both the narrow particularity of my avowed purpose in this book and a healthy abhorrence of redundancy: these arguments are millennia old, and the literature upon them is so compendious that I cannot imagine what I could add to it apart from yet another very partial distillation of certain of their elements. Presuming permission, therefore, I shall once again simply wave a limp, lethargic hand in the direction of my postscript.

I will say this much, however: the general argument from the contingent to the absolute, or from the conditioned to the unconditioned, is a powerful and cogent one. No attempt, philosophical or otherwise, to show that it is a confused argument, or logically insufficient, or susceptible of some purely physical answer has ever been impressively successful. Even if one does not accept its conclusions one still has absolutely no rational warrant for believing that materialism has any sort of logical superiority over theism; the classical argument is strong enough to show that naturalism is far and away a weaker, more incomplete, and more willfully doctrinaire position than classical theism is. Naturalism, as I have said repeatedly, is a philosophy of the absurd, of the just-there-ness of what is certainly by its nature a contingent reality; it is, simply enough, an absurd philosophy. As I have also said, however, there is a certain circularity in that claim, inasmuch as naturalism, if it is true, renders all reason debile; so it is possible to believe that what has the appearance of absurdity may in fact be the reality of things, even if one cannot consistently act upon that belief, or even conceive what it would mean. I, at least, am willing to grant naturalism its proper dignity as a kind of pure, unreasoning faith: absolute fidelity to an absolute paradox. Theism has nothing so magnificently wild and rhapsodically anarchic to offer; the faith it supports depends at some point upon a consistent set of logical intuitions, and so lacks the sheer intellectual brio of that sort of madly, romantically adventurous absurdism. In a few of my more purely passionate moments I find myself a little envious of materialism's casual audacity and happy barbarism.

I think, moreover, that most philosophical debate on these matters soon becomes more a distraction from the obvious than an aid to reflection. I may be something of a superstitious romantic myself, but it seems to me that one's meditations on the world's contingency should end more or less where they begin: in that moment of wonder, of sheer existential surprise, of which I spoke at the outset of this chapter. It can be a fairly taxing spiritual labor, admittedly—it is, in the end, a contemplative art—but one should strive as far as possible to let all complexities of argument fall away as often as one can, and to make a simple return to that original apprehension of the gratuity of all things. From that vantage, one already knows which arguments about reality are relevant or coherent and which are not, whether or not one has the conceptual vocabulary to express what one knows. In that moment of remote immediacy to things—of intimate strangeness—there may be some element of unreflective innocence, even something childlike; but any philosophy that is not ultimately responsible before what is revealed in that moment is merely childish. That sudden instant of existential surprise is, as I have said, one of wakefulness, of attentiveness to reality as such, rather than to the impulses of the ego or of desire or of ambition; and it opens up upon the limitless beauty of being, which is to say, upon the beauty of being seen as a gift that comes from beyond all possible beings. This wakefulness can, moreover, become habitual, a kind of sustained awareness of the surfeit of being over the beings it sustains, though this may be truly possible only for saints. For anyone who experiences only fleeting intimations of that kind of vision, however, those shining instants are reminders that the encounter with the mystery of being as such occurs within every encounter with the things of the world; one knows the extraordinary within the ordinary, the supernatural within the natural. The highest vocation of reason and of the will is to seek to know the ultimate source of that mystery. Above all, one should wish to know whether our consciousness of that mystery directs us toward a reality that is, in its turn, conscious of us.

⬛

CHAPTER FOUR

Consciousness (*Chit*)

I

In those moments when our experience of the world awakens us to the strangeness—the utter fortuity and pure givenness—of existence, we are confronted by two mysteries simultaneously, or at least by a mystery with two equally inscrutable poles. No less wonderful than the being of things is our consciousness of them: our ability to know the world, to possess a continuous subjective awareness of reality, to mirror the unity of being in the unity of private cognizance, to contemplate the world and ourselves, to assume each moment of experience into a fuller comprehension of the whole, and to relate ourselves to the world through acts of judgment and will. In a single movement of thought, the mind is capable of receiving the world in both its integrity and its diversity, of holding past, present, and future together, of contemplating reality at once under both its particular (or concrete) and its general (or abstract) aspects, of composing endless imaginative and conceptual variations upon experience, of pondering itself as it ponders the outer world—and all the while preserving that limpid and silent presence to itself in which it indivisibly abides. Being is transparent to mind; mind is transparent to being; each is "fitted" to the other, open to the other, at once containing and contained by the other. Each is the mysterious glass in which the other shines, revealed not in itself but only in reflecting and being reflected by the other.

To a convinced materialist, all of this is a reality essentially physical in nature, and probably entirely mechanical (in the broadest sense): even if the science as yet eludes us, consciousness must be explicable entirely in terms of the interaction between our neural constitution and the concrete world around us. Even the materialist would acknowledge, of course, that the powers of the mind cannot be exhaustively accounted for solely in terms of the mechanics of sensory stimulus and neurological response, if for no other reason than the fairly obvious truth that neither stimulus nor response is, by itself, a mental phenomenon; neither, as a purely physical reality, possesses conceptual content or personal awareness. I would go further, however, and say that consciousness is a reality that cannot be explained in any purely physiological terms at all. All our modern "scientistic" presuppositions may tell us that mind must be entirely a mechanical function or residue of the brain's neuronal processes, but even the most basic phenomenology of consciousness discloses so vast an incommensurability between physical causation and mental events that it is probably impossible that the latter could ever be wholly reduced to the former. It may well be, in fact, that the widely cherished expectation that neuroscience will one day discover an explanation of consciousness solely within the brain's electrochemical processes is no less enormous a category error than the expectation that physics will one day discover the reason for the existence of the material universe. In either case, the problem is not one of pardonably exaggerated hope but of fundamental and incorrigible conceptual confusion.

For one thing—and this is no small matter—considered solely within the conceptual paradigms we have inherited from the mechanical philosophy, it is something of a conundrum that such a thing as consciousness should be possible for material beings at all. Absolutely central to the mechanistic vision of reality is the principle that material forces are inherently mindless, intrinsically devoid of purpose, and therefore only adventitiously and accidentally directed toward any end. Complex rational organization, so we are told, is not a property naturally residing in material reality, but is only a state imposed upon material reality whenever matter is assumed into composite structures whose essentially disparate parts, as a result of design or chance, operate together in some kind of functional order. Nothing within the material constituents of those structures has the least innate tendency toward such order, any more than the material elements from which a watch is composed have any innate tendency toward horology. And, if complex rational order is extrinsic to what matter essentially is, how much more so must rationality itself be; for consciousness would appear to be everything that, according to the principles of mechanism, matter is not: directed, purposive, essentially rational. The notion that material causes could yield a result so apparently contrary to material nature is paradoxical enough that it ought to give even the most convinced of materialists pause.

Certainly, at the dawn of the mechanistic age the difficulty seemed obvious to most scientists and philosophers, and they were for the most part content simply to draw a demarcation between the distinct realms of material mechanism and rational soul, and leave the operations of each to its own proper sphere. They could do this with untroubled consciences, however, only because they were not metaphysical materialists or "naturalists" of the late modern kind, and so did not regard matter as some sort of grand monistic principle, beside which there can be no other. Today the dominant prejudices all tend in quite the opposite direction; now the circle must be squared, however improbable the task may seem, if we are to "save the appearances" without abandoning our convictions about reality. The result is an almost endless variety of particularly thorny problems. Cartesian dualism—the idea that the soul and the body are two conjoined but ontologically distinct kinds of substance—suffered from a great many explanatory deficiencies, perhaps, but at least it was a coherent position and made it possible to find a place for consciousness in a cosmos stripped of formal and final causes. After all, if one truly believes that matter is, as the mechanical philosophy says, nothing more than mass and force, and that all material actions are nothing more than exchanges of energy accomplished by undetermined movement, immediate contact, direct force, and direct resistance, then it makes a good deal of sense to regard mind—with its seeming indivisibility, intentional orientation toward formal and final objects of thought, incommunicable privacy of perspective, capacity for abstract concepts, and all its other mysterious powers—as essentially separate from the economy of material interactions. Admittedly, the question of precisely how two essentially alien orders of reality might interact with one another, or be united in some *tertium quid,* may be a vexing one; but, considered in purely mechanistic terms, it is nowhere near so baffling as the question of how any combination of diverse material forces, even when fortuitously gathered into complex neurological systems, could just somehow add up to the simplicity and immediacy of consciousness, to its extraordinary openness to the physical world, to its reflective awareness of itself, or to the liberty of its conceptual and imaginative powers from the constraints of its material circumstances.

Most attempts to provide an answer without straying beyond the boundaries of materialist orthodoxy are ultimately little more than vague appeals to the power of cumulative complexity: some-how, the argument goes, a sufficient number of neurological systems and subsystems operating in connection with one another will at some point naturally produce unified, self-reflective, and intentional consciousness, or at least (as strange as this may sound) the illusion of such consciousness. This is probably just another version of the pleonastic fallacy, another hopeless attempt to overcome a qualitative difference by way of an indeterminately large number of gradual quantitative steps. Even if it is not, it remains a supposition almost cruelly resistant to scientific investigation or demonstration, simply because consciousness as an actual phenomenon is entirely confined to the experience of a particular mind, a particular subject. It is a uniquely "first person" phenomenon—the very phenomenon of the "first person" as such, actually, the sole act whereby someone is anyone at all—with no directly objective "third person" aspect available to research. My thoughts and feelings are my own, yours are yours, and all of theirs are theirs, and none of us has access to anyone's but his or her own. One can observe behaviors associated with consciousness in others, but none of those affords any immediate intuition of the subjectivity that lies behind them. One can conduct an exhaustive surveillance of all those electrical events in the neurons of the brain that are undoubtedly the physical concomitants of mental states, but one does not thereby gain access to that singular, continuous, and wholly interior experience of being *this* person that is the actual substance of conscious thought. One can even alter, confuse, or interfere with particular conscious states by intruding upon the activities of the brain, chemically, surgically, traumatically, or otherwise; but one can never enter into, let alone measure, the persistent and irreducibly private perspective of the subject in whom these states inhere.

This should be obvious, even to the most committed believer in empirical method, but its implications often prove strangely difficult to grasp (perhaps they are altogether too obvious): there is an absolute qualitative abyss between the objective facts of neurophysiology and the subjective experience of being a conscious self, and so a method capable of providing a model of only the former can never produce an adequate causal narrative of the latter. While one may choose to believe that the brain's objectively observable electrochemical processes and the mind's subjective, impenetrably private experiences are simply two sides of a single, wholly physical phenomenon, there is still no empirical way in which the two sides can be collapsed into a single observable datum, or even connected to one another in a clear causal sequence. The purely physical nature of those experiences remains, therefore, only a conjecture, and one that lacks even the support of a plausible analogy to some other physical process, as there is no other "mechanism" in nature remotely similar to consciousness. The difference in kind between the material structure of the brain and the subjective structure of consciousness remains fixed and inviolable, and so the precise relation between them cannot be defined, or even isolated as an object of scientific scrutiny. And this is an epistemological limit that it seems reasonable to think may never be erased, no matter how sophisticated our knowledge of the complex activities of the brain may become; we will never be able to examine, from any objective vantage, the simple act of thought in its proper aspect: the conscious awareness of a subject. And the impotence of traditional scientific method here indicates a conceptual aporia that is irresoluble in mechanical terms: How could it be that, in this instance alone, the essential aimlessness of matter achieves so intense and intricate a concentration of its various random forces that, all at once, it is fantastically inverted into the virtual opposite of everything modern orthodoxy tells us matter is? In the end, there will always remain that essential part of the conscious self that seems simply to stand apart from the spectacle of material causality: pure perspective, a gaze in upon reality that is itself available to no gaze from beyond itself, known to itself only in its act of knowing what is other than itself. For a scientific culture that believes true knowledge of anything can be gained only by the systematic reduction of that thing to its simplest parts, undertaken from an entirely third person stance, this inaccessible first person subjectivity—this absolute interiority, full of numberless incommunicable qualitative sensations and velleities and intuitions that no inquisitive eye will ever glimpse, and that is impossible to disassemble, reconstruct, or model—is so radically elusive a phenomenon that there seems no hope of capturing it in any complete scientific account. Those who imagine otherwise simply have not understood the problem fully.

None of this, however, is to denigrate the very real advances that have been achieved in neuroscience over the past several decades. It is quite wonderful that we seem to be finding so many correlations between certain portions of the brain and certain elementary cognitive functions. But that has little bearing on most of the more difficult questions consciousness raises: how matter can produce subjective awareness, how abstract processes of reasoning or deliberation could possibly correspond with sequences of purely physical events in the brain, and so on. That there is a deep and integral connection between brain and mind no one doubts; but, again, since the brain can be investigated only mechanically while consciousness admits of no mechanical description, the nature of that connection is impossible to conceive, let alone identify. To put the matter a little absurdly, if one did not know that such a thing as subjective consciousness existed, one would never discover that it did through any empirical investigation of the structure and activities of the brain, however comprehensive or exact; one could map out the whole magnificent machinery of the brain for everyone to see, in all its intricacy, and compile a complete catalogue of all its typical processes of stimulus and response, all its systems and functions, and yet still never guess that a privately conscious self inhabited it. Electrochemical events are not thoughts, even when they may be inseparably associated with thoughts, and no empirical inventory of such events will ever disclose for us either the content or the experiential quality of an idea, a desire, a volition, or any other mental event. This being so, we have no better warrant for saying that the brain produces the mind than that the mind makes use of the brain; and in neither case can we imagine how this happens.

To be as clear as possible here: I am not saying simply that the brain is far too complex for us ever to understand its relation to consciousness fully; if that were my argument, it would amount to nothing more than a vapid prognostication based entirely upon personal incredulity. The problem is not one of the relative quantity of our knowledge of the brain. Not that it does any harm to remind ourselves just how complex the brain really is, given the extravagant claims regarding our current understanding of its workings frequently made by excited neuroscientists, psychologists, philosophers of mind, and journalists, and given the wild expectations those claims often inspire. A great many scientists, psychologists, and philosophers even go so far as to dismiss our common understanding of the mind—that it is a unified subject of real experiences that possesses ideas, intentions, and desires and that freely acts upon them—as mere "folk psychology," in need of correction by neurobiology. And there is no pseudoscientific fad more vigorous these days than the production of books that attempt to turn neuroscience into an explanation for every imaginable aspect of human behavior and experience. All of that merits not only considerable skepticism but a good measure of ridicule as well. Even so, putting all exaggerations aside, sound neuroscience really is providing us with an ever richer picture of the brain and its operations, and in some far distant epoch may actually achieve something like a comprehensive survey of what is perhaps the single most complex physical object in the universe. That is all entirely irrelevant to my argument, however. My claim here is that, whatever we may learn about the brain in the future, it will remain in principle impossible to produce any entirely mechanistic account of the conscious mind, for a great many reasons (many of which I shall soon address), and that therefore consciousness is a reality that defeats mechanistic or materialist thinking. For the intuitions of folk psychology are in fact perfectly accurate; they are not merely some *theory* about the mind that is either corrigible or dispensable. They constitute nothing less than a full and coherent phenomenological description of the life of the mind, and they are absolutely "primordial data," which cannot be abandoned in favor of some alternative description without producing logical nonsense. Simply said, consciousness as we commonly conceive of it is quite real (as all of us, apart from a few cognitive scientists and philosophers, already know—and they know it too, really). And this presents a problem for materialism, because consciousness as we commonly conceive of it is also almost certainly irreconcilable with a materialist view of reality.

II

The question of consciousness as it is usually posed today is not, by the way, an ancient question to which modern scientific method is at last beginning to provide promising answers; it arises specifically from a set of metaphysical assumptions only accidentally associated with that method. Within the mechanistic view of reality, material reality is no more than mindless mass, and physical causality is no more than mindless force, and so the causal power of seemingly immaterial things like conceptual abstractions or volitions or final purposes creates a deep problem, one that seems to allow of only two possible solutions, neither of which is particularly convincing: either some version of Cartesian dualism (according to which the body is a machine centrally operated by an immaterial homunculus called the "soul") or a thoroughgoing mechanical monism (according to which mind or "soul" is an emergent result or epiphenomenon of unguided physical events). Between the looming escarpments of these two options lies a very narrow pass indeed. And, given so stark a set of alternatives, it is only natural that so many materialist philosophers or neuroscientists assume that it is enough to have disposed of the Cartesian soul to establish the supremacy of the physicalist position. If one can only find a sufficient number of instances in which the brain operates without immediately conscious supervision on the part of any purely rational and cognizant agency within—if, that is, one can find significant instances when the homunculus appears to be asleep at the controls—then surely one has proved that everything, mind included, is only a form of mechanism after all.

Take, for example, a fairly famous series of experiments conducted by Benjamin Libet in the 1970s: human test subjects were placed before an oscilloscope timer and asked to perform some minor motor action, such as twitching a wrist, whenever they felt the desire to do so, and then to report precisely at what point, as recorded by the timer, they had been aware of consciously deciding to act; at the same time, electrodes attached to their scalps recorded the electrical impulses presumably motivating the decision. A minuscule but measurable difference (say, two hundred milliseconds) was repeatedly found between the time at which the physiological impulse was recorded and the time at which the test subject, as far as he or she could tell, had chosen to act. In the years since Libet's experiments other researchers have repeated the test, often with considerable refinements, generally reporting the same results and occasionally reporting a more significant delay between the unconscious and conscious moments within the subject's "choice." All of which is very interesting, but none of which warrants the moral that many have drawn from the story. It is not at all uncommon for cognitive scientists and philosophers of mind to claim that Libet and his successors, by demonstrating that certain kinds of conscious choices are typically preceded by certain unconscious neuronal actions, have proved that free will is an illusion. But this is nonsensical. For one thing, the method employed in the original experiments was a bit incoherent: one cannot really make a direct comparison between a conscious subject's sense of when something happened in relation to a visible external timer—the act of observing which must take more than a few hundred milliseconds for the nerves and brain to process properly—and a mechanical register of events in objective time. For another, we have no notion whatsoever of how these electrical firings in the cerebral cortex relate to the conceptual contents of a decision to do something, because as objectively observable events they possess no mental content; we certainly cannot say that they themselves constitute the act of decision, or that they are anything more than physiological tendencies that the deliberative will might still have the power either to obey or to suppress. And in fact, as it happens, under laboratory conditions the measurable brain events never infallibly indicate that the expected action will actually occur; the neuronal impulse may or may not be followed by the twitch of a wrist (or its equivalent), and the impulse is followed by the expected action usually only around an unimpressive six times out of ten. Whatever that impulse is, then, it constitutes at most a physiological potential for action, not a decision to act. So, even taken entirely on their own terms, these experiments tell us little that we did not already know: that the impulse to act frequently comes before we consciously choose to comply with or resist that impulse. One might almost say that our free decisions seem to act as formal causes of action, imposing determinate order upon the otherwise inchoate promptings of our neurons.

The deeper problem with these experiments, however, or at least with the way in which their results have often been inter-preted, is not the methods the researchers employed, but the metaphysical scheme they seem to have presumed. Only if one starts from the assumption that all natural causality is mechanistic can one possibly imagine that it makes sense to take a single physi-cal act in isolation from any larger context of actions and determi-nations, look for a discrete physiological concomitant apparently prior to that act, and then claim that one has found a physical explanation of the act that renders all the prospective, conceptual, and deliberative powers of the will causally superfluous. As should not need to be said, if one approaches all human acts simply as discrete mechanical movements, located within a sequence of other such movements, which one can explain merely by isolating one specific mechanical spring among others, then one has already prescinded one's investigations from the continuous context of intentional activity within which each of those actions takes place. Yet it is only in that context that the question of free will can be intelligibly asked. In its narrow way, an approach like Libet's might cast some small doubt upon the direct and constant supervision of human actions by a Cartesian homunculus within; but who in his or her right senses actually believes in that fabulous and anxiously alert little imp to begin with? We already know that most of our physical actions are not determined moment to moment by our conscious minds. For instance, as I made my daily climb this morning up the wooded mountain trail near my home, I was not constantly issuing conscious instructions to the muscles, sinews, nerves, and organs of my body, or telling my body how to react to stones unexpectedly slipping underfoot or to the prick of the unseen thorn that drew blood from the back of my hand. Clearly my conscious mind would not know how to command such things. If free will is the issue, the pertinent question is whether going for that walk up that trail—conceiving of it, choosing to do it, persisting in doing it, for reasons (that is, final causes) of which I had some intentional grasp—was a rationally free activity, integrated within a larger intentionality directed toward some end. And the answer does not depend upon whether the individual physiological constituents of the experience were directly determined by a wholly conscious controller incorporeally residing in, say, my pineal gland.

Freely rational human activities involve complex behaviors, which comprehend any number of moving somatic and mental parts—many unconscious, but certainly not all—within a single and determinate totality of purposive operations. In the case of the Libet experiments, for instance, everything that happened in the laboratory had been decided upon in advance, in accord with purely abstract instructions ("Move your wrist whenever you wish to do so") and purely deliberative undertakings ("I *will*"); from the initial decision onward, everyone had acted to a single end. There is simply something banal in trying to extricate a single moment of physiological activity from that totality and thereby prove anything about the rational liberty of the mind. More to the point, if the very same experiment had been undertaken from an entirely different conceptual vantage, the results might just as easily have been taken as triumphant proof of the reality of free will. How amazing, the researchers might have concluded, that a person has the rational power to command his or her body to behave spontaneously at a future date—"I shall let the promptings of physiological impulse pass through my nerves like breezes through the strings of an Aeolian harp"—and then bring it to pass. The mind, it turns out, is so potent that it can even ordain the responsive quiescence of the flesh. There could scarcely be a more glorious vindication of the truth of rational freedom. Nor, for that matter, could there be a better illustration of the power of a final cause to bring about physical effects: the movement of the subject's wrist occurred within a continuous activity directed toward a rational end consciously sought, apart from which it would not have happened at all; the whole structure of the act was teleological, which is precisely how a mechanistic view of reality says physical reality cannot behave. How even more amazing, then, that a future purpose could dictate material results at the most fundamental and pre-conscious level of an organism's operations. Perhaps nature is something of an Aristotelian at heart.

In the end, experiments of this sort might tell us about the connection between certain neural impulses and certain brain events, but the attempt to draw some conclusion from them regarding human free will proves only that ideology often makes us believe that we are seeing more than in fact we are, and that it is insidiously easy to confuse our genuine empirical discoveries with our metaphysical premises. That we are rational agents—that a great many of our actions are not merely the results of serial physiological urges but are instead dictated by coherent conceptual connections and private deliberations—is one of those primordial data I mentioned above that cannot be reduced to some set of purely mechanical functions without producing nonsense. That a number of cognitive scientists should be exerting themselves to tear down the Cartesian partition between body and soul, hoping to demonstrate that there is no Wonderful Wizard on the other side pulling the levers, is poignant proof that our mechanistic paradigms trap much of our thinking about mind and body within an absurd dilemma: we must believe either in a ghost mysteriously animating a machine or in a machine miraculously generating a ghost. Premodern thought allowed for a far less restricted range of conceptual possibilities.

In Western philosophical tradition, for instance, neither Platonists, nor Aristotelians, nor Stoics, nor any of the Christian metaphysicians of late antiquity or the Middle Ages could have conceived of matter as something independent of "spirit," or of spirit as something simply superadded to matter in living beings. Certainly none of them thought of either the body or the cosmos as a machine merely organized by a rational force from beyond itself. Rather, they saw matter as being always already informed by indwelling rational causes, and thus open to—and in fact directed toward—mind. Nor did Platonists or Aristotelians or Christians conceive of spirit as being immaterial in a purely privative sense, in the way that a vacuum is not aerial or a vapor is not a solid. If anything, they understood spirit as being more substantial, more actual, more "supereminently" real than matter, and as in fact being the pervasive reality in which matter had to participate in order to be anything at all. The quandary produced by early mod-

ern dualism—the notorious "interaction problem" of how an immaterial reality could have an effect upon a purely material thing
—was no quandary at all, because no school conceived of the interaction between soul and body as a purely extrinsic *physical* alliance between two disparate kinds of substance. The material order
is only, it was assumed, an ontologically diminished or constricted
effect of the fuller actuality of the spiritual order. And this is why
it is nearly impossible to find an ancient or mediaeval school of
thought whose concept of the relation of soul and body was anything like a relation between two wholly independent kinds of
substance: the ghost and its machine (which, for what it is worth,
was not really Descartes' understanding of the relation either).

In Platonic tradition, the soul was not conceived of merely as
a pure intellect presiding over the automaton of the body. The
soul was seen as the body's life, spiritual and organic at once, comprising the appetites and passions no less than rational intellect,
while the body was seen as a material reflection of a rational and
ideal order. Matter was not simply the inert and opaque matter of
mechanistic thought but rather a mirror of eternal splendors and
verities, truly (if defectively) predisposed to the light of spirit. For
Aristotelian tradition, the human soul was the "form of the body,"
the very essence and nature of a human being's whole rational and
animal organism, the formal and vital power animating, pervading, and shaping every person, drawing all the energies of life into
a living unity. For Stoic tradition as well, the indwelling mind or
"logos" of each person was also the rational and living integrity of
the body, and was a particular instance of the universal logos that
animates, shapes, and guides the whole cosmos. For pagans, Hellenistic Jews, and Christians alike, the soul was the source and im-

manent entelechy of corporeal life, encompassing every dimension of human existence: animal functions and abstract intellect, sensation and reason, emotion and ratiocination, flesh and spirit, natural aptitude and supernatural longing. Gregory of Nyssa, for instance, spoke of the soul not only as intellect but also as a gathering and formative natural power, progressively developing all of a person's faculties, physical and mental, over the entire course of a life. Such an understanding of the soul may be analogous in some ways to the pure rational consciousness of the "Cartesian" soul, but in other ways it is also analogous to the "information" that is encoded in DNA or embodied in epigenetic systems. And at either end of the continuum of the soul's powers, thus conceived, there is much that does not lie at the surface of thought and that rarely appears within ordinary awareness: rational consciousness is neither directly in control of all the body's physiological functions nor, without intense spiritual discipline, aware of the highest intellect's perpetual openness to the light of the divine. And this richer conception of the soul is hardly unique to Western intellectual tradition. Consider (to take an example more or less at random) the *Taittiriya Upanishad*'s wonderful delineation of the various levels of mind: the material (*anna*), vital (*prana*), mental (*manas*), purely conscious (*vijñana*), and blissful (*ananda*).[1]

Within the mechanistic picture of reality, however, the problems of consciousness are not only very real, but also depressingly numerous, and attempts to solve them in materialist terms frequently devolve into absurdity, and seem inevitably only to exchange one explanatory deficiency for another. The most daring of these attempts, a line of thought known as "eliminativism," works a series of curious variations on the notion that all truths about the world can be entirely reduced to, and so more correctly described by, the facts of physics. The genuine, fully developed eliminativist position—and I am not exaggerating or indulging in spiteful caricature here—is that there really is no such thing as consciousness at all, and that all talk about minds, intentions, ideas, convictions, thoughts, and so forth belongs to the quaintly primitive patois of folk psychology. Ideally, we should be able to dispense with such language altogether and instead speak solely in terms of discrete physical processes and material elements, "eliminating" all pre-scientific allusions to persons and mental events entirely. Consciousness and thoughts and the like are just figments of folklore; they no more have any real existence in themselves than the images in a pointillistic painting have any real existence in addition to the canvas and the minuscule motes of paint composing them: in either case, if one will but look closely enough, the illusion of unity will dissolve. And even this simile probably concedes too much to our conventional mythology of consciousness, given that a painting can reasonably be said—though the eliminativist would ultimately have to deny this as well, come to think of it—to have been arranged by some sort of formal principle and agency beyond its material components and physical genesis, whereas eliminativism seeks to dispense with language of formal principles and agencies altogether, in favor of a purely particulate and physically causal description of reality. Such a description, once it is perfected, will supposedly do away with the problem of consciousness because it will have done away with consciousness itself.

Clearly this is not a position that should be taken very seriously, even if a number of academic philosophers treat it as if it should be. It is little more than the genetic fallacy monstrously amplified into an interminable succession of reductiones ad absurdum, and its guiding premise—the arcane idea that somewhere out there, in principle at least, there exists an infinite narrative of physical particularities that could supplant all references to unified states of consciousness, without any empirical remainder—is not so much audacious as hallucinatory. At the apex of the mind, so to speak, there is the experience of consciousness as an absolutely singular and indivisible reality, which no inventory of material constituents and physical events will ever be able to eliminate. Here again, and as nowhere else, we are dealing with an irreducibly primordial datum. That said, it would be wrong to dismiss eliminativism as just an absurdist fantasy. It should at least be commended for its intellectual honesty, and even for the fearless consistency of the reasoning behind it. Eliminativists grasp—as many materialists are unable or unwilling to do—that a truly consistent materialism must inevitably reach just such a logical terminus. It is an extreme position, admittedly, almost beyond the point of parody, but it is also the inevitable result of an unfailing adherence to naturalist principles. If all those formal structures that seem to constitute the reality we know, and all the manifest purposes that seem to call them into being, are in fact not genuinely causal forces but only the posterior results of unguided physical processes, then in the end they really do have no substantial reality *in themselves.* Any description of them, then, must be not only reducible to but also eliminable by more fundamental descriptions of a purely physical, purely impersonal kind. To allow for even the slightest deviation on this point—to suggest, perhaps, that personal consciousness or culture or ideas possess any features or produce any effects that cannot in principle be more correctly described without reference to consciousness, culture, ideas, or anything else of that kind—is to surrender materialism's moral advantage over "transcendental" or "supernatural" thinking. Any incoherence in eliminativist theory, therefore, lies not in the theory itself—which is supremely internally coherent—but rather in the naturalist principles to which it is obedient.

To make sense of that claim, however, one needs to consider how numerous and deep the problems that consciousness poses for the naturalist view of reality truly are.

III

Even to begin to do the topic justice, admittedly, would require a book of its own, which obviously I cannot produce here, since my ultimate concerns lie elsewhere. What I *can* do, however, other than gesture insouciantly in the direction of my postscript once again, is list a few of the more notable and irksome difficulties that the phenomenology of consciousness creates for materialist models of the mind, and thus for attempts to devise naturalistic or mechanistic explanations of consciousness.

So, then:

1. *The qualitative dimension of experience.* Nothing is more basic to consciousness than what philosophers of mind call *qualia*. A *quale* (the singular form of the noun) is that irreducibly subjective feeling of "what it is like" to experience something, the "phenomenal" aspect of knowledge, the private impression one has of a sensible reality (a color, a musical tone, a fragrance, a shock of

pain, and so on), or of a more impalpable but still perceptible reality (an emotional atmosphere, a memory, a fantasy, an aesthetic effect, a personal mood). Qualia are what define and differentiate our experiences, what make it possible to distinguish blue from red or yellow or green as sensible properties, or a sound from a sight, what determine our tastes and distastes, pleasures and displeasures, what endow the things of the world with this or that character *for us*. They constitute the purest, most immediate, most inalienable dimension of personal awareness, without which there could be no private experience and no personal identity at all; apart from qualia there is no such thing as subjective consciousness. They are often said to be, in philosophical parlance, intrinsic properties, because they cannot be wholly reduced to a relation to some other kind of thing, beyond themselves or beyond the subject who experiences them; they simply are what they are. Your shock of pain may be caused by an objective encounter between the heel of your left foot and a sharp pebble, but your subjective experience of that pain as your own is not an objective item open to general scrutiny, nor is it even a functionally necessary aspect of your body's system of stimulus and response. Qualia seem to exist in excess of all the objectively detectable physical processes with which they are associated: they do not inhere in the objects of experience themselves but only in our act of perceiving those objects, and they seem to differ from one another far more radically than any one neuronal event differs from any other. In mechanistic terms, they cannot be directly correlated with, let alone identified with, the electrochemical impulses in the brain's synapses, because the objective nature of those impulses is so very different in kind from the phenomenal events of subjective awareness. In materialist terms, they cannot be directly correlated with, let alone identified with, the physical realities they presumably reflect, because those realities as objectively measured lack any of the purely relative features of qualitative experience—whether, for example, I find the tea in the blue willow cup before me too tepid, too hot, or exactly right—but possess only absolute values—such as can be measured by the Fahrenheit or Celsius scale. In themselves, physical realities are not invested with the perceptible qualities available to a person's senses, sensibility, and temperament; the red you see "in" a rose is not in the rose itself, considered as an ensemble of quantifiable particles, processes, and aggregations, but only in your perception of it. And mechanistic metaphysics tells us that only the quantitative physical properties of the world are *really* real. A computer equipped with the right instrumentation could record all the physical facts about, say, a sunset quite exhaustively as far as scientific method is concerned, despite its incapacity for any qualitative experience of the "what it is like" of that sunset. At the same time, my personal experience of what that sunset "is like" is not an additional objective fact about the event itself, but only a subjective fact about me.

Or so many have argued. The question of qualia is a remarkably prominent concern in much modern philosophy of mind, though the philosophers most concerned with the issue are often talking at cross-purposes. The most obvious mystery about qualia is simply that there seems to be no conceivable causal model, of the sort credible to modern scientific method, that could seamlessly, intelligibly explain to us how the electrochemistry of the brain, which is mechanically uniform and physically causal, could generate the unique, varied, and incommunicable experience of a particular person's inner phenomenal world. The first-person perspective is not dissoluble into a third-person narrative of reality; consciousness cannot be satisfactorily reduced to physics without subtracting something. The redness of the red, red rose in my garden, as I consciously experience it while gazing at the rose in a poetic reverie, has objective existence not in the molecules or biochemical events that compose those petals, that stem, or those thorns, or that compose my synapses, my sensory apparatus, or the electrochemical reactions going on in my brain. The phenomenal experience is in my mind but has no physical presence in my brain or in the world around me; no visible "red plasm" detaches itself from the petals of the rose and nimbly slips in through my optic nerves and then across the axons of my brain, retaining its visible redness all along the way. And, as I have suggested, it is probably logically impossible to address this issue meaningfully in purely quantitative and physicalist terms. This is because the essential mystery here is not that the encounter between a particular physical object and a particular kind of sensory apparatus should generate data of a very particular kind. Yes, the rose is "red" because it has certain properties that reflect light in a way that is chromatically legible, so to speak, when translated through the human eyes and optic nerves and brain. But the real mystery lies on the other side of that process, entirely in the subjectivity that is the site of those impressions, and hence in their irreducibly subjective character.

Some of the current naturalist attempts to explain away the problems qualia pose for a mechanistic understanding of reality are of the "functionalist" or instrumental variety: qualia have a causal role in the integrated physiological systems of organisms, it is argued; they can serve, for instance, to prevent us from attempting to hold fire in our hands, or perhaps from running heedlessly toward the open jaws of a bear. Hence, they are not purely intrinsic properties of the mind, but objective properties of an integrated system of physiological and mental operations, with distinct functions. There are many problems with such arguments, and they have been pointed out often enough: for instance, the difficulty in showing how the qualitative dimension of experiences adds anything indispensably causative to the information those experiences convey. Could not a very sophisticated automaton or even some kind of "soulless" human replicant have all the same functional relations without possessing subjective awareness as well? Could not either be programmed to withdraw its titanium pincers or biotechnical digits from the flame or to flee wildly before the teeth of the bear, in either case uttering the appropriate howls of pain or terror, even though within each of them there existed only an absolute affective void? (For all I know, all of you whom I imagine as reading and understanding this text are just such beings, because—once again—one subjectivity has no access to any other, by any avenue whatsoever.) Is not the qualitative dimension of experience, then, still something ontologically distinct from and additional to the objective functional relations of a mechanical system of stimulus and response? And, then again, are there not also innumerable qualia that seem clearly to have no functional purpose at all, but simply are—such as that odd and poignantly buoyant melancholy that I derive from a great deal of music written in the key of D-minor? And so on. Most of the debates on these matters are probably irresoluble, because they all take place in a shadowy borderland between a nonexistent science and an inadjudicable logic, where the meanings of terms drift about shape-lessly like billows of mist. The deeper problem with a functionalist account, however, is that it persistently fails to say anything about the real enigma of consciousness, which is subjectivity as such; the functional account is only a conjecture regarding what purpose subjective phenomena might serve, and not an explanation of how those phenomena are possible despite how obviously they differ from all the ponderable *quanta* of which the physical world is sup-posedly made.

Some theorists have argued that all perplexities on the matter can be dispelled by the postulate that qualia are nothing more than how the brain registers and "represents" the objects it en-counters through the senses. That is to say, a great many philoso-phers of mind take for granted the position that the world as it appears to us is not a direct apprehension of the world in itself, but only the "picture" or "representation" of the world produced by the brain processing the perceptions translated through the nerves of the body and then reconstructing the objects of percep-tion as mental images. When I look at a red rose, I am not seeing the rose "in itself," but only a portrait of the rose composed by my optical and cerebral equipment and then presented to my mind. Perhaps, moreover, qualia are nothing but elements of the brain's representational palette, aspects of the way in which the intricate machinery of brain and body respond to the data of objective properties in the things perceived; they are entirely reducible to the ways our minds "intend" or "aim at" the reality around us (and I shall say more about such "intending" below), and so are not in-trinsic realities distinct from the objects of experience. My sup-posedly subjective experience of the rose's redness is actually the way in which objective aspects of the rose are known to me, and so qualia are not really subjective mental realities, but exist objectively as features of the things themselves. Some even argue that our conscious experience is "transparent" to the objects of perception, and has no content not received from them. These are contentious claims, and many cogent arguments have been raised against reducing qualia to aspects of representation: Are there not qualia that seem clearly associated with no representational content at all, for instance, or that seem far to exceed any of the information an object imparts (and so forth)? For myself, I am largely indifferent to these debates, since all of them seem at once minutely technical and conceptually vague, and often involve a constant and dubious redefinition of terms.

More to the point, it seems to me that these arguments also fail to engage the truly essential and abiding mystery of qualitative experience. I have to say, I have no idea how a materialist or physicalist understanding of the world allows for such a thing as the "transparency" of experience before the world, not simply because whatever the brain knows of things has to be mediated and translated through an apparatus of perception (the sensible red that I perceive in the rose really is not present in the rose *as* that shade of red in any objective, quantitative sense) but also because—and here, once again, is the crux of the matter—the form and manner of qualitative experience remain subjective in precisely the way that material quanta are not. According to certain premodern metaphysical schemes, it might make perfect sense to say that experience can constitute some kind of immediate communion between consciousness and objective things, because both mind and matter can be *informed,* in their differing modes, by one and the same rational form: the form of the rose is an ideal reality that is simultaneously conceivable and creatively causal, subjective and objective at once, simultaneously shaping both my thoughts and the material substrate of the rose. But, from a modern naturalist perspective, it simply cannot be the case that my qualitative experience of a rose's redness just *is* the same thing as a property quantitatively present in a physical object out there; there is no "higher cause" uniting the subjective and objective poles of experience in some sort of ontological identity or harmony. Even if that phenomenal redness is derived from some objective feature of that rose, that redness is not in that rose in the form of subjective awareness; for me, that redness exists as a feeling of "what it is like," and no such feeling is any part of the rose itself. And it is that subjectivity, the qualitativeness as such of the experience, that remains unaccounted for by any attempt—functionalist, representationalist, or other—to naturalize consciousness in a way conformable to materialism.

Again, the problem of subjectivity requires not some explanation of what purpose qualitative personal experience might conceivably serve, evolutionary or physiological or otherwise, but some account of how it is that the alleged aimlessness and mechanistic extrinsicism of matter can produce the directedness, self-presence, and introspective depth of the personal vantage, the pure perspective of the I. It is remarkable how often this rather obvious and quite, quite indubitable reality—that I possess a unique, immediate, and incommunicable subjectivity, a private perspective and self-reflective identity—is obscured rather than illumined by the debates regarding qualia. Daniel Dennett, for instance, has argued that there are no such things as qualia, on the grounds that what we think of as qualia are not immediately self-verifying or immune to third-person explanations of their content, and therefore cannot be truly "intrinsic." For instance, he says, take two coffee drinkers whose attitudes toward their coffee change over time, one believing the change has occurred in the coffee itself, the other believing that it has occurred in his feelings about the coffee; neither, it seems, could determine from direct introspection whether indeed the alteration in his tastes is really physiological or only aesthetic, and so it would require some third-person examination of the facts to confirm or dispel his suspicions; so clearly neither man has any infallibly direct access to his private intuitions, and hence (and the logic of this step is somewhat eerily elusive) there are no qualia at all. But this is simply a non sequitur. No one doubts that qualitative states of consciousness can be altered by changes both in the objects of perception or in one's organs of perception, or that they may not be constant throughout one's life; but that does not mean that such states do not exist.

If the red of the rose in my garden should all at once turn to gray, for example, I should indeed need some sort of third-person explanation to apprise me of whether some change in the environment has caused the rose to lose its pigmentation or whether instead I am suffering from some kind of dyschromatopsia induced by, say, a peculiar variant of optic neuritis. That in no way, however, diminishes the immediacy, indubitability, irreducible subjectivity, and qualitative nature of my experience of either that red or that gray in the moment I am having it. Whatever peculiar weight we give to the term "intrinsic" (and there is room for much tiresome debate here), it certainly applies properly to this indissoluble privacy of qualitative awareness. Perhaps, in fact, there are no roses in my garden at all and I am hallucinating the entire episode, along with the environmental scientist or physician trying to explain the situation to me. Whatever the case, though, my experience is definitely invested with intrinsically subjective qualities. If anything, Dennett's arguments seem simply to reinforce the claim that the qualitative dimension of experience in itself does not merely convey *objective* information, about the world or about one's own brain states, but is thoroughly subjective, thoroughly of itself, and thus ontologically distinct from the objectively mensurable physical processes with which it is associated. A particular quale in the present may not be sufficient to tell me whether it is my coffee or my gustatory standards that time has altered (and so does not simply represent some objective feature of perception), but it certainly testifies to itself in an absolutely immediate, private, and undeniable way.

I do not want to dwell on this at unnecessary length. The reality of subjectivity is another primordial datum—the primordial datum par excellence, in fact—that cannot be denied without a swift descent into nonsense. One of the distinct oddities of physicalist approaches to the problem, however, is that they generally involve some attempt to reduce qualitative consciousness to some other aspect of the mind's processes, such as representation, on the bizarre assumption that these processes can then be explained in purely physical and mechanical terms, once we have mastered the neurology underlying them. But this is an inversion of logic, because processes like representation are ultimately contingent upon subjective consciousness and so cannot be invoked as explanations of consciousness. Purely physical systems can translate physical realities into different kinds of data, perhaps: a camera, for example, can store patterns of light and color in an analogue or digital form, and a recording device can do the same thing with sounds. But nothing a camera or a recording device produces constitutes a representation of anything at all unless there is a subjective consciousness present to interpret it as a picture or recording *of* some other thing. There must be a real intention—a real directedness—of the mind toward the picture or the recording *as* representing something beyond itself, and toward the thing depicted *as* represented, and this is an intellective act of subjective awareness. To confirm this, one need only consider what the mind does when it thinks about the world, or about anything at all. For instance:

IV

2. *Abstract concepts.* It is extremely difficult to explain how any set of purely physical actions and interactions could possibly invest consciousness with the immaterial—which is to say, purely abstract—concepts by which all experience is necessarily interpreted and known. It is almost impossible to say how a purely material system of stimulus and response could generate universal categories of understanding, especially if (and one hopes that most materialists would grant this much) those categories are not mere idiosyncratic personal inflections of experience, but real forms of knowledge about reality. In fact, they are the very substance of our knowledge of reality. As Hegel argued perhaps more persuasively than any other philosopher, simple sense-knowledge of particular things, in itself, would be utterly vacuous. My understanding of anything, even something as humbly particular as that

insistently red rose in my garden, is composed not just of a collection of physical data but of the conceptual abstractions that my mind imposes upon them: I know the rose as a discrete object, as a flower, as a particular kind of flower, as a kind of vegetation, as a horticultural achievement, as a biological system, as a feature of an ecology, as an object of artistic interest, as a venerable and multifaceted symbol, and so on; some of the concepts by which I know it are eidetic, some taxonomic, some aesthetic, some personal, and so on. All of these abstractions belong to various kinds of category and allow me, according to my interests and intentions, to situate the rose in a vast number of different sets: I can associate it eidetically not only with other flowers, but also with pictures of flowers; I can associate it biologically not only with other flowers, but also with non-floriferous sorts of vegetation; and so on.

It is excruciatingly hard to see how any mechanical material system could create these categories, or how any purely physical system of interactions, however precisely coordinated, could produce an abstract concept. Surely no sequence of gradual or particulate steps, physiological or evolutionary, could by itself overcome the qualitative abyss between sense experience and mental abstractions. Even the purely eidetic resemblances between two objects would be unrecognizable to a merely material system of surveillance. A wholly mechanical process of morphological sifting and filtering, cumulative retention and comparison—even one developed over vast phylogenic epochs and operating through an equally vast series of neurological subsystems—could never by itself generate the sense of resemblances and general kinds that give us our ability to recognize anything at all. To think otherwise is to commit just another version of the pleonastic fallacy. Before any conscious recognition of even an elementary likeness between different things is possible, certain abstract concepts must already be in operation. To see how the rose in my garden resembles another flower, I must already have not only some notion of flowers in the abstract but also some grasp of the abstract concept of resemblance, as well as some concept of discrete objects as discrete objects of mental focus, and some set of conceptual rules regarding what sorts of similarity or dissimilarity to look for or ignore. And no order of empirical magnitude changes this fact: no matter how many times a purely mechanical sensory apparatus might encounter similar objects, all of those accumulated instances taken together would not yield a single glimmer of awareness of the likeness between two things were there not some kind of conscious grasp of a universal absolute—that is, a concept already "absolved" of any attachment to this or that particular object, logically prior to any empirical encounter—already in place: likeness, flower, object, substance, shape . . . There are no hybrid intermediaries here, half empirical and half abstract, that could bridge the difference. The world can appear to us as the world only because it comes to us formally abstracted, defined for us by general types that cannot just be gathered from physical reality, like pollen from flowers. Not even the simplest abstractions, such as the resemblance between different shapes or patterns, can arise from mere physical condensations of experience, spontaneously generating conceptual algorithms of reality, because the synthesizing work of comparison is only possible by way of some prior conceptual grammar, which is not wholly dependent on the senses, and which can direct consciousness toward specific defining features of likeness and unlikeness. Simply said, there is no wholly cogent objective "percept" without a concept—though, as it happens, there is many a concept without a corresponding percept.

This last consideration, moreover, is a still more difficult problem for materialist models of the mind. Even if one imagines that somehow, given a sufficiently varied evolutionary history and sufficient neural complexity, a responsive organism could arrive by physical processes at some sort of eidetic consciousness, and some notion of similarity in the abstract, the levels of abstraction at which the mind works far exceed those merely morphological similarities between material things that the senses might somehow detect. A classic example, going back to antiquity, is that of geometric figures, like a perfect circle or a perfectly straight line. There may exist indistinct analogies of such figures in nature, but no real instances; and even those analogies are recognizable only because the mind synthesizes them through the concept to which they correspond. It is hard to see how the idea of a perfect isosceles triangle, for instance, could be arrived at physiologically, as a rarefaction of sense experience into geometry, unless it were already there to assist the mind in finding its imperfect reflection in certain physical patterns. And then, of course, there are more elaborate figures of which we possess logical concepts, but no intuition in either empirical experience or the imagination (how many faces can my mental picture of a polyhedron have before it melts into an indistinct haze, and how far can my mental image of an infinite straight line really extend, and how well can I summon up a picture of a punctiliar absence of extension?). And even if one insists on believing that geometrical abstractions are genetically derived from sensory impressions of physical shapes, which the apparatus of perception is somehow able to recognize in the natural world without the initial assistance of even the abstract concept *shape,* there is the still more daunting and astounding reality of pure mathematics. That the human intellect is capable of discovering mathematical truths, which (among many other things) again and again prove themselves able to describe the realities that physics explores, is a marvel that might very well exceed anyone's best powers of exaggeration.

I sometimes think we fail to be nearly as surprised and baffled by mathematical knowledge as we ought to be largely because we tend to think of the world as vaguely "arithmetical," in the sense that its parts are enumerable and measurable, and because we lazily think of pure mathematics as just some sort of immense amplification of arithmetic, rather than the angelic language of nearly limitless intelligibility that it is. So we are not particularly astonished to find that nature appears to be only "a spume that plays upon a ghostly paradigm of things." Even if one could wholly ground mathematics in empirical experience (which one cannot), it would still give evidence of abstractive powers in the human mind so far in excess of what the physical forces of mechanized matter or the requirements of evolution could produce that it would be hard not to view the whole phenomenon as a kind of miracle. All attempts to produce a naturalist philosophy of mathematics—by way of different kinds of formalism, constructivism, fictionalism, or what have you—have consistently failed to account adequately for what mathematics actually can accomplish. Especially hopeless are attempts to give an evolutionary account of mathematics: inasmuch as advances in mathematical knowledge unfold from mathematical premises, entirely outside of any physical context, and are not subject to natural selection; and inasmuch as mathematical truths are necessary truths, whose authority depends upon no physical reality at all. It is no great surprise then that so pronounced a majority of mathematicians are realists (or perhaps one should say Platonists) in regard to mathematical truths. The power of mathematics' abstract and immaterial language to make reality ever more transparent to reason and reason ever more transparent to reality is not readily (or even imaginably) susceptible of any reduction to physical causes.

In any event, the human aptitude for mathematical truth is merely one of the more acute examples of a faculty that is revealed in every aspect of rational life: in the ability to form and use abstract concepts like "beauty" or "justice," for instance, or in the mind's capacities for reasoning about unrepresentable but intelligible ideas like "infinity," or for grasping logical truths, or for fantasy and fancy, or for speculative thought, or for letting one concept lead to another under its own momentum. And this leads naturally into the next topic.

3. *Reason.* If there is such a thing as rational thought, which I like to think there is, it must consist in the use of a logical syntax containing real semantic content (that is, it must contain meanings that can be joined together by conceptual connections). To reason about something is to proceed from one premise or proposition or concept to another, in order ideally to arrive at some conclusion, and in a coherent sequence whose connections are determined by the semantic content of each of the steps taken— each individual logical syntagma of the argument, each clause or sentence or symbol. In a simple syllogism, for example, two premises in conjunction inevitably produce a conclusion determined by their logical content. "Every rose in my garden is red; the rose I am looking at now is in my garden; therefore, the rose I am looking

at now is red." But then the series of steps by which the mind arrives at the conclusion of a series of propositions simply cannot be identical with a series of brute events in the biochemistry of the brain. If the mechanical picture of nature is correct, after all, any sequence of physical causes and effects is determined entirely by the impersonal laws governing the material world. One neuronal event can cause another as a result of physical necessity, but certainly not as a result of logical necessity. And yet the necessary connection that exists between the addition of two numbers and the sum thereby yielded is one produced entirely by the conceptual content of the various terms of the equation, and not by any set of biochemical contingencies. Conversely, if the tenets of mechanistic materialism are sound, the mere semantic content of a thought should not be able to affect the course of physical events in the cerebrum. Even if the long process of human evolution has produced a brain *capable* of reason, the brain cannot produce the actual *contents* of reasoning; the connections among the brain's neurons cannot generate the symbolic and conceptual connections that compose an act of consecutive logic, because the brain's neurons are related to one another organically and therefore interact physically, not conceptually. Clearly, then, there are mental events that cannot be reduced to mechanical electrochemical processes.

Although, to be fair, I should note that the enterprising materialist can get around this argument by the simple expedient of arguing that there is no such thing as reason. And, strange to say, there are some who have made precisely that claim. It may be that each of the two discrete thoughts "Every rose in my garden is red" and "The rose I am looking at now is in my garden" is really just a physical event among my brain's neurons, as is the belief that they are connected to one another semantically and logically rather than merely conjoined electrochemically. And perhaps, also, their apparent logical connection to the thought "The rose I am looking at now is red" is really just another physical event prompted by its neuronal antecedents. Perhaps, moreover, my introspective sense that there is a clear rational order uniting this sequence of mental events is itself yet another electrochemical incident, just a little to the left of that area in the cerebral cortex where this utterly enchanting mirage of a cogent syllogism has taken up its momentary residence. Perhaps nothing really means anything; even the logical ligatures uniting a word (spoken or written) to the concept or object it represents and then to the community of language-users—what is sometimes called language's triadic semeiotic structure—may in fact be nothing more than extrinsic neurological associations. This may seem a somewhat preposterous position for the materialist to take, since it would mean that no rational argument is actually determined by its logical syntax; in fact, it would mean that there is no such thing as logical syntax, or syntax of any kind, or even words with meanings. It would even mean that no process of reasoning—not even the reasoning that produces the argument that there is no such thing as reason—is rationally coherent. But perhaps that is not too high a price to pay for someone emotionally committed to materialism (though, of course, in this view of things there would really be no such thing as materialism, since if there were it would be a concept with consecutive logical contents). Most materialists or physicalists or naturalists, however, like to see themselves as flinty rationalists rather than mad fanatics with an infinite appetite for paradox, and so this line of argument remains something of a boutique item among atheist fashions.[2]

4. *The transcendental conditions of experience.* To understand the world, the mind must in some sense compose the world, by which I mean supply the conditions necessary for its comprehension. So said Immanuel Kant (1724–1804), at least, and the point seems fairly difficult to dispute. One does not have to embrace Kantian epistemology as a whole (as I certainly do not) to recognize the truth that it is only as organized under a set of a priori categories that experience becomes intelligible; and those categories are not impressed upon the mind by physical reality but must always precede empirical experience. This is a point closely related to the issue of abstract concepts, as described above, though it is slightly more radical; the issue here is not just how the mind understands reality but how the mind has any continuous experience of anything at all. We can see easily enough how certain transcendental categories (that is to say, categories not bound to particular things, but abstractly applicable to all particular things) are necessary for the formation of rational judgments about things. For instance, a series of mere sense impressions of consecutive events, like smoke rising from a fire, can be synthesized into the judgment that the relation between the two events is one of causality only because the mind already possesses the concept of cause. Hence what the senses perceive as only a sequence the mind understands as a real consequence. And the category of cause could not be abstracted from nature were it not already present in the mind's perception of nature. In a broader sense, however, one can say that apart from the rational organization of experience in an

articulated and continuous order, under concepts formally prior to empirical data, the world would be for us nothing more than a sea-storm of sense impressions. The senses would not even perceive sequences of events because they would not be able to perceive distinct events at all. The mind interprets reality so as to have a reality to interpret, and the order of priority is irreversible. The categories that connect all things in a rational arrangement cannot be the noetic residues of sensuous experiences that, through sheer accumulation, arrange and interpret themselves; the coherence and intelligibility of experience is conditional upon those categories. This is a problem from a physicalist perspective, of course, in a way it was not for most ancient and mediaeval schools of thought (for which mind and world were both intrinsically informed by the same order of rational causes, and so were essentially open to one another). It is a problem that I do not want to linger over, however, because I would rather subsume the further considerations to which it points under what I take to be two still more insurmountable obstacles for any attempt at a naturalistic account of consciousness. To wit:

v

5. *Intentionality.* The Latin verb *intendere* means, among other things, to "direct toward," "aim at," or "reach for." In the philosophy of mind, the term "intentionality" refers not simply to a volitional tendency, but to the fundamental power of the mind to direct itself toward something. Intentionality is the mind's capacity for "aboutness," by which it thinks, desires, believes, means, rep-

resents, wills, imagines, or otherwise orients itself toward a specific object, purpose, or end. Intentionality is present in all perception, conception, language, cogitation, imagination, expectation, hope, and fear, as well as in every other determinate act of the conscious mind. It is what allows for conscious meaning, for references to or propositions about or representations of anything. The term was introduced into modern philosophy (drawing on scholastic precedent) by the brilliant Franz Brentano (1838–1917), a thinker more often invoked than read. For Brentano, intentionality is the very "mark of the mental," and is of its nature something entirely absent from the merely material physical order. Moreover, for Brentano there is no real act of consciousness that is not in some sense informed by this intentionality, not even the barest act of cognition.

At the simplest phenomenological level, it is not difficult to demonstrate that a certain degree of conscious and purposive attentiveness is needed for the mind to know clearly even the content of sense impressions. For instance, if one takes up a cup and drinks from it expecting to taste a dark ale, only instead to swallow a draught of wine, the immediate effect is not one of recognition but of cognitive dissonance; only as one adjusts one's intentional orientation does one taste the wine as wine rather than as just a confusing contradiction of one's expectations. What has happened is that at first the content of one's intentionality was met only in part by the content of one's experience—one experienced the drink as a liquid but not as ale—and so the mind had to retreat for an instant and intend the experience anew, so that the sense data could be organized (rather as if by a kind of formal cause) into a coherent act of consciousness. Much the same thing occurs in the case of optical illusions, of the sort one can choose to see in more than one way, as one consciously decides to do: as a result of a very specific intentional act, one can make oneself see the same figure as either a duck or a rabbit, or as either a vase or a pair of counterposed human profiles. These, however, are fairly trivial and local examples of the far deeper and more ubiquitous truth that the mind knows nothing in a merely passive way, but always has an end or meaning toward which it is purposively directed, as toward a final cause. In every act of representation, the intending mind invests perception with meaning by directing itself toward a certain determinate content of experience, and by thus interpreting each experience as an experience *of* this or that reality. Physical reality, however, according to mechanistic metaphysics at least, is intrinsically devoid of purpose, determinacy, or meaning. It is not directed toward any ends at all, it has no final causes, it cannot intend anything. Among many other things, this means that, in themselves, physical events cannot produce our representations of them, because it is we who supply whatever meaning or intelligibility those representations possess. The physical reality that impinges upon our organs of perception is a limitless ocean of causal sequences, neither beginning nor ending at any point in our experience, without discrete aspects or intrinsic orientation, pouring in upon us ceaselessly; our intentionality, by contrast, is finite, directed at a particular set of limits and a particular set of aspects, and imposes discrete forms upon our perceptions, thereby isolating objects of attention and interpretation amid the endless flow of physical cause and effect. Intentionality is, therefore, an abstract and conceptual operation entirely contrary to the logic of purely physical causation.

This cannot be stressed too forcibly. John Searle (as consistent a naturalist in philosophy as one can find, as it happens) usefully identifies three distinct kinds of intentionality: the intrinsic, the derived, and the "as-if" varieties. The first is the sort of real intentionality that the mind exercises toward objects of thought, desire, knowledge, or what have you. The second is the kind of directedness or meaning that exists in objects like diagrams, words, or signs when (and only when) they are employed by conscious minds capable of representing them as indications *of* something else. In themselves, as combinations of paper and ink, the marks on a diagram *mean* nothing. The third is not real intentionality at all but only the metaphorical purposiveness we ascribe to physical events that are in reality unguided, such as the flowing of a river down to the sea; the river does not *intend* the sea but flows thither simply on account of the force of gravity. And, needless to say, there can be no penumbral areas in the interstices of these distinctions, where one kind of intentionality gently merges into another; each is absolutely separate in nature from the other two. Nevertheless, there are those who claim that a real basis for intrinsic intentionality can be found in unconscious physical processes. Fred Dretske, for instance, has suggested that the needle of a compass pointing toward magnetic north constitutes a physical instance of intentionality, one that clearly "means" something beyond itself, in a particular way or in regard to a particular aspect of its object, and that therefore it is reasonable to see the intentionality of the mind as merely a far more elaborate form of the same phenomenon. It would be hard to imagine a more striking example of the pleonastic fallacy than this. Considered as a purely physical event, the needle of a compass does not *point* north, but is merely aligned at a certain angle by magnetic forces; as a physical object, it has no real "point" in that sense at all, nor certainly any reference beyond itself, and its behavior is at most an example of "as-if" intentionality, which is to say it is intentional in a purely figurative sense. Considered as an instrument constructed and used by human minds, of course, the compass does indeed have a kind of intentionality about it, but only of the derived variety; but that means that it receives its meaning entirely from a mind exercising intrinsic intentionality and so cannot in any sense provide a physical model of how intrinsic intentionality works.[3]

All attempts to naturalize the intentional powers of the conscious mind in a mechanical or materialist fashion—to show how, by a series of innumerable and agonizingly gradual advances, a diversity of purely physical forces could somehow add up to rational intellect's intentional aptitude—tend to make the same mistake, with greater or lesser sophistication. The qualitative difference between intrinsic intentionality and any other sort of "directedness," real or metaphorical, is absolute; even an infinite number of quantitative steps up from the mire of material forces toward the starry firmament of consciousness will prove inadequate to span the distance. The mind's "aboutness" truly is the unique "mark of the mental," and it indelibly marks the mental as irreducible to the physical. To see this, one need only remember that there is absolutely no intentional reciprocity between the mind and the objects of its intentions. Thoughts can be directed toward things, but (if the modern picture of nature is true) things cannot be directed toward thoughts, and so the *specific* content of the mind's intentions must be determined by consciousness alone. One could never derive the specific *meaning* of a given physical event from the event itself, not even a brain event, because in itself it *means* nothing at all; even the most minute investigation of its physical constituents and instances could never yield the particular significance that the mind represents it as having. John Haldane uses the example of a single geometrical figure that can be contemplated as either a triangle or a trilateral; as drawn on a sheet of paper, there is nothing in its physical composition that could possibly determine which of these intentional meanings has been brought to bear upon it. To take another example: I can contemplate the dark green vase standing before me, in which my wife has placed several red roses brought in from the garden, as a container for flowers, as an aesthetic artifact, as a variation upon certain Chinese decorative motifs, as a lovely abstract shape, as deceptively similar in its sheen to spinach-leaf jade, or as any number of other things, and none of those meanings in its precise specificity is imposed upon me by the simple physical event of the vase. And, of course, while the physical differences between the *Don Quixote* of Miguel de Cervantes and that of Pierre Menard might be nonexistent, still the latter is, as Borges notes, immeasurably richer in allusions, ironies, and evocations. And these examples do not begin to convey how radically basic to consciousness intentionality really is. Even to recognize a geometrical figure, or vase, or volume of *Don Quixote* as a discrete object, the mind must represent it as such, extracting it from the roiling tumult of ceaselessly changing impressions that crowd in upon the senses, isolating it and situating it within a coherent picture of the world; the mind must attend to it as having a specific meaning, a particular intentional content, toward which thought may be directed. In fact, intentionality does not necessarily require a physical object "out there" at all; its contents can be wholly imaginary, entirely conceptual, or purely prospective. My hopes for this man's respect or that woman's love depend not on any physical "meanings" I have received from beyond myself, but only on my subjective disposition toward him or her. And nothing in the whole ensemble of physical realities that constitute the world and the brain, understood purely as material occurrences, can determine precisely how and why thought should or can be directed at any end, concrete, abstract, or fanciful. Intentionality, therefore, is not a physical relation, not even a relation between external objects and the internal structure of the brain, but a mental event in excess of all physical relations. (Though, again, this is true only if nature is what our mechanistic metaphysics tells us it is.)[4]

6. *The unity of consciousness.* In the mechanical view of nature, the physical realm is devoid of simple unities, at least at the level of continuously subsistent things; nature consists in composites, with extension in space and time. Nonetheless—and despite the claims of many materialist philosophers to the contrary—consciousness is, in its subjectivity, one and indivisible. This is not to say that brain states cannot be altered, or that the mind cannot be confused, or that either the operations of the brain or the actions of the mind cannot be multiple. But in order for there to be such a thing as representation, or reason, or conceptual connections, or coherent experience, or subjectivity, or even the experience of confusion, there must be a single unified presence of consciousness to itself, a single point of perspective that is, so to speak, a vanishing point, without extension or parts, subsisting in its own simplicity. Actually, rather profound arguments in support of this claim can be drawn from thinkers as diverse as Plotinus, Shankara, and Kant.

It is unimportant here, however, whether one wants to speak of this unity as the *nous* that abides within and beyond our ordinary psychic operations, or as the *atman* within and beyond the finite mind wandering in *maya*, or as the transcendental apperception that is distinct from the ego's empirical apperception, or in altogether different terms. However one describes it, it is that luminous continuity and singleness of consciousness that underlies all the variety of perception, knowledge, memory, or even personal identity. It is in and by this unity that the incalculable diversity of the brain's processes, as well as the plurality and complexity of the world perceived, are converted into the fused awareness of a single subject; but this unity cannot have arisen from that diversity.

Before that claim can be understood, however, it is necessary to grasp that what is at issue here is not mere psychological unity or the integrity of personal identity or of private memory over time. These can be diminished, impaired, or largely destroyed by deep psychosis, brain damage, cortical surgery, drugs, amnesia, and so forth. The unity of consciousness, however, is immune to all disruption. When I say that consciousness cannot be reduced to material causes I am not denying that the regular operations of consciousness in corporeal beings are dependent upon the workings of the brain, or that the contents of consciousness can be radically changed or disrupted by physiological events. I am talking here only about the transcendental condition of consciousness, a simple and perhaps anonymous singularity of vantage, which makes subjective awareness and mental activity possible. It is present even when the ego's psychological or cognitive operations have been disoriented, clouded, or shattered. It is the failure to make this distinction—between, on the one hand, the unity of this transcendental perspective within the mind and, on the other, the integrity of personal mental states—that occasionally leads to assertions of the divisibility and hence materiality of consciousness. Claims of that sort are, I suppose, further evidence of the curious dilemma that the mechanical philosophy has created for us in forcing us to choose between a Cartesian dualism and a materialist monism. But a living embodied mind is neither simply an incorporeal intellect nor a mechanical function; it is a power that exceeds material causality without being free of the conditions of corporeal life; and it is a mistake to think that the unity of consciousness—or, if one prefers, the indivisibility of the soul— is called into doubt by cases of severe psychological or cognitive disorder.

We know, for instance, that a commissurotomy performed on the corpus callosum (a now largely abandoned treatment for severe epilepsy) can produce strange disjunctions between the cognitive functions of the brain's hemispheres. As a rule, a person who has undergone the procedure shows no signs of mental disintegration; but under certain test conditions, in which each hemisphere is "addressed" separately, one side of the brain can recognize and respond to stimuli without the other side's "knowledge." The results of these tests are somewhat ambiguous in many cases, and in the popular accounts it is often hard to sort out the empirical from the anecdotal; but in general it seems clear that the dominant left hemisphere, usually the seat of language skills, and the more subordinate and inexpressive right hemisphere can each accomplish certain specific cognitive tasks without any conscious communication (if that is the right word) between the two. This has led many to conclude that the operation has either created or discovered the existence of two distinct "minds" and that, therefore, conscious-ness is clearly a physiological and entirely frangible reality. That is a considerable exaggeration of the clinical findings. There is no real evidence that (as is sometimes claimed) a commissurotomy actu-ally produces two distinct subjects with discrete self-awarenesses and entirely different personal identities, or that these two selves are often in conflict, with the orderly intentions of the left hemi-sphere often being thwarted by the impish antics and designs of the right. Claims that such evidence exists prove, when the find-ings are viewed impartially, to involve as much interpretation as observation. They might equally well be taken, for example, as in-stances of a single consciousness trying and failing to integrate the experiences and behaviors that each hemisphere makes possible. As I have said, those who have had the operation remain largely normal and psychologically whole individuals, and only under special experimental conditions exhibit certain cognitive disjunc-tions. Even, however, if surgery or psychosis (if, say, multiple per-sonality disorder really exists) can create divisions within person-ality, the disorder of the empirical ego does not detract from the unity of the subjective perspective that is expressed in each "iden-tity" to the degree that there is true consciousness present.

At a minimum, though, experiments on commissurotomy patients do definitely seem to show that, in certain constrained circumstances, a disruption of the brain's functional integrity can force consciousness to exercise its attention upon each hemisphere's cognitive and behavioral functions separately, within the limits of what each hemisphere can naturally do now that it is deprived of its normal connections to the other hemisphere. This can perhaps create a kind of parallel and synchronous amnesia, so to speak, in which the mind cannot properly integrate the cognitive powers of the brain in a continuous experience, but must attend to each separately. But there is no reason to doubt that these cognitive disjunctions still exist within a single subjectivity, just like any other cognitive or psychological discontinuities brought about by neurological or emotional pathologies, or just like conscious and subconscious mental activities in a person with an undamaged brain. The results of these experiments are fascinating, needless to say, but it is not clear that they tell us anything *entirely* new about the relation between consciousness and discrete cognitive activities in the brain. We know, for instance, that it is possible to drive an accustomed route in one's car while thinking intently about something else, only to discover at the end of the journey that there is no trace of an affective awareness of the actual journey left in memory; and it may be that the whole cognitive task of driving that route had been consigned throughout to a capable but mostly subliminal level of awareness. We know also that it is possible to hear without hearing a dull political oration or fatuous sermon while one's conscious thoughts are elsewhere, enjoying the blessed liberty of some other cognitive dimension. We know how little conscious direction is exercised in the coordination of the two hands of a pianist. We know that our psychological identities are mutable and often full of internal tensions and multiple impulses. We already know, in short, that the conscious self is not a simple empirical unity but a plurality of powers and faculties, with many strata reaching far beneath—and perhaps others reaching far above—the level of ordinary awareness. We all contain multitudes. This is and has always been a problem for the more unsophisticated formulations of Cartesian dualism, but not for those nonmaterialist models of the mind that presume an intimate union between body and soul, comprising degrees of association and interdependency and different levels of "soul." Whatever the case, moreover, it is still only the transcendental unity of consciousness—its irreducible, inescapable subjectivity of perspective—that makes even the disjoined experiences of commissurotomy patients possible as acts of awareness (assuming, that is, that the operations in the right hemisphere of the brain are usually fully conscious operations to begin with, which is not entirely clear). Only the "vanishing point" of a subjective perspective allows the diversity of reality to appear to the mind as a unified phenomenon, to which consciousness can attend.

This, and not just the psychological integrity of the "empirical ego," is the unity of consciousness—the "I think" that underlies any mental representation of reality as a coherent phenomenon—that seems irreconcilable with a purely mechanical picture of the mind, even one that allows for a physiological convergence of the disparate faculties of the brain in some privileged panopticon located at some executive hub of the brain's neurology. However modular the structure of the brain may or may not be, the attempt to discover the unity of consciousness in a final supervisory cerebral module suffers from a number of simple logical difficulties. For one thing, as a physical reality that organizing module would itself be a composite thing whose power to unify experience could not arise from its various parts and functions, but would have to precede them and organize them into a single point of view also. Even if every part of that faculty were in some sense partially aware, there would still have to be a simple awareness of the whole ensemble of impressions organizing them, a prior intention and capacity to view that whole as *one*. Neuroscientists tend not to believe in a central locus of thought within the brain in any event; but even if there were such a thing it could unify the disparate forms of knowledge drawn from the various parts of the brain and nervous system only by synthesizing them through its own faculties; and these too would have to be unified by some other central faculty, which itself would have to be unified, and so on without end. Any physical thing that might be able to integrate experience into a conscious unity would somehow already have to possess a unified "knowledge" of the diverse realities that it is supposed to gather into a totality, a transcendental grasp of the empirical data as a consonant totality, toward which it would be intentionally inclined; and so it would already have to be informed by a unity of perspective logically prior to its own physiological complexity. It would have to be dependent upon, and hence could not be the source of, the principle of unity; and, apart from that principle and its perfect simplicity, all the diverse faculties of perception, in all their splendid richness and variety, would never be combined in a coherent act of knowledge. Any attempt to arrive at the unity of thought from the complexity of material structures leads to an infinite regress, an infinite multiplication of pleonastic insufficiencies.[5]

VI

Take these observations as you will. They are meant as inductive approaches to a nonmaterialist conception of the mind, not deductive demonstrations of some particular theory of the relation between soul and body. None of these issues is ever settled, in any event. As an academic discipline, philosophy of mind may be, of its nature, especially immune to conclusive statements of any kind; there really is no other area in philosophy in which the outlandish, the vague, the willfully obscure, and the patently ridiculous are tolerated in such lavish quantities. This may be inevitable, though. Perhaps it really is the case that, as "new mysterians" like Colin McGinn have argued, our brains simply have not been equipped by evolution to think about thought, or at least to understand it. I think it much more likely, however, that our conceptual limitations are imposed upon us not just by our biology but also by the history of intellectual fashions. What makes the question of consciousness so intractable to us today, and hence so fertile a source of confusion and dashingly delirious invention, is not so much the magnitude of the logical problem as our inflexible and imaginatively constrained loyalty to a particular ontology and a particular conception of nature. Materialism, mechanism: neither is especially hospitable to a coherent theory of mind. This being so, the wise course might be to reconsider our commitment to our metaphysics.

Whatever picture of reality we choose to cling to, however, we should at least be able to preserve some appropriate sense of the sheer immensity of the mystery of consciousness—just a humble sense of how much it differs from any other, *obviously* material phenomenon—no matter how far afield our speculations might carry us. We should be able to notice that we are talking about something that is so unlike anything else known to us empirically that, if it can be explained in physical terms, it also demands a

radical revision of those terms. To account for subjective consciousness in a way that shows some grasp of its apparent resistance to
the mechanistic understanding of things, it simply cannot suffice
to offer hypotheses concerning what functions consciousness might
serve in the general mechanics of the brain. J. J. C. Smart, an atheist philosopher of some real acuity, dismisses the problem of consciousness practically out of hand by suggesting that subjective
awareness might be some kind of "proprioception" by which one
part of the brain keeps an eye on other parts of the brain, rather as
a device within a sophisticated robot might be programmed to
monitor the robot's own systems; and one can see, says Smart,
how such a function would be evolutionarily advantageous. So
the problem of how the brain can be intentionally directed toward
the world is to be explained in terms of a smaller brain within the
brain intentionally directed toward the brain's perception of the
world. I am not sure how this is supposed to help us understand
anything about the mind, or how it does much more than inaugu-
rate an infinite explanatory regress. Even if the mechanical metaphors were cogent (which they are not, for reasons mentioned
both above and below), positing yet another material function
atop the other material functions of sensation and perception still
does nothing to explain how all those features of consciousness
that seem to defy the physicalist narrative of reality are possible in
the first place. If I should visit you at your home and discover that,
rather than living in a house, you instead shelter under a large roof
that simply hovers above the ground, apparently neither supported
by nor suspended from anything else, and should ask you how this
is possible, I should not feel at all satisfied if you were to answer,

"It's to keep the rain out"—not even if you were then helpfully to elaborate upon this by observing that keeping the rain out is evolutionarily advantageous.[6]

This is the great non sequitur that pervades practically all attempts, evolutionary or mechanical, to reduce consciousness wholly to its basic physiological constituents. If there is something structurally problematic about consciousness for a physicalist view of things, a strictly genetic narrative of how consciousness might have evolved over a very long time, by a very great number of discrete steps, under the pressure of natural selection, cannot provide us with an answer to the central question. What, precisely, did nature select for survival, and at what point was the qualitative difference between brute physical causality and unified intentional subjectivity vanquished? And how can that transition fail to have been an essentially magical one? It makes sense to say that a photosensitive cutaneous patch may be preserved by natural selection and so become the first step toward the camera eye; but there is no meaning-sensitive or category-sensitive patch of the brain or nervous system that can become the first step toward intentionality, because meanings and categories are not physical things to which a neural capacity can correspond, but are instead products of intentional consciousness. By the same token, these questions are not answered by trying to show how consciousness can be built up from the raw accumulation of the purely physical systems and subsystems and modular concrescences constituting conscious organisms. At some stage of organic complexity in that process— amoeba, cephalopod, reptile, viviparous mammal, Australopithecines, what have you—a qualitative abyss still must be bridged. It might be tempting to imagine that we could imaginatively dissolve consciousness into ever smaller and more particular elements, until we reached the barest material substrate, and then conceptually reconstitute it again without the invocation of any immaterial aptitudes, just as we can make the image on that pointillist canvas I mentioned above dissolve before our eyes simply by drawing as near to it as possible and can then make it reappear simply by stepping sufficiently far back again. There is no magic in any of that, no matter what those credulous savages stupefied by the superstitions of "folk psychology" might believe. But, then again, there is something usefully recursive about this metaphor: Who does the standing back, after all? Where is this point of perspective that allows for the appearance of an ordered unity located? At what point does the chaos of sensory processes somehow acquire a singular point of view of itself? These are not facetious questions. There is a troubling tendency among materialist philosophers of mind and cognitive scientists to indulge in analogies that, far from making consciousness more intelligible, are themselves intelligible only because they presume the operations of consciousness. It is not uncommon to find cameras or televisions mentioned as mechanical analogies of the mind's processes of representation; but, of course, a camera does not look at pictures and a television does not watch itself, and there is nothing even remotely representational in their functions apart from the intentions of a conscious mind, which is to be found not in those devices but in a person. Something very similar is true of attempts to explain human thought in terms of computers, as I shall discuss shortly. All such analogies terminate precisely where they began: in the living mind, imperturbable in its incommunicable subjectivity and awareness, still the mysterious glass in which being shines forth as *thought*.

There is nowhere else to go, really. Even so, the project of "naturalizing consciousness" will continue so long as there seems even a shimmer of a hope of reducing the qualitative difference between material and mental events to a quantitative difference between different kinds of physical causality. The history of modern intellectual dogma dictates that it must. Daniel Dennett—for whom, as for most late modern philosophers of mind, the only options open are materialism and Cartesian dualism—deals with matters like representation by proposing a "homuncular decomposition" of our customary picture of unified intentional consciousness into a plurality of disparate but integrated sensory, neurological, and discriminatory systems. Rather than a single brilliant and omnicompetent Cartesian homunculus seated at the center of the self, perhaps there are a great many rather stupid and minimally competent homunculi whom evolutionary history has collected into a vastly complex confederation of largely cooperative but still diffuse functions. Rather than a unified intentional feat of representation, perhaps one's knowledge of the world consists in a great number of information states that are never resolved into a single presentation or located in any single place in the brain, but that instead spill over and modify one another a little untidily. This, at any rate, is Dennett's "Multiple Drafts Model" of the mind: not only is there no unique and indivisible spiritual subject within— no soul—but neither is there some central control room in the brain, some "Cartesian theatre" where the mind enjoys the fully composed spectacle of the represented world. Rather, data enter the brain in a large variety of ways, not absolutely coordinated or synchronous with one another, in a ceaseless flow of shifting and not entirely consonant "drafts" of reality. And from the multiplic-

ity and generality of brain activity we can conclude, Dennett suggests, that there is no single locus of consciousness and so no such
thing as subjective consciousness at all, or any real intentionality;
there is only the illusion of consciousness, as a sort of after-effect
produced by the variegated physical and functional machinery of
the body and brain.

If that last move seems somewhat incoherent . . . well, in fact
it is. The very notion that the idea of "multiple drafts" has any
bearing on the "question" of whether subjective consciousness really exists—which, again, is not a question at all, because subjective consciousness is an indubitable primordial datum, the denial
of which is simply meaningless—is just a confusion of issues. It is
a mistake to think that the quite obvious reality that the brain
processes sensations and perceptions through several distinct aspects of its apparatus, not always perfectly harmonized with one
another, entitles us to deny the reality of the consciousness in
which those sensations and perceptions—in all their conjunctions
and disjunctions—are experienced from a unified perspective. We
know and have always known that the senses and our modes of
perception and judgment are multiple and occasionally confused;
that does not mean that there is not still a unified subjectivity in
which both the continuities and discontinuities of perception are
integrated into a single awareness. The eye may see something at a
great distance well before the ear hears it, but that does not mean
there is not a discrete I in whom the two perceptions are joined in
a continuous representation. The unity of intentional subjectivity
does not depend on the perfect synchronicity of the senses; but the
recognition of the lack of such synchronicity, or the recognition
of anything else for that matter, most definitely depends upon the

unity of intentional subjectivity. In fact, if Dennett is right about just how diffusely distributed all the receptive and discriminative faculties of the brain are, then he has provided a powerful argument for the reality of the immaterial soul. After all, the spatially extended and mechanically plural operations of the brain as a physical structure clearly cannot account for the existence of the unity of consciousness. And yet, for all that, consciousness is very real, in all its intentionality and unity, as we confirm for ourselves beyond any shadow of a doubt when we engage in such intentional activities as trimming the hedges or writing books denying the reality of consciousness. Where then, if not in the brain, is that point of perspective located?

In the end, it makes no sense to draw any sort of real distinction between appearance and reality when discussing our sense that we are conscious subjects; the illusion of consciousness would have to be the consciousness of an illusion, and so any denial of the reality of consciousness is essentially gibberish. That said, putting the extravagances of rhetoric aside, might there not still be some value in the modest and seemingly plausible suggestion that representation and intentionality and the like could in principle be decomposed into a hierarchical arrangement of subordinate and diminishingly capable faculties? Perhaps, as one descends into the stratified systems and subsystems of the brain and body, one finds aptitudes that are able to represent less and less of reality, fewer and fewer aspects of what the senses can detect, until one arrives at a level where what we took to be the power of representation or intention turns out to be just a responsive system of physical impulses. And, for all the reasons I have given above, my surmise is that this is impossible. Intention is intention, representation is representation; the directedness of the mind toward specific ends, apart from which the mind does not know anything at all, is not something dissoluble into relative degrees of physical causality; it either exists or does not. The sensory and cognitive apparatus of the brain consists in a multiplicity of faculties and functions, unquestionably; parts of the eye associated with parts of the brain may be capable of only certain hues or intensities or lateral configurations or what have you, and so provide only partial and subordinate aspects of the larger reality of vision. But none of those faculties and functions is some discrete part of an intention that can be combined with others, all adding up to a complete subjectivity. Intentionality is a mental act that, contrary to the behavior of purely physical mechanisms, is specifically and finitely directed to an end, specifically "about" reality as composed of meanings, and apart from that act no sensory datum amounts to an object of knowledge. Between the objective causality that affects the brain's physiology and the subjective intentionality that produces representation and personal experience, the qualitative difference remains absolute. No physical stimulus amounts to a perception of anything unless there is already consciousness there to interpret its disclosures intentionally. No mere sensory aptitude is in any sense a form of conscious intention, and no conscious intention can be reduced to mere sensory aptitude. And so, if subjective consciousness makes its first appearance anywhere within the continuum of our physiological systems, it must do so all at once, without physical premise, as a transition that constitutes nothing less than a miraculous reversal of physical logic (if, yet again, matter really is what modern metaphysical prejudices say that it is).

None of these claims is incontestable, and all of them have been contested; and I doubt I can carry the day with just my richly resonant tone of personal conviction. Even so, I think that any perfectly scrupulous consideration of consciousness as the unique phenomenon it is leads quite naturally toward the supposition of a "spiritual" dimension of the mind, the simple and necessarily immaterial perspective of a noetic or transcendentally apperceptive power that abides, that knows, that holds reality together from some vantage of unassailable subjectivity. The conviction among many that this must be false is dictated not by logical considerations but only by an earnest devotion to a certain picture of the world; and, with regard to the mystery of consciousness no less than with regard to the mystery of being, the materialist position is the least coherent metaphysical position on offer, and the one that suffers from the greatest explanatory poverty. This is why I have a certain sincere sympathy for Dennett and even for the eliminativists. Since consciousness cannot really be satisfactorily explained in purely physical terms, and since it would be dogmatically and emotionally impossible for them even to consider abandoning the materialist view of reality, it becomes necessary for them to deny the reality of consciousness as traditionally understood, in its every distinctive feature. To anyone who objects that the existence of consciousness is as indisputable a fact of experience as experience itself (because, simply said, it *is* experience), for now it must suffice to issue promissory notes on those innumerable future scientific discoveries that will one day conjure away all the seemingly insurmountable logical obstacles to the naturalist project.

What else is to be done? There are materialist or naturalist alternatives to eliminativism, but they simply do not do enough to prevent "supernaturalism" from insinuating itself back into the philosophy of mind. One can, for instance, argue that consciousness is real, but that it emerges from purely material forces. This, however, creates far more questions than it answers. A true physicalism makes no allowance for emergent properties in nature that are not already implicit in their causes. Unless, then, one is positing the existence of proto-conscious material elements, particles of intentionality and awareness that are in some inconceivable way already rational and subjective, and that can add up to the unified perspective of a single conscious subject (which seems a quite fantastic notion), one is really just talking about some marvelously inexplicable transition from the undirected, mindless causality of mechanistic matter to the intentional unity of consciousness. Talk of emergence in purely physical terms, then, really does not seem conspicuously better than talk of magic. Nor does it improve matters to assert that consciousness "supervenes," in one way or another, on material forces. According to this approach, consciousness really exists and really operates through its own inherent properties, and so cannot be "eliminated" in favor of purely physical descriptions of things; at the same time, however, it is wholly dependent upon its material basis or substrate, and there can be no change of state at the level of consciousness without a corresponding change of state at the physical level. Unfortunately, there is no way of making this a coherent position from a naturalist perspec-

tive. It makes sense to speak of one reality supervening upon another if one is talking about two genuinely distinct orders of causality; thus one could speak of a formal cause "supervening" upon
a material cause in order to bring about a particular substance.
But materialist theories of supervenience have nothing to do with
this kind of complementary causality, but concern only some sort
of obscure parallelism between different levels of reality, the physical and the mental: one mental event can cause another only if the
physical reality underlying the former also causes the physical reality underlying the latter. But how is that possible? How, in physicalist terms, could mental events operate as causes in any real sense
in this scheme? They would really only float upon the surface of a
stream of physical causality that could not actually be interrupted
in its flowing by any power from above. Such a picture of the relation of the physical to the mental, no matter how subtly conceived,
would surely have to succumb to the problems posed by the logical syntax and semantics of rational thought, as described above.

Another option is "epiphenomenalism," a theory that says that
consciousness is quite real, that it arises from physical processes,
but that it is not itself a cause of anything; it is merely a phenomenal residue of processes that it cannot influence. In this view of
things, all physical events belong to a closed causal continuum,
but some of those events have the curious effect of generating the
ghostly epiphenomenon of personal consciousness, which—not
being itself material—cannot enter back into the continuum from
which it arises. This would mean that, though you might imagine that it is your consciousness of desiring to eat a cherry that
prompts you to take one from a bowl and place it in your mouth,
or your conscious belief in epiphenomenalism that prompts you to

speak the words "I believe in epiphenomenalism," nothing of the sort is true: consciousness cannot make your hand move toward that cherry, or part your lips to eat, or part them again to utter your strange profession of belief, because all of those bodily actions belong to the realm of physical causality, and occur entirely as a result of physical forces. As strange as it seems, this position does have some very serious defenders (though in small numbers). I suppose this is because it obliges one neither to deny the undeniable reality of consciousness nor to abandon the naturalist dogma that the physical universe is causally closed. It suffers, however, from some considerable logical deficiencies, not the least of which is that it is self-evidently false. There is no need to be coy here. Your desires, beliefs, ideas, ambitions, plans, hopes, fears, and intentions of every other kind clearly do play a causal role in your actions, physical and mental, and only a lunatic or a philosopher of mind could be so removed from reality as to doubt this.

Alternatively, one could opt for the naturalist version of "panpsychism" (naturalist, that is, rather than dualist or idealist). This theory claims that consciousness is not a unique property of organisms with brains, but is a fundamental property of the universe at large, present in all physical reality in some form: perhaps as, say, a natural accompaniment to the exchange of "information states" that occurs whenever one material reality affects another (so that a thermometer or a coffee spoon could be said to be conscious, presumably at a fairly idiotic level, of a change in room temperature or of stirring cream into coffee). In this view of things, there is a qualitative and intentional dimension to everything, no less fundamental than the particles of matter, though entirely different from them in nature. This approach to things does, at least,

relieve one of the burden of explaining the existence of mind—
why, it's everywhere!—but few committed philosophical naturalists will wish to solve the mystery of consciousness by invoking
some ubiquitous quintessence more mysterious still. And, in any
event, the whole notion, when posed in naturalist terms, merely
conflates the distinct realities of information and our consciousness
of information, which is both logically illicit and explanatorily
vacuous. (For the record, I find some versions of panpsychism
quite attractive, but am also quite certain that the idea is irreconcilable with materialism.)

Better, then, to forge bravely ahead and try to prove that subjective consciousness is not real to begin with, but only a phantom
effect of the brain's systems. And, really, why should it surprise us
to discover that thought is ultimately just a collection of mechanized functions? Are we not now perfectly familiar with thinking
machines? Why should we not think of the brain as a computer,
perhaps, and of what we call "mind" as nothing more than the
unfolding of the mechanical algorithms embedded in the "software" that the brain processes? This is the view largely endorsed
by the Strong Artificial Intelligence factions among cognitive scientists and philosophers of mind: rather than consciousness, understood in the common sense as the intentional act of an indivisible subject, the mind contains only flows of data and behavior, in
and out, functional relations, discriminatory filters, information
states, all erected upon a simple digital platform, binary or some
other kind, operating by way of a few simple physiological switches
that can be turned on and off. For some theorists this implies that
an artificial computer comparable in complexity to the human
brain and nervous system could achieve something like our con-

scious states; to others, like Daniel Dennett, it is more correct to say that neither we nor our computers possess conscious states as commonly conceived; we and they merely have functions that, seen from a certain naive vantage, look like consciousness.

Unfortunately, the entire theory is an incorrigible confusion of categories, for a very great number of reasons, foremost among them the absolute dependency of all computational processes upon the prior reality of intentional consciousness. I do not mean this simply in the sense that computers and their programs happen to be designed by human minds, which is an important but ancillary issue. After all, one could argue that the brain too has been designed and programmed, perhaps by an Intelligent Designer or perhaps purely by natural selection (though, in the latter case, the intentional content of the programming would be a miracle). I mean rather that—as John Searle has correctly argued—apart from specific representations produced by intentional consciousness, the operations of a computer are merely physical events devoid of meaning. The physical brain may be something very remotely like the physical object we use to run software programs, but to speak of the mind in terms of computation is really no better than speaking of representation in terms of photography. The analogy is momentarily compelling, in a purely pictorial way at least, but it cannot help us make sense of what consciousness is, because it involves comparing the mind to a device that exists only relative to the logically prior and mysteriously irreducible reality of mind itself.

This would perhaps be more immediately obvious to us if we were not the victims of our own metaphors. We have become so accustomed to speaking of computers as artificial minds and of their operations as thinking that we have forgotten that these are mere figures of speech. We speak of computer memory, for instance, but of course computers recall nothing. They do not even store any "remembered" information—in the sense of symbols with real semantic content, real meaning—but only preserve the binary patterns of certain electronic notations. And I do not mean simply that the computers are not aware of the information they contain; I mean that, in themselves, they do not contain any semantic information at all. They are merely the silicon parchment and electrical ink on which we record symbols that possess semantic content only in respect to our intentional representations of their meanings. A computer no more remembers the files stored in it than the paper and print of this book remember my argument to this point. Nor can one credibly argue that, even though computer "memory" may have no intentional meaning, still the "higher functions" of the computer's software transform those notations into coherent meanings by integrating them into a larger functional system. There are no higher functions and no programs as such, either in the computer considered purely as a physical object or in its operations considered purely as physical events; there are only the material components of the machine, electrical impulses, and binary patterns, which we use to construct certain representations and which have meanings only so long as they are the objects of the representing mind's attention. Call it a vicious circle, the circuit of irony, the dialectic of projection, or what you will: we have imposed the metaphor of an artificial mind on computers and then reimported the image of a thinking machine and imposed it upon our minds. If you address a letter to yourself and post it, it will almost certainly come back to you; but you would be foolish eagerly to tear the envelope open in the hope of finding something unexpected inside.

Computational models of the mind would make sense if what a computer actually does could be characterized as an elementary version of what the mind does, or at least as something remotely like thinking. In fact, though, there is not even a useful analogy to be drawn here. A computer does not even really compute. We compute, using it as a tool. We can set a program in motion to calculate the square root of pi, but the stream of digits that will appear on the screen will have mathematical content only because of our intentions, and because we—not the computer—are running algorithms. The computer, in itself, as an object or a series of physical events, does not contain or produce any symbols at all; its operations are not determined by any semantic content but only by binary sequences that mean nothing in themselves. The visible figures that appear on the computer's screen are only the electronic traces of sets of binary correlates, and they serve as symbols only when we represent them as such, and assign them intelligible significances. The computer could just as well be programmed so that it would respond to the request for the square root of pi with the result "Rupert Bear"; nor would it be wrong to do so, because an ensemble of merely material components and purely physical events can be neither wrong nor right about anything—in fact, it cannot be *about* anything at all. Software no more "thinks" than a minute hand knows the time or the printed word "pelican" knows what a pelican is. We might just as well liken the mind to an abacus, a typewriter, or a library. No computer has ever used language, or responded to a question, or assigned a meaning to anything. No computer has ever so much as added two numbers together, let alone entertained a thought, and none ever will. The only intelligence or consciousness or even illusion of consciousness in the whole computational process is situated, quite incommutably, in us; everything seemingly analogous to our minds in our machines is reducible, when analyzed correctly, only back to our own minds once again, and we end where we began, immersed in the same mystery as ever. We believe otherwise only when, like Narcissus bent above the waters, we look down at our creations and, captivated by what we see reflected in them, imagine that another gaze has met our own.[7]

As for those, then, who are committed to the practical project of producing genuine artificial intelligence built upon computational models of thought, theirs is a poignantly hopeless enterprise. When, in 1997, Garry Kasparov at last lost a chess match to the computer Deep Blue, frissons of excitement coursed through the artificial intelligence community and the press; it was blazoned abroad that the computer had defeated the chess master and had done so by "thinking" with greater agility than its human opponent. But it had done neither of these things, as became clear in 2003 when Kasparov faced the far more formidable Deep Junior and played to a draw. This mystified many true believers in artificial intelligence. The computer's program could process three million possible strategies every second, whereas Kasparov was able to consider only a few at any given juncture; but, as Kasparov remarked, whichever options he considered were the best conceivable. This is because what Kasparov was doing was precisely what the computer, in running through millions upon millions of unconscious computational configurations, was not doing, even for an instant: thinking. Not a single thought passed through its pretty

little circuit board. Nor did it have intentions, or anything remotely like intentions. Nor did it play chess. All of its putatively
mental actions were actually derivative consequences of the conscious intentions of its programmers, who used its circuitry to run
algorithms that were largely the distillation of a vast archive of
past chess matches, some of them Kasparov's own; the computer
was merely the alembic through which the distillate flowed. When
Kasparov lost his game in 1997, he was defeated not by a machine
but by a large alliance of human opponents, himself among them.
And nowhere in that process was there some intelligent entity
called Deep Blue. Conversely, when Kasparov thought about and
made his moves upon the board, he may have employed certain
functions in his brain analogous to the functions of a computer,
but his conscious act of thinking was not itself a kind of computation. His mind was not merely mechanically repeating every
imaginable configuration of the chessboard and then automati-
cally selecting those moves statistically most likely to meet with
success; rather, he *understood* what he was doing, subjectively and
intentionally, and his ability to understand—to grasp at once the
principles of chess strategy, his memory of his previous experiences,
his volitional purposes, and a host of other things—allowed him
to accomplish ends that a mindless device like a computer never
could. Just as no computer program will ever likely be devised that
could, say, adequately translate a poem from one language to another, no program will ever "play" chess, even if its synthesis of the
skills of its inventors should prove invincible by a human master
of the game. Rational thought—understanding, intention, will,
consciousness—is not a species of computation.

To imagine that it is involves an error regarding not only what the mind does, but what a computer does as well. One of the assumptions underlying artificial intelligence theory is that the brain, like a computer, uses algorithms in the form of complex neuronal events, which translate neural information into representational symbols. If we were to undertake a "homuncular decomposition" of the mind in computationalist terms, supposedly, we would descend through a symbolic level of operations down to a level of something like binary functions, then down further until we reached the simple "switches" in the brain that underlie those functions. But this reverses the order of causality on both sides of the analogy. Neither brains nor computers, considered purely as physical systems, contain algorithms or symbols; it is only as represented to consciousness that the physical behaviors of those systems yield any intentional content. It is in the consciousness of the person who programs or uses a computer, and in the consciousness that operates through the physical apparatus of the brain, that symbols reside. In fact, it is only for this reason that symbolic translation is possible, because the metabolism of data into meaning, or of one kind of meaning into another, is the work of an intentional subjectivity that already transcends the difference between the original "text" and its translation. A computer programmer can translate meanings or functions into algorithms because, being intentionally conscious, he or she is capable of representing the operations of the computer not merely as physical events but as intelligible symbolic transcriptions of something else; it is in his or her consciousness, at either end of the process, that the physical serves the purposes of the mental. If the brain produces "symbols" of the world perceived by the senses, for instance, it is not a physical transaction but a mental act of representation that already intends perception as an experience of a world beyond. And it is solely there, where symbolic meaning exists, that anything we might call thinking occurs. Thus, even if we could imaginatively or deductively descend from the level of consciousness down through strata of symbols, simple notational functions, and neural machinery, we would not be able then to ascend back again the way we came. Once more, the physicalist reduction of any phenomenon to purely material forces explains nothing if one cannot then reconstruct that phenomenon from its material basis without invoking any higher causes; but this no computational picture of thought can ever do. Symbols exist only from above, as it were, in the consciousness looking downward along the path of that descent, acting always as a higher cause upon material reality. Looking up in the opposite direction, from below to above, one finds only an untraversable abyss, separating the intentional nullity of matter from the intentional plenitude of mind. It is an absolute error to imagine that the electrical activity in a computer is itself computation; and, when a believer in artificial intelligence claims that the electrochemical operations of a brain are a kind of computation, and that consciousness arises from that computation, he or she is saying something utterly without meaning. All computation is ontologically dependent on consciousness, simply said, and so computation cannot provide the foundation upon which consciousness rests. One might just as well attempt to explain the existence of the sun as the result of the warmth and brightness of summer days.

This also means, incidentally, that it is equally silly to speak of minds as collections of "memes" constituting a "virtual machine" or a "program" running in the structure of the brain, as Dennett and others like to do. This term "memes"—a word coined by Richard Dawkins and beloved by a small cadre of cognitive and evolutionary theorists—refers to a kind of cultural analogue of genes: a meme is supposedly a unit of shared behavior or thought, like a style of clothing or an architectural fashion or a tune or an idea or a turn of phrase, which is transmitted from one person to another by imitation and variation. More to the point (and this is the analogy between genetics and "memetics"), memes supposedly replicate *themselves* in some sense, colonizing the ecology of the brain, adapting, surviving, displacing less robust memetic populations, and thereby creating and determining the contents of consciousness. Now, as an ironic metaphor, meant as a slightly caustic comment upon the human tendency toward conformism, talk of "memes" might be either a fetching or an annoyingly cute way of describing the genealogy of popular culture. As a serious proposal regarding how consciousness works—how it acquires its "programs" or its mental intentions—it is pseudoscientific and pseudophilosophical twaddle. It would certainly be convenient, for a computational model of the mind, if one could discover some sort of preconscious form of intentional content that proliferates on its own, that is situated within the brain the way DNA is situated within the cells of the body, and that thereby constitutes the "information" of consciousness in something like the way genetic codes contribute "information" to organisms. The notion is nonsense, however. Genetic materials are propagated by physical transactions because they themselves are physical realities; at their level, no conscious acts need be present. Whatever else "memes" might be, however, if such things really did exist, they would most definitely be composed of intentional content and would exist only as objects of mental representation. They would not therefore be metaphorically "selected" by nature, in the way the units of biological evolution are said to be, but would literally be chosen (even if often a little passively) by a conscious mind. They might be objects of intentionality, but they certainly could not explain intentionality; the existence of a cause cannot be explained by its own contingent effects. As it is, the word "memes" is simply faddish jargon, a somewhat precious name for the vagaries of human taste, curiosity, imagination, and desire for community. When used in this context, moreover, there may be no more conspicuous example of an analogy that is meant to explain consciousness but that is itself intelligible only in light of the reality of consciousness (in all its perennial inexplicability).

VIII

In any event, my topic is not really the philosophy of mind, though by this point it may seem as if I have forgotten that. I am concerned not simply with the mystery of consciousness but with the significance of that mystery for a proper understanding of the word "God." I admit that I have taken my time in reaching this point, but I think defensibly so. My claim throughout these pages is that the grammar for our thinking about the transcendent is given to us in the immanent, in the most humbly ordinary and familiar experiences of reality; in the case of our experience of consciousness, however, the familiarity can easily overwhelm our sense of the essential mystery. There is no meaningful distinction between the subject and the object of experience here, and so the mystery is hidden by its own ubiquity. One extremely good way, then, to appreciate the utter strangeness of consciousness—the hither side, so to speak, of that moment of existential wonder that wakens us to the strangeness of all things—is to consider the extraordinary labors required to describe the mind in purely material terms. We have reached a curious juncture in the history of materialism, which seems to point toward a terminus that is either tragic or comical (depending on where one's sympathies lie). For a number of "naturalist" theorists it has become entirely credible, and even logically inevitable, that the defense of "rationalistic" values should require the denial of the existence of reason. Or, rather, intellectual consistency obliges them to believe that reason is parasitic upon purely irrational physical events, and that it may well be the case that our nonexistent consciousness is only deluded in intentionally believing that there is such a thing as intentional belief. Or they think that what we have mistaken for our rational convictions and ideas are actually only a colony of diverse "memes" that have established themselves in the ecologies of our cerebral cortices. Or whatever. At such a bizarre cultural or intellectual juncture, the word "fanaticism" is not opprobrious, but merely descriptive. We have reached a point of almost mystically fundamentalist absurdism. Even so, what is really astonishing here is not that some extreme proponents of naturalist thought accept such ideas but that any person of a naturalist bent could imagine that his or her beliefs permit any other conclusions. If nature really is what mechanistic metaphysics portrays it as being, then consciousness is, like being itself, *super naturam;* and that must be intolerable to any true believer in the mechanistic creed. Materialism is, as I have said, the least rationally defensible and most explanatorily impoverished of metaphysical dogmas; but, if materialism is one's faith, even reason itself may not be too great an offering to place upon its altar. If one is to exclude the supernatural absolutely from one's picture of reality, one must not only ignore the mystery of being but also refuse to grant that consciousness could possibly be what it self-evidently is.

Still, at the beginning and end of all our philosophizing mind remains a mystery that resists reduction to material causes. Perhaps this cannot be proved irrefutably (so very few things can be, outside the realm of mathematics), but it is far and away the most logically plausible conclusion one can reach. Inasmuch, then, as reality is one, a totality embraced within the unity of being, and inasmuch as matter seems to be insufficient as a principle to account for all the differing dimensions of that reality (being, consciousness . . .), perhaps we really should look elsewhere for the source and sustaining principle of that unity. And there is no good reason not to accord serious consideration to the ancient intuition that the true order of ultimate causes is precisely the opposite of what the materialist philosopher imagines it is, and that the material realm is ultimately dependent upon mind rather than the reverse: that the fullness of being upon which all contingent beings depend is at the same time a limitless act of consciousness. What could we possibly imagine we know about matter or mind that would preclude such a possibility? That the concept of incorporeal or extraphysical consciousness is unintelligible? That, as it happens, is a vacuous assertion: we have no plausible causal model for how consciousness could arise from mechanistic physical processes, and therefore no reason at all to presume some sort of necessary bond between mind and matter. And, truth be told, we have far better warrant for believing in mind than we do for believing in matter. Of the material world we have compelling evidence, of course, but all of it consists in mental impressions and conceptual paradigms produced by and inhabiting the prior reality of consciousness. Of consciousness itself, however, our knowledge is immediate and indubitable. I can doubt that the world really exists, but I cannot doubt that I have intentional consciousness, since doubt is itself a form of conscious intention. This certitude is the imperturbable foundation of my knowledge of anything else. We have and share a world only because each of us has this incommunicable and integral subjectivity within. That whole rich inner universe of experience and thought is not only real, but more real than any physical object can be for us—more real, for instance, than this book you hold in your hands, which exists for you only within the far deeper, fuller, and more certain reality of your consciousness. Once again, we can approach nature only across the interval of the supernatural.

When one looks inward, moreover, toward that vanishing point of unity that makes the whole of mental life possible, perhaps one looks toward something more real still. Contemplative and philosophical traditions, Eastern and Western, insist on this: that the source and ground of the mind's unity is the transcendent reality of unity as such, the simplicity of God, the one ground of both consciousness and being. For Plotinus, the oneness of *nous,* the intellective apex of the self, is a participation in the One, the divine origin of all things and the ground of the openness of mind and world one to another. For Sufi thought, God is the Self of all selves, the One—*al-Ahad*—who is the sole true "I" underlying the consciousness of every dependent "me." According to the *Kena*

Upanishad, Brahman is not that which the mind knows like an object, or that the eye sees or the ear hears, but is that by which the mind comprehends, by which the eye sees, by which the ear hears; *atman*—the self in its divine depth—is the eye of the eye, the ear of the ear, the ground of all knowing. Augustine, on looking inward, found a light within that flowed not from himself but from above, creating and sustaining him, illuminating his mind and calling his mind to itself. According to Moses de León (c. 1250–1305), to turn the eye of the mind inward is to find that, in their inner essences, all things are a chain caught in the oneness of the indivisible being and knowledge of God. For the Rhineland mystics—as for the contemplatives of all the great theistic traditions, really—more inward to consciousness than consciousness itself is that "scintilla" or "spark" of divine light that imparts life and truth to the soul, and the mind's interior journey toward its own wellspring brings it to a place where it finds itself utterly dependent upon the sublime simplicity of God's knowledge of all things in his knowledge of himself. This is not, however, a contemplative teaching only.

What precisely is the relation between the being of the world and our knowledge of it? Is it purely extrinsic, a purely physical interaction between material things? Or is there some more intimate and interdependent relation between them? It is a question for which a truly mechanistic age should have no patience, I suppose; but arguably it is the basic question underlying all the other questions of philosophy. It is a very old metaphysical puzzle whether being and consciousness are entirely severable concepts. Could something exist, for instance, in such a manner that it could not be perceived or thought about in any way at all, not even by itself, even in principle? In what sense would it be distinct from absolute nothingness? It certainly seems reasonable to say that being is manifestation, that real subsistence is revelation, that to exist is to be perceptible, conceivable, knowable. And so, perhaps, to exist fully is to be manifest to consciousness. If there were a universe in which consciousness did not exist, in what sense precisely would that universe itself exist? Certainly not as a fully articulated spatial and temporal reality filled with clearly discrete objects, concretely and continuously flowing from a vanished past to an as-yet unrealized future, like the universe that exists in our minds: the reality we find represented in our thoughts, in which intensities and densities and durations and successions are arranged in such magnificently complex but diverse order, exists only relative to consciousness; in a universe devoid of mind, at the phenomenal level—the level of reality as it appears to intentional awareness—nothing would exist at all. In itself, if it had any reality in itself, this "mindless" universe would be only a plenum or totality of particles or quantum potentialities "extended" relative only to one another, but in a way quite different from the kinds of extension in space and time of which we conceive. Even then, however, it seems fair to say that such a universe, if it existed, would exist exactly to the extent that it *could* be known to consciousness of some kind. There is no such thing as ontological coherence that is not a *rational* coherence. There is a point then, arguably, at which being and intelligibility become conceptually indistinguishable. It is only as an intelligible order, as a coherent phenomenon (sensible or intellectual), that anything is anything at all, whether an elementary particle or a universe; perhaps it is true that only what could in principle be known can in actuality exist.

So, at any rate, we have to believe. The human striving to know the truth of things, as far as possible and in every sphere, is sustained by a tacit faith in some kind of ultimate coincidence or convertibility between being and consciousness. There is a natural orientation of the mind toward a horizon of total intelligibility—a natural intellectual appetite for immediate knowledge of what is— that requires us to venture our time, our hopes, our labors, and our contentions on the assumption that rational thought and coherent order are two sides of a single reality, or at least somehow naturally fitted to one another. If we believe that the structure of reality can truly be mirrored in the structure of our thinking, then we must also believe that there is an ideal or abstract or purely intelligible dimension of reality that corresponds to the categories and concepts that allow us to understand the world. It is possible to deny this philosophically—at least, some philosophers have done so—but entirely impossible to live by that denial. There is a wonderful transparency of the world to thought, and a wonderful power of thought to interpret reality coherently through forms and principles that are of an entirely noetic nature. The world yields itself to our abstractions, and we cannot help but work upon the assumption that it always will precisely because being in itself is pure intelligibility. We do not need to imagine that we will ever fully understand all of reality, but we certainly need to believe that in principle all of reality is rationally comprehensible. The progress of physics over the past few centuries, for instance, has taken a great number of unexpected turns, and every substantial advance in the field has tended to multiply rather than reduce perplexities, and a single unifying theory as yet eludes us. Molecular biology has made magnificent discoveries in the past several decades but seems to have created a great number of new complications in, for example, our concept of what a gene is. But both sciences continue in their very different ways to discover ever deeper layers of intelligibility, and both are inspired by a faith in the rational lawfulness of nature, and in the power of conceptual paradigms to reflect the rational truths upon which reality is built. No scientist imagines that, at the probably unattainable end of the mind's journey toward full understanding, reality will turn out to be essentially irrational.

If none of this is an illusion, and if in fact world and mind really are open to one another, and if reason is real and not a fantasy generated by fortuitous regularities in sequences of physical events in our brains, then it is perfectly rational to accord a certain causal priority to mind over matter in our picture of reality. If the materialist understanding of nature were essentially correct, it would be difficult enough to account for the existence of consciousness; but it would be far more difficult still to say how consciousness, in all its exorbitant difference from the purposeless welter of physical causality, could actually capture the truth of physical reality in the exquisite trammels of its concepts. Yet it certainly seems that, in abstracting experience into various kinds of ideal content—formal, mathematical, moral, aesthetic, and so on—the mind really does extract knowledge from what would otherwise be nothing but meaningless brute events. In fact, reality becomes more intelligible to us the more we are able to abstract it into concepts, and to arrange it under categories, and then to arrange our concepts under ever simpler, more comprehensive, more unconditioned concepts, always ascending toward the simplest and most capacious and most unconditional concept our minds can reach. To say that something has become entirely intelligible to us is to say that we have an *idea* of it that can be understood according to the simplest abstract laws and that leaves no empirical or conceptual remainder behind. This is the highest form of intelligibility. We may or may not be Platonists in our metaphysics, but we certainly must be practical idealists in our epistemology. This being so, it makes perfect sense that so many ancient and mediaeval philosophers took it as a given that the ideal dimension of things, their intrinsic intelligibility, was not only a real property of their existence but in some sense was identical with existence itself. What, however, is an idea other than the product of a mind? What is a concept other than the expression of a rational intentionality? And how, therefore, could being be pure intelligibility if it were not also pure intelligence—the mind of God, so to speak? The Christian philosopher Bernard Lonergan (1904–1984), in fact, proposed an argument that was intended, in a very complicated and ingenious way, to transform this venerable philosophical intuition into something like a comprehensive philosophical proof, one that moved from the "unrestricted intelligibility" of reality to the reality of God as the one "unrestricted act of understanding." It is a powerful and evocative argument, actually, and inductively persuasive in many ways; but it is not definitive or unanswerable.[8]

Not that it needs to be for my purposes here. The essential truth to which Lonergan's argument points is that the very search for truth is implicitly a search for God (properly defined, that is). As the mind moves toward an ever more comprehensive, capacious, and "supereminent" grasp of reality, it necessarily moves toward an ideal level of reality at which intelligibility and intelligence are no longer distinguishable concepts. It seems to me we all really know this, in some sense: that we assume that the human mind can be a true mirror of objective reality because we assume that objective reality is already a mirror of mind. No other comportment toward truth as a desirable end is existentially possible. The ascent toward ever greater knowledge is, if only tacitly and secretly and *contre cœur,* an ascent toward an ultimate encounter with limitless consciousness, limitless reason, a transcendent reality where being and knowledge are always already one and the same, and so inalienable from one another. To believe that being is inexhaustibly intelligible is to believe also—whether one wishes to acknowledge it or not—that reality emanates from an inexhaustible intelligence: in the words of the *Shvetashvatara Upanishad,* "pure consciousness, omnipresent, omniscient, the creator of time."[9]

IX

However compelling one may or may not find such reasoning, at least it serves to elucidate certain vital dimensions of the classical conception of God. What is most definitely not at issue here is the demiurgic god of Deism, the Intelligent Design movement, or New Atheist polemic. God is not, in any of the great theistic traditions, merely some rational agent, external to the order of the physical universe, who imposes some kind of design upon an otherwise inert and mindless material order. He is not some discrete being somewhere out there, floating in the great beyond, who fashions nature in accordance with rational laws upon which he is dependent. Rather, he is himself the logical order of all reality, the ground both of the subjective rationality of mind and the objective rationality of being, the transcendent and indwelling Reason or Wisdom by which mind and matter are both informed and in which both participate. If indeed to exist is to be manifest—to be intelligible and perceptible—and if to exist fully is to be consciously known, then God, as infinite being, is also an act of infinite knowledge. He is in himself the absolute unity of consciousness and being, and so in the realm of contingent things is the source of the fittedness of consciousness and being each to the other, the one ontological reality of reason as it exists both in thought and in the structure of the universe. At least, according to almost all the classical metaphysical schools, East and West, the marvelous coincidence between, on the one hand, our powers of reason and, on the other, the capacity of being to be understood points to an ultimate identity between them, in the depths of their transcendent origin. God's being—*esse, on, sat, wujud*—is also consciousness—*ratio, logos, chit, wijdan.* As Ramanuja would have it, Brahman, as the fullness of all being, must possess immediate knowledge of all reality within himself, and so be the fullness of all consciousness as well, the "personal" source in whom being achieves total manifestation, total actuality. Or, in the language of Plotinus, the One ceaselessly generates the eternal reflective consciousness of the divine mind, *nous,* from which emanates all the rationally coherent diversity of the cosmos. Or, in the terms of Philo of Alexandria or the Gospel of John, God is never without his Logos, the divine Wisdom, in and through whom the world is created, ordered, and sustained.

I suggested above that, in many classical metaphysical traditions, the concept of being is one of power: the power of actuality, the capacity to affect or to be affected. To be is to act. This definition already implies that, in its fullness, being must also be consciousness, because the highest power to act—and hence the most unconditioned and unconstrained reality of being—is rational mind. *Absolute* being, therefore, must be *absolute* mind. Or, in simpler terms, the greater the degree of something's actuality, the greater the degree of its consciousness, and so infinite actuality is necessarily infinite consciousness. That, at least, is one way of trying to describe another essential logical intuition that recurs in various forms throughout the great theistic metaphysical systems. It is the conviction that in God lies at once the deepest truth of mind and the most universal truth of existence, and that for this reason the world can truly be known by us. Whatever else one might call this vision of things, it is most certainly, in a very real sense, a kind of "total rationalism." Belief in God, properly understood, allows one to see all that exists—both in its own being and in our knowledge of it—as rational. It may be possible to believe in the materialist view of reality, I suppose, and in some kind of mechanical account of consciousness, but it is a belief that precludes any final trust in the power of reason to reflect the objective truths of nature. I happen to think that a coherent materialist model of mind is an impossibility. I think also that the mechanistic picture of nature is self-evidently false, nothing more than an intellectual adherence to a limited empirical method that has been ineptly mistaken for a complete metaphysical description of reality. I believe that nature is rational, that it possesses inherent meaning, that it even exhibits genuine formal and final causes, and that therefore it can be faithfully mirrored in the intentional, abstractive, formal, and final activity of rational consciousness. If I am wrong about all of these things, however, I think it also clear that what lies outside such beliefs is not some alternative rationalism, some other and more rigorous style of logic, some better way of grasping the truth of things, but only an abandonment of firm belief in any kind of reasoning at all. God explains the existence of the universe despite its ontological contingency, which is something that no form of naturalism can do; but God also explains the transparency of the universe to consciousness, despite its apparent difference from consciousness, as well as the coincidence between reason and reality, and the intentional power of the mind, and the reality of truth as a dimension of existence that is at once objective and subjective. Here, just as in the realm of ontology, atheism is simply another name for radical absurdism—which, again, may be a perfectly "correct" view of things, if reason is just a physiological accident after all, and logic an illusion. That is an argument that I shall not revisit just now, however.

Instead, I shall simply observe that, if reason's primordial orientation is indeed toward total intelligibility and perfect truth, then it is essentially a kind of ecstasy of the mind toward an end beyond the limits of nature. It is an impossibly extravagant appetite, a longing that can be sated only by a fullness that can never be reached in the world, but that ceaselessly opens up the world to consciousness. To speak of God, however, as infinite consciousness, which is identical to infinite being, is to say that in him the ecstasy of mind is also the perfect satiety of achieved knowledge, of perfect wisdom. God is both the knower and the known, infinite intelligence and infinite intelligibility. This is to say that, in him, rational appetite is perfectly fulfilled, and consciousness perfectly possesses the end it desires. And this, of course, is perfect bliss.

CHAPTER FIVE

Bliss (*Ananda*)

I

Consciousness does not merely passively reflect the reality of the world; it is necessarily a dynamic movement of reason and will toward reality. If nothing else is to be concluded from the previous chapter, this much is absolutely certain: subjective consciousness becomes actual only through intentionality, and intentionality is a kind of agency, directed toward an end. We could never know the world from a *purely* receptive position. To know anything, the mind must be actively disposed toward things outside itself, always at work interpreting experience through concepts that only the mind itself can supply. The world is intelligible to us because we reach out to it, or reach beyond it, coming to know the endless diversity of particular things within the embrace of a more general and abstract yearning for a knowledge of truth as such, and by way of an aboriginal inclination of the mind toward reality as a comprehensible whole. In every moment of awareness, the mind at once receives and composes the world, discerning meaning in the objects of experience precisely in conferring meaning upon them; thus consciousness lies open to—and enters into intimate communion with—the *forms* of things. Every venture of reason toward an end, moreover, is prompted by a desire of the mind, a "rational appetite." Knowledge is born out of a predisposition and predilection of the will toward beings, a longing for the ideal comprehensibility of things, and a natural orientation of the mind toward that infinite horizon of intelligibility that is being itself.

That may seem a somewhat extravagant way of describing our ordinary acts of cognition, but I think it so obviously correct as to verge on a truism. The mind does not simply submissively register sensory data, like wax receiving the impression of a signet, but is constantly at work organizing what it receives from the senses into form and meaning; and this it does because it has a certain natural compulsion to do so, a certain interestedness that exceeds most of the individual objects of knowledge that it encounters. The only reason that we can regard the great majority of particular things we come across with disinterest, or even in a wholly uninterested way, and yet still experience them as objects of recognition and reflection is that we are inspired by a prior and consuming interest in reality as such. There simply is no such thing as knowledge entirely devoid of desire—you could not make cognitive sense of a glass of water or a tree on a hill apart from the action of your mind toward some end found either in that thing or beyond that thing—and so all knowledge involves an adventure of the mind beyond itself. Again, as Brentano rightly saw, this essential direct-edness of consciousness sets it apart from any merely mechanical function. Desire, moreover, is never purely spontaneous; it does not arise without premise out of some aimless nothingness within the will but must always be moved toward an end, real or imagined, that draws it on. The will is, of its nature, teleological, and every rational act is intrinsically purposive, prompted by some final cause. One cannot so much as freely stir a finger without the lure of some aim, proximate or remote, great or small, constant or evanescent. What is it that the mind desires, then, or even that the mind loves, when it is moved to seek the ideality of things, the intelligibility of experience as a whole? What continues to compel thought onward, whether or not the mind happens at any given moment to have some attachment to the immediate objects of experience? What is the horizon of that limitless directedness of consciousness that allows the mind to define the limits of the world it knows? Whatever it is, it is an end that lies always beyond whatever is near at hand, and it excites in the mind a need not merely to be aware, but truly to know, to discern meaning, to grasp all of being under the aspect of intelligible truth.

Perhaps this is all only the special predicament and glory of a remarkably fortunate primate, and we have become the rational possessors of the world only because we have somehow acquired a pathetic hunger for an illusory end—"truth as such"—that transcends all those merely concrete objects of awareness in which we might or might not have some interest. Perhaps it is only the accidental exaggeration in our species of an animal capacity for recognizing danger or noticing something comestible slinking through the forest shade that has somehow produced in us this paradoxical longing for an ultimate abstraction, and rendered us not merely responsive to our physical environment but obsessively conscious of it as well, insatiably transforming the real into the conceptual, arranging experience into webs of associations, ideas, and words. It seems unlikely, however. Nature could scarcely have implanted that supreme abstraction in us, at least not according to any physicalist calculus of material causation, because abstract concepts are not natural objects. And so an essential mystery lies at the very heart of rational life: in all experience there is a movement of the self beyond the self, an ecstasy—a "standing-forth"—of the mind, directed toward an end that resides nowhere within physical nature as a closed system of causes and effects. All rational experience and all knowledge is a kind of rapture, prompted by a longing that cannot be exhausted by any finite object. What, then, do we really seek in seeking to know the world? What lures us on into reality? Is it only an illusion, or is it something that opens the world to us precisely because it is a genuine dimension of reality, in which the mind and the world together participate?

There are, very broadly speaking, two ways of desiring a thing: as an end in itself or for an end beyond itself. This seems quite obvious. But, if one thinks about it, there appears to be no actual object among finite things that we can truly desire—if we desire it at all—except either in both ways at once or in the second way only. That is to say, no finite thing is desirable simply in itself, if only in the trivial sense that whatever we find desirable about that thing must correspond to some prior and more general disposition of the appetites and the will. I might, for example, conceive a longing for some particularly beautiful object out of the purest aesthetic motives; but this still means that I cannot regard that object as its own index of value. Rather, I am moved by a more constant and general desire for beauty as such, as an absolute value of which I have some sort of intentional grasp and in light of which I am able to judge the object before me as either beautiful or not. The object itself pleases me, perhaps, but only because the appetite it appeases, without wholly satisfying, is a more original and expansive longing for the beautiful. If not for that rather abstract and exalted orientation of the will—if, that is, I were a person entirely lacking in aesthetic longings of any kind, refined or coarse, passionate or tepid—I would not desire that object at all. There is always a kind of deferral of finite desire toward ultimate ends, and there is always a greater and more remote purpose for the sake of which one wants whatever one wants. This is true even when one's interest in an object is inspired by some perfectly mundane concern, such as its monetary worth. One desires money not in itself but only for what it can purchase; and one desires the things money can purchase not simply as ends in themselves but because they correspond to more general and abstract longings for comfort, prestige, power, diversion, or what have you; and one desires all such things out of a still deeper and more general desire for happiness itself, whatever that may be, and for a fuller share in the goodness of being. In this world, the desirable is always desirable in respect of some yet more elementary and comprehensive need or yearning. All concretely limited aspirations of the will are sustained within formally limitless aspirations of the will.

In the end, the only objects of desire that are not reducible to other, more general objects of desire, and that may therefore truly be said to be desirable entirely in and of themselves, are a small number of universal, unconditional, and extremely abstract ideals that, according to a somewhat antique metaphysical vocabulary, are called "transcendentals." Traditionally, these are said to be predicates or properties that in some way apply to all existing things, because they are essential aspects of existence as such: the intrinsic perfections of being in its fullness. There are both purely ontological transcendentals, such as being and unity, and critical or "criteriological" transcendentals, such as truth, goodness, and beauty; ultimately, though, they are distinct from one another only conceptually, from our necessarily limited vantage, but in themselves are wholly convertible with one another, each being only one name for the single reality of being itself. Precise scholastic enumerations and definitions of the various transcendentals, however, do not concern me here. What interests me is the simple but crucial insight that our experience of reality does in fact have a transcendental structure. Our minds and our wills are, in an absolutely necessary way, related to being—to everything that exists and to existence itself—always under the forms provided by certain absolute orientations of imagination, desire, and (for want of a better word) faith. Whatever ontological or metaphysical substance one may or may not be willing to accord to such immense generalities as truth, goodness, and beauty, the very shape of conscious intentionality is entirely determined by them; they constitute an absolute orientation for thought, that horizon of being of which I spoke above, toward which the mind is always turned and against which every finite object is set off, in clear and distinct outlines, in the great middle distance of the phenomenal world.

I am not speaking here, however, about one or another mood or private disposition, of which one must be continuously conscious. It is not the case that, in every instant of experience, one is immediately aware of seeking truth, goodness, or beauty in its transcendent plenitude. The vocation of the mind to absolute ends is no more a simple psychological state than the unity of consciousness is a simple condition of psychological integrity; in both cases, what is at issue is a transcendental condition of thought, which is in some sense logically prior to the finite identity and diverse impulses of the ego. The vanishing point of the mind's inner coherence and simplicity is met by the vanishing point of the world's highest values; the gaze of the apperceptive "I" within is turned toward a transcendental "that" forever beyond; and mental experience, of the self or of the world outside the self, takes shape in the relation between these two "supernatural" poles. The rational mind is able to know reality with the fullness it does because of its singular ability to go beyond each object of experience, and thereby to comprehend that object within more capacious conceptual categories; and ultimately the mind knows the world as a whole because it has always already, in its intentions, exceeded the world. Consciousness contains nature, as a complete and cogent reality, because it has gone beyond nature. And the mind possesses the capacity to understand and to judge because it is obedient to absolute values that appear as concrete realities nowhere within the physical order. Just as the contingency of our existence points ultimately toward some unconditioned source of being, so the contingency of our desires points toward unconditioned final causes. And, again, whether one believes these values are in some sense actual, ontological constituents of reality, or one believes instead that they are only fortunate illusions that have in some unimaginably improbable way emerged from the hypertrophy of our animal brains, it is by their transcendence of all finite conditions that they give us a world. As ever, we approach nature only across the interval of the supernatural.

II

From a physicalist perspective, I should think, there is a very real enigma here to be dealt with. This rational capacity to think and to act in obedience to absolute or transcendental values constitutes a dependency of consciousness upon a dimension of reality found nowhere within the physical order. It is a capacity for something that nature cannot "see," and a desire at once inexhaustible and often remarkably impractical. The mind stretches out toward and prospectively takes hold of an ultimate "object" that is neither concrete nor immediate, and only in that way interprets and judges the world. There is here a mysterious commerce of the will and imagination with forces that, whether they exist in themselves or only in our thoughts, can never be contained within the economies of natural prudence. In their commanding abstractness, our transcendental ideals—the true, the good, the beautiful, and so on—have the power to move us not only toward objects that are imperfectly desirable in themselves, but even toward objects that we regard as intrinsically undesirable, or even repugnant and terrifying. We often find ourselves moved to act in defiance of our own best interests solely because that absolute horizon commands our unremitting attention and compliance, and makes us submit ourselves to contingencies we would otherwise avoid. We may, for example, force ourselves to hear and to accept an unwelcome truth, not because it pleases or attracts us, but because we are driven by a deeper devotion to truth as such. We can be compelled by conscience to undertake extraordinary labors in the service of others, even perfect strangers, often contrary to every sound practical consideration, and occasionally at great personal cost, all on account of an always deeper longing for a transcendent goodness whose demands are irresistible and indifferent to our frailties. We can be drawn toward objects of aesthetic contemplation that possess no practical value for us—that cannot nourish, protect, strengthen, or enrich us—because we delight in a certain transcendent splendor that shines through them.

There is always room for a measure of "Nietzschean" suspicion here, of course. Our motives are rarely entirely pure. Our longing for truth, goodness, beauty, or any other exalted end, in many or most cases, may well be mixed with selfishness or a will to power or what have you. Conversely, though, even our impure intentions are sustained by our primordial orientation toward ends that cannot be reduced to merely private interests. Before we can want anything for ourselves we must come to know it conceptually, through our openness to purposes that lie outside ourselves and even, in some sense, outside the cosmos. Individual psychology is complicated, but subjective consciousness is simple. In even our most ordinary acts of cognition we commit ourselves to the unconditional: the ultimate truth for which we yearn and in light of which we judge the content of experience; the ideal of absolute intelligibility that drives us to extract as much knowledge as we can from experience; the transcendent that imparts to us the gift of the immanent. Speaking purely phenomenologically, the structure of rational consciousness is ecstatic: our minds are capable of reflecting the world because there is a kind of elation in our thinking, a joy, or at least anticipation of joy, which seeks its fulfillment in an embrace of truth in its essence. Every movement of the intellect and will toward truth is already an act of devotion, or (again) of faith, in a number of related senses. In a quite undeniable way, for instance, almost everything we know about the greater world is something we have to take on trust, from the testimony of others; even our scientific knowledge is, for most of us, the report of those in whom we vest our confidence because we must, knowing that they will undertake the work of experiment and theory that the rest of us cannot. At a far more elementary level, however, even the personal knowledge possessed by a trained expert in some field, or by an immediate witness to some fact or other, is a knowledge acquired in the light of an original trust in the simple givenness of reality, a primal belief in a genuine conformity of the mind to the world and in the power of reality to disclose itself to reason. No intellectual endeavor—not even, shockingly enough, mathematics —can provide the logical ground of its own governing premises and principles; every act of the intellect is sustained by a fiduciary trust in the transparency of reality to consciousness. The mind has some sort of awareness—some "fore-grasp"—of truth, one that apprises it constantly of the incompleteness of what it already understands, or of the contingency of what it believes. And what the mind seeks in attempting to discover the truth is a kind of delight, a kind of fulfillment that can supersede the momentary disappointments or frustrations that the search for truth brings. Even when one suffers some immense "shift of paradigm" in one's understanding of reality, and comes to believe that one must radically alter one's beliefs about things, one continues to act toward the world out of a deeper and unalterable confidence in the (so to speak) nuptial unity of mind and world, and out of an ineradicable joy in the experience of that unity. The indissoluble bond between the intellect and objective reality is forged by this faith that is also a kind of love—a kind of adherence of the will and mind to something inexhaustibly desirable.

Seen from the perspective of a variety of theistic traditions, this is nothing less than the reflection of absolute reality within the realm of the contingent. It is bliss that draws us toward and joins us to the being of all things because that bliss is already one with being and consciousness, in the infinite simplicity of God. As the *Chandogya Upanishad* says, Brahman is at once both the joy residing in the depths of the heart and also the pervasive reality in which all things subsist.[1] The restless heart that seeks its repose in God (to use the language of Augustine) expresses itself not only in the exultations and raptures of spiritual experience but also in the plain persistence of awareness. The soul's unquenchable eros for the divine, of which Plotinus and Gregory of Nyssa and countless Christian contemplatives speak, Sufism's ʿ*ishq* or passionately adherent love for God, Jewish mysticism's *devekut,* Hinduism's *bhakti,* Sikhism's *pyaar*—these are all names for the acute manifestation of a love that, in a more chronic and subtle form, underlies all knowledge, all openness of the mind to the truth of things. This is because, in God, the fullness of being is also a perfect act of infinite consciousness that, wholly possessing the truth of being in itself, forever finds its consummation in boundless delight. The Father knows his own essence perfectly in the mirror of the Logos and rejoices in the Spirit who is the "bond of love" or "bond of glory" in which divine being and divine consciousness are perfectly joined. God's *wujud* is also his *wijdan*—his infinite being is infinite consciousness—in the unity of his *wajd,* the bliss of perfect enjoyment. The divine *sat* is always also the divine *chit,* and their perfect coincidence is the divine *ananda.* It only makes sense, then—though, of course, it is quite wonderful as well—that consciousness should be made open to being by an implausible desire for the absolute, and that being should disclose itself to consciousness through the power of the absolute to inspire and (ideally) satiate that desire. The ecstatic structure of finite consciousness— this inextinguishable yearning for truth that weds the mind to the being of all things—is simply a manifestation of the metaphysical structure of all reality. God is the one act of being, consciousness, and bliss in whom everything lives and moves and has its being; and so the only way to know the truth of things is, necessarily, the way of bliss.

In any event, I do not believe the physicalist narrative of reality can ever really account for consciousness and its intentionality (or, alternatively, coherently eliminate the concepts of consciousness and intentionality from our thinking); still less do I believe that it can account for the conscious mind's aptitude for grasping reality by way of abstract concepts; and I am quite certain it can have nothing solvent or significant to say about the mind's capacity for absolute values or transcendental aims. All of these things lie outside the circle of what contemporary physicalism, with its reflexively mechanistic metaphysics, can acknowledge as real. In one's every encounter with the world, one is immersed in the twin mysteries of being and consciousness; and, in the very structure of that encounter, a third mystery appears: that of the absolute, those ultimate ends toward which consciousness is oriented in its primal embrace of being, those intelligible forms of nature that nature (at least as we conceive of it today) cannot comprehend. In the very midst of our quotidian acts of awareness we are already placed before the transcendent, the infinite horizon of meaning that makes rational knowledge possible, and thereby presented with the question of God. And this orientation is also, in some sense, a moral disposition of the will and imagination. At some level—not necessarily at the surface of one's awareness from moment to moment, but on a very personal level nonetheless—the human longing for truth involves moral constancy, a loyalty to an ultimate ideal that beckons from beyond the totality of beings. We are all, of course, prone to egoism, and often choose to believe what we want to believe because it soothes or aggrandizes us; often we believe we are right because we refuse to believe we are wrong. Even then, however, we would not care at all about beliefs and persuasions were it not for a deeper need to possess the truth. Even the materialist who ardently clings to his or her absurd system of belief thereby exhibits the piety of a mind responsive to the summons of the transcendent. The atheist who proudly and persistently strives to convince others that there is no God does so out of a devotion to the absolute, to the highest of values, to the divine. It is an old maxim—one that infuriates many unbelievers, but that happens to be true nonetheless—that one cannot *meaningfully* reject belief in the God of classical theism. If one refuses to believe in God out of one's love of the truth, one affirms the reality of God in that very act of rejection. Whatever image of God one abjures, it can never be more than an idol: a god, but not God; a *theos*, but not *ho Theos*; a being, not Being in its transcendent fullness. I will not argue the point here, however. I shall simply say that any dedication to truth as an absolute or even preeminent value is at best a paradoxical commitment for a person of naturalist bent; and yet such a commitment is at some level inseparable from all rational life. Anyone who sincerely believes that truth ought to be honored, and that

the mind should desire to know the truth as a matter of unconditional obligation, thereby assents to a very ancient metaphysical
proposition: that the true is also the good.

III

Among the mind's transcendental aspirations, it is the longing
for moral goodness that is probably the most difficult to contain
within the confines of a naturalist metaphysics. Epistemic desire—
the hunger for truth—is problematic enough for a materialist account of things, but ethical desire raises questions that are not only
hard to answer but fraught with all kinds of "existential" peril.
One can deceive oneself that it is possible to believe in facts without believing in some sort of transcendent "Truth as such" (even
though the very concept of "fact" is entirely dependent on the
mind's prior devotion to such Truth). It is far harder, however, to
deceive oneself that it is possible to believe in ethical imperatives
without reference to some sort of absolute "Goodness as such."
Cognition, after all, is an act of the rational intellect but not really
a matter of personal choice; even if we should conclude that there
is no such thing as transcendent truth, we cannot as a result simply
cease to experience a rational cognizance of the world. Ethics, by
contrast, necessarily involves volition; if we should conclude that
there is no such thing as real goodness, we can certainly cease to
behave in a spirit of charity, or to feel any sense of moral responsibility toward others. Most persons of a naturalist persuasion, commendably enough, refuse to believe—or refuse to act as if they
believe—that ethical values are illusory, and are no more willing

to abandon belief in moral imperatives than they are to abandon belief in empirical facts. The charming hopelessness of the situation should be obvious to anyone, however. A naturalist morality is a manifest absurdity, something rather on the order of a square circle, and it requires almost heroic contortions of logic to make the notion seem credible. Fortunately, the human will to believe is indefatigable.

The most common strategy for "naturalizing" ethics is a sort of evolutionary utilitarianism, with two distinct moments: first, the attempt to reduce the human ethical sense to a variety of traits that, by virtue of the evolutionary advantages they confer, have been implanted in us by natural selection; and then, second, a vague but earnest assertion that, for this very reason, ethical imperatives ought to be accorded real authority. This is entirely contradictory, of course, but every utilitarian ethics inevitably is. The knowledge that certain fortuitously acquired behaviors may have proved evolutionarily advantageous in the past entails no binding demand upon any person to adopt those behaviors in the present. Quite the opposite, in fact. If morality really is nothing more than a useful biological adaptation with a wholly contingent genealogy, it can, like any other useful instrument, be taken up or laid down as one chooses. What has been generally beneficial to the species over many ages may not be particularly beneficial to an individual in the present, after all; and, if morality is really a matter of benefit rather than of spiritual obligations transcending personal concerns, no one has any sound motive to act in accord with anything other than private prudence. An ethical desire exists only so long as the will is obedient to a "deontological" dimension of moral truth: a dimension, that is, of moral imperatives that have the power to command the will on no authority but their own. Conscience subsists only on absolutes; it knows nothing of merely conditional goods. But what else is a materialist to do? The only alternative is the more "pragmatic" tactic of those philosophers (such as Richard Rorty) who frankly acknowledge that from a materialist position there can be no such thing as moral truth in any ultimate sense, but who nevertheless advocate certain ethical principles simply as expressions of our shared cultural preferences and habitual sympathies. But that is utterly vacuous. Any ethical "preference" will always turn out to be, on closer scrutiny, a preference for practices that cannot be reduced purely to self-interest, which means to a choice that is clearly more than *merely* preferential; in its very form, such a preference invokes an absolute end, however that end may be dissembled as some kind of purely elective affinity. Nor can one get around this logic with vague talk of "sympathy," since sympathy is a moral emotion only when the one who feels it interprets it in light of a prior commitment to moral goodness; a feeling of pity for others does not by itself amount to a sense of moral obligation. So, really, in the end the conscientious naturalist has no choice but to try to have it both ways: morality is a contingent product of brute amoral nature; morality is binding upon the conscience of any rational man or woman. Ask no further questions.

The classical theistic perspective, if nothing else, does not burden one with so embarrassing a paradox. The equation, in fact, is quite simple: the good is an eternal reality, a transcendental truth that is ultimately identical with the very essence of God. God is not some gentleman or lady out there in the great beyond who happens to have a superlatively good character, but is the very ontological substance of goodness. The good is nothing less than God himself, in his aspect as the original source and ultimate end of all desire: that transcendent reality in which all things exist and in which the will has its highest fulfillment. To exist is to be entirely contingent upon absolute being, and every particular being craves ever more of the riches of being in itself, and so to exist is to be drawn toward the absolute, where alone one's nature can find its own perfection. Thus ontology and ethics are one "science," and the desire for being is inseparable from the desire for the good. Ethical codes may vary from culture to culture, but the human need to regard goodness as an absolute end in itself does not. And whenever one acts in accord with moral desire one acts in relation to unconditional reality. The least gesture of the will toward a moral end, no matter how vehemently one may insist otherwise, is necessarily a confession of a natural longing for God. Or so the ancient story goes. And, in some sense, it is a story from which we can never wholly escape. We are free to try to tell it differently— to attempt to reverse the order of its episodes and readjust the relative prominence of its dramatis personae ("What we call the natural desire for God is simply a mythic misrepresentation of a tendency toward certain behavioral patterns that have aided our species in surviving down through the evolutionary epochs!"). But even then we can never really invert the teleological structure of moral conduct. Any truly ethical act is an act toward the transcendent, a decision of the will reached *sub specie aeternitatis,* and a task undertaken for the sake of something beyond the fold of nature as we know it. Ethics, like knowledge, has a necessarily transcendental logic. Every deed performed for the sake of its moral goodness is an act of faith.

What else could it be? One occasionally hears atheists complaining that religious apologists assume one must believe in God in order to be an ethical person. I do not know if this is true, as it happens, since I am not sure I have ever heard anyone make that claim; and, for what it is worth, it is a claim explicitly denied by every classical theistic tradition of which we have records. Whatever the case, though, it is most definitely true that believers in God have a far easier time believing that there really is such a thing as goodness, and that moral truth is not just an illusion generated by biological history, cultural prejudice, or personal psychology. If religious faith is any aid to moral life, it is so simply in making it possible to persevere in the certitude that real goodness not only truly exists but also can reveal itself to us. It allows one to think that—as Plato might have it—our minds may really have glimpsed the form of the good, and so we can recognize goodness when we see it because it has left its impress and its fragrance and its sparks in our souls. The grand or (occasionally) homely phrases by which believers seek to assure themselves of this—"God is love," "Love your neighbor as yourself," "Do unto others as you would have them do unto you," "Judge not lest you be judged," and so on—both express and fortify the conviction that, in a world of cruelty, tragedy, tyranny, self-love, and violence, our moral longings and the reproaches of our consciences truly show us something of the eternal truth of being. But the condition of the religious believer here differs from that of the moralizing unbeliever not in kind, but only in degree. Try though the atheist might to ground the ethical in the purely practical, and the practical in a larger consideration of what benefits the species or the planet, the effort is ultimately nonsensical. Every act *for the sake of* the good is a subversion of the logic of materialism.

Moreover, practical concerns never adequately account for the actual content of ethical actions. The evolutionary utilitarian speaks of the social need for, say, *cooperation* among persons as indispensable for the survival and flourishing of humanity as a whole; but "cooperation" as an evolutionary concept is devoid of moral content and might just as well describe the practice of slavery (an eminently cooperative system) as any other functional social order. And, even if one could devise an account of human morality in evolutionary terms that seems to lead toward certain ineluctable "ethical" claims, such as "Slavery is bad for human society on the whole," one still cannot account for the sense of responsibility that this knowledge might instill in any particular person. The ethical dimension of one's judgment regarding one's actions at any given moment is, of necessity, open to a realm that a purely materialist picture of nature cannot comprise. Whenever conscience commands a thing, it does so in the intonations of an unconditional obligation, directed toward a strictly transcendental end. The structure of any meaningful ethics, no matter how encumbered it may be with utilitarian or pragmatic obfuscations, is invariably "religious." It is prompted by concerns that, in evolutionary terms, are "unnatural" or (better) "supernatural." Simply said, if there were no God, neither would there be such a thing as moral truth, nor such a thing as good or evil, nor such a thing as a moral imperative of any kind. This is so obviously true that the need to argue the point is itself evidence of how inextirpable our hunger for a transcendent moral truth is, even when all our metaphysical convictions militate against the existence of that truth. So, yes, it certainly is not the case that one needs to believe in God in any explicit way in order to be good; but it certainly *is* the case, as classical theism asserts, that to seek the good is already to believe in God, whether one wishes to do so or not.

IV

Again, I know that many atheists find assertions of that kind deeply annoying. This does not much concern me, I have to admit, but I ought to note that I am not attempting to start an argument regarding what atheists do or should *really* believe; my purpose is merely to make clear how the classical concept of God differs from the rather inane anthropomorphisms that proliferate in contemporary debates on the matter, both among atheists and among certain kinds of religious believers. And to this end I think it worth pointing out how very deep a conceptual problem a moral phenomenon such as, say, altruism poses for a materialist metaphysics. The difficulty is not genetic, strictly speaking: I assume that, if one confines one's thinking on such matters to a mechanistic understanding of material causality, one can certainly show that altruism has immense evolutionary benefits for certain groups of organisms, and so can be said to have developed along with the species. Rather, the real problem is structural: the question most worth asking about altruism is not whether it has measurable natural consequences that can aid certain populations in survival (surely it does), but whether in itself it can be made to fit seamlessly into a purely materialist account of reality, or whether instead it inevitably leaves open a path beyond the merely material. Certainly the typical naturalist attempts to explain altruism in entirely evolutionary terms create as many questions as they seem to answer. Part of the reason for this is that a great deal of evolutionary biology, as is not the case with physics or chemistry, takes the form of an historical reconstruction rather than a controlled experimental regimen, and so involves far more conjecture about past contingencies than any other modern science, and employs a theoretical language with more than its fair share of ill-defined concepts (such as "fitness"). There is nothing reprehensible in this; not all sciences should operate in the same way. The once reasonable hope that a deeper understanding of genetics would make evolutionary theory as precise as physics, by disclosing the secrets of a kind of basic biological particle analogous to the atom, seems to have been dashed by advances in molecular and cellular biology, which have tended to complicate rather than simplify our concept of genes. But biology has never really been dependent upon that sort of logic, and so its failure to isolate a basic particle all of its very own is hardly something to be lamented. Still, that said, the one great drawback of the reconstructive nature of much of evolutionary science is that ideology and pseudoscience can insinuate themselves into evolutionary theory somewhat more easily than into other scientific fields.

It is a pity, really, since there are few scientific queries more mysteriously beautiful than those that concern the origins and evolution of organic life. But there are also few areas of scientific endeavor more easily distorted in the public imagination by metaphysical commitments disguised as scientific principles (such as the persistence of a narrowly mechanistic view of nature that is almost certainly wholly inadequate as a model of how organisms and ecologies function) and by certain partisan theoretical loyalties (such as the purely dogmatic insistence that practically all biological phenomena must be understood according to a rigid adaptationism). When a particular scientific method becomes a metaphysics, and when that metaphysics masquerades as empirical rigor, it becomes exceedingly difficult to identify the real demarcations between genuine discoveries and arbitrary interpretations. All too often, evolutionary terms are employed not to identify what is actually known or unknown about the structure of life, but solely to advance a materialist mythology. Consider, for example, the profoundly foolish metaphor of the "selfish gene"—foolish, that is, simply because a metaphor is useful only when it elucidates its topic. This one does just the opposite: it actually obscures any clear picture of the genetic determination of organisms, and ultimately produces an alternate picture that cannot possibly be accurate. As a result, it is more an invitation to error than anything else. To be honest, talk of selfish genes does not even really qualify as a form of scientific language—although, admittedly, it possesses just enough of a ghostly trace of scientific content to have provoked a number of purely scientific debates. The idea that genes are the primary units of natural selection is, to put it mildly, a contentious one among evolutionary biologists, and the notion that DNA should be thought of as some kind of deterministic digital code that constructs vehicles for itself—"survival machines," to use a popular phrase—seems to be falling irretrievably into ever greater disfavor. There no longer appears to be a perfectly fixed concept of what a gene is, and a great deal of epigenetic theory and systems biology now presents us not with a unilinear picture of the gene as a kind of master program, which inexorably unfolds into the three-dimensional structure of the organism, but instead with a multilinear picture of genetic material as something whose functions are in many ways determined by the context of an organism's proteins and complex cellular processes. This is probably very old news by now. Anyone who had a decent biology teacher in school knows that there is not really any such thing as a "gene for" anything as such, so much as a kind of pluripotential genetic record of the evolutionary past that, in the present, is largely subordinate to the proteins encoded by the genome, and that can be used in vastly differing ways by cells, organisms, species, and ecologies.[2]

That, however, is not my complaint. The picture will continue to shift, in any event. Scientific paradigms are intrinsically provisional and dispensable. But it does not really matter what the ultimate status of "genetocentric" evolutionary theory will prove to be, because the metaphor of selfish genes is inept in any possible scientific context. The problem lies in applying the imagery of agency—of hidden motives and purposes and designs—to what are, after all, only biochemical constituents of immeasurably more complex organic structures (many of which truly do possess the sort of real intentionality that genes do not). The result is pictorial, mythological, but certainly not "scientific" in any meaningful sense. Take, for instance, the famous (or notorious) passage in which Richard Dawkins most memorably describes what genes do: "Now they swarm in huge colonies," he writes, "safe inside gigantic lumbering robots, sealed off from the outside world, communicating with it by tortuous indirect routes, manipulating it by remote control. They are in you and me; they created us, body and mind; and their preservation is the ultimate rationale for our existence." Then compare this to Denis Noble's elegant inversion of its central conceits: "Now they are trapped in huge colonies, locked inside highly intelligent beings, moulded by the outside world, communicating with it by complex processes, through which, blindly, as if by magic, function emerges. They are in you and me; we are the system that allows their code to be read; and their preservation is totally dependent on the joy we experience in reproducing ourselves. We are the ultimate rationale for their existence." Now, what precisely is the difference between these two approaches to genetic theory? Dawkins has graciously granted that Noble's revision of his text is every bit as plausible as the original, and that it really is all a matter of perspective in the end (which is a significant concession, since it means that the original text is making claims that are not empirical but only, at best, picturesque). In fact, though, the two passages are not comparably plausible at all. Colorful though it is, Noble's language is largely literally true. That of Dawkins, by contrast, is metaphorical all the way down: lumbering robots, manipulation, remote control, "they created us"— all of this is winsome enough, and even a little quaint (in a 1950s science fiction sort of way), but more or less nonsensical as well. Rhetorically speaking, it is a splendid example of the "pathetic fallacy," the naive habit of attributing human motives and intentions to nonhuman objects. It certainly describes nothing real, or even analogously real. Especially fanciful are those ridiculous robots, since they are precisely the sorts of things that we human beings—capable as we are of conscious intentions—most definitely are not. The image does, however, make obvious how very mechanistic a metaphor the "selfish gene" really is. At least, it is difficult not to notice that Noble's language has a vaguely (very vaguely) Aristotelian quality about it, what with its invocation of a kind of higher causality, descending from complex systems toward more primitive elements, while Dawkins is describing an essentially

Cartesian model of organisms: large automata governed by some more primal agency deep within (in this case, not a soul or ghost or homunculus but a host of self-interested imps discreetly nestled in organic cells).[3]

If it seems that I am being willfully humorless here, and refusing to take a metaphor for what it is, I can only once again insist that a metaphor must be genuinely germane to the reality it is meant to illustrate if it is to have any point. Talk of genetic selfishness, however, is simply a fundamental misrepresentation of reality. There is no value in speaking as if the ultimate seat of purposive agency in nature were situated in a material realm where intentionality does not exist, and as if all other causal levels—even those where real intentionality is to be found—are merely its deterministic residue. We are, after all, talking only about macromolecules that provide codes for proteins, the actions of whose products are, as Michel Morange says, "expressed only indirectly through an organizational and structural organic hierarchy—protein machines, organelles, cells, tissues, organs, organisms, and populations."[4] To his credit, Dawkins is not in fact a believer in total genetic determinism; he even speaks of human beings as having the unique capacity to resist the selfishness of their genes; but that very admission shows how ill-chosen the original metaphor was. A more accurate description of the matter might be to say that the "codes" contained in genetic materials are transcriptions of the histories of organisms that, in a quite passive way, have been preserved from generation to generation by virtue of the distinctive traits of the organic wholes into which they have been assumed and to which they make their vital but pluripotential contribution. Since natural selection is a theory regarding the opportune survival of fortuitous mutations, it would probably be far better to speak of the "fortunate," "privileged," or perhaps "graced" gene. After all, a man can be selfish, a rabbit might be selfish in some remotely analogous sense, but a gene can no more be selfish than can a teacup. Genes should always be qualified by objective, not subjective, adjectives.

Again, though, where is the harm in a mere figure of speech? But images often shape our concepts far more thoroughly than dialectical arguments can. It may not be *entirely* the fault of Dawkins that the language of genetic selfishness has spread so far as it has, but the damage has been considerable nonetheless. It has become an irritating commonplace to hear it asserted that, for instance, the *real* reason for a mother cherishing and protecting her young is that her genes have engineered her for their own survival. This is simply an absurd way of thinking about the matter. There is neither agency nor motive at the genetic level of organisms: "genes" do not "recognize" kindred beings, they do not "seek" to survive, they do not see or "program" any organism, they do not guide evolution, they are not the "rationale" for anything at all. The powerful but in many ways indeterminate causality found at the molecular level of physiological potentialities cannot begin adequately to account for behavioral effects at higher levels of organic, mental, and social complexity; but what happens at those higher levels can certainly determine what becomes of those macromolecular materials. To put things in the correct order, it is only because a mother has a desire to protect her young (let us be quaint here and call this desire "love") that the mindless genetic material contained in her cells—whose functions are as much determined as determining—is blessed with a derivative survival. It is only because the larger conditions of the world we share make it possible for a creature capable of love to evolve and flourish that life's notation of its organismic history (the "codes" inscribed in genes) can continue to be passed down stably from one generation to the next. Our DNA might well be characterized as an enduring record of our moral achievements, rather than as some secret truer text or hidden deterministic program subversive of those achievements. And, as explanatorily vacuous as the language of selfishness is in the case of maternal love (which, at the phenomenologically real level of actual intentionality, is frequently among the most selfless of rational emotions), in the case of altruistic deeds that extend beyond oneself or one's immediate group it can only generate bizarre distortions of reality.

A perfect example of what I mean would be the writings of the popular journalist Robert Wright, a mild-mannered, well-meaning, and influential purveyor of painfully simplistic accounts of evolutionary theory. Take, for instance, a short article he wrote for *Time* magazine back in 1996 called "Science and Original Sin." In one sense, it is a deeply incoherent essay, full of flawed reasoning from beginning to end, but in another sense there is a certain impressive logical inexorability in the way in which it unfolds from a single misguided premise: that everything in organic nature is reducible to the master "program" of genetic selfishness. Wright believes that altruism, for instance, is essentially an evolutionary strategy, which can always be traced back to a more fundamental (and mostly merciless) struggle for survival; it is basically a mechanism of survival, whose *real* purpose is to procure reciprocal benefits from those whom one assists. Below all conscious charity, therefore, lies a substrate of unalloyed selfishness, which is somehow more real or authentic than the superstructure of behaviors it supports. Wright at one point even illustrates his claim with the almost lunatic assertion that, when we contribute money for the relief of far distant famine victims, it is because our discriminatory "equipment"—which is meant to calculate the quid pro quo possibilities in any situation—has been "fooled" by the ubiquity of modern communications media into mistaking those victims for immediate neighbors, and this in turn leads us to send them aid in the pragmatic (if entirely tacit) expectation that we will receive some benefit from them in return. Altruism is in fact only selfishness deceived. I do not know if it would be possible to exaggerate how utterly ludicrous this argument is. Starting from some wholly metaphorical "selfishness" in our genes, Wright has extrapolated to some supposedly literal selfishness unconsciously but discreetly present in all our conscious intentions. What, concretely, can this possibly mean? This sort of confusion between the metaphorical and the actual is akin to a belief in sympathetic magic—rather like imagining that an allegorical image of Asclepius has the power to restore the health of a cancer patient. When we give money for the relief of the victims of a distant famine, the only intentional agencies at work are our conscious minds, which are quite aware that our benevolence will never be reciprocated in any way that can truly profit us. Our "equipment" has not made any mistake on that score at all. There may be some element of psychological duplicity involved in the act, such as the hope that others will think better of us, or that we will think better of ourselves; but that hardly outweighs the essentially uneconomic supererogation of our act. At the level of real experience and real thought—which is the *only* level at which motivations and decisions are to be found—

altruism is quite often really, truly, unambiguously altruistic. To suppose that it is even rational to talk about some phantom intentionality behind one's apparent intentionality, or some secret motive hiding deep below the surface of one's ostensible motives, is majestically silly. It transforms a defective metaphor regarding the "behaviors" of mindless physiological elements into an occult psychology regarding some inner mental faculty within us that has both the ability cunningly to deceive our conscious minds and the ability to be idiotically deceived by images flowing in from the world beyond. Who precisely is this homunculus, and where does he live? Where does this *real* intentionality that weaves the iridescent veils of our illusory intentionality ply its loom? In the pineal gland perhaps? Or perhaps in the right hemisphere of the brain?[5]

Anyway, as strange as such reasoning is, maybe it is somewhat pardonable. If one is constantly told that genetic codes are "programs" (which is a bad metaphor) and that organisms are "robots" (a worse metaphor) and that genes are "selfish" (a catastrophically worse metaphor), one might be forgiven for forgetting that intentionality belongs to consciousness, not to mere physical events. Even if one insists on speaking of the persistence of certain genetic materials down the ages as "selfish," one can never meaningfully translate such language into a coherent psychological account of human motives. The attempt to do so can lead only to a kind of deliriously indiscriminate paranoia: everything—even kindness—is struggle; everything—even charity—is selfishness. Not only is this a perverse and unwarranted picture of reality; it opens a vast phenomenological abyss between our actual experience of life and the allegedly more fundamental reality that this story of a primordial selfishness describes.

If one absolutely must make sense of moral phenomena in purely evolutionary terms, one can always, I suppose, allow for a degree of epiphenomenal surfeit in one's account of evolutionary adaptation. Perhaps one can argue that, while most of our natural capacities exist because they are clearly advantageous, some exist accidentally, as "spandrels" or "pendentives" formed in superfluous intervals in the architecture of our natures. Or perhaps one could argue that our more disproportionate displays of conscience are merely "memetic" variations on our natural aptitudes that have accidentally exceeded all practical purposes, because vagrant units of cultural transmission have colonized our evolutionarily advantageous capacity for beneficial cooperation and metastasized into a predisposition to act not only in ways that confer no real evolutionary benefit on us (like trying to feed famine victims), but even in ways that militate against our evolutionary interests entirely (like risking our lives to, say, save a cat trapped down a well). This is, at least, an approach almost impossible to falsify: whatever our native capacities for moral actions may be, we can always claim that either they are really only expressions of special selfishness or they are only the accidental epiphenomena of such selfishness; any apparent discord between pure adaptationism and our living experience of our own moral acts can be avoided by a simple but deftly nimble leap from one explanation to the other. For myself, however, I find it all rather unsatisfactory. I cannot believe that any explanatory model can really be powerful enough to explain both what it does explain and what it does not. This is only slightly better than those exuberantly impressionistic fables that evolutionary psychology—the phrenology of our day—invents in order to provide evolutionary rationales for every observable form of behavior, no matter how seemingly contrary to adaptive imperatives. But I suppose this is the best explanation of moral desire that a materialist picture of things can provide: there is no such thing as selflessness; and, anyway, if there is it is merely an accidental accretion upon a more essential selfishness.

In the end, the incongruity speaks for itself. No explanation of ethical desire entirely in terms of evolutionary benefit can ever really account for the sheer exorbitance of the moral passion of which rational minds are capable, or for the transcendentally "ecstatic" structure of moral longing. If nothing else, one has to wonder what the need for the whole ethical illusion of personal selflessness really is, after all. Whom does evolution need to deceive? What is the benefit we derive from needing to misunderstand our true motives? Why should we have such moral expectations of ourselves in the first place? Why should not natural selection have fashioned us for a perfectly rational capacity for prudent cooperative selfishness, without the additional stage-trickery of this odd inner conviction that our motives should be prompted by more than self-interest? What is the need for a conscience so uncompromising in its demands that it must be continually deluded? In a sense, these are all meaningless questions—or, rather, their meaning lies in their capacity to show how inherently contradictory is the premise on which the "selfish" reading of morality rests. Logically, conscience cannot possibly be deceived in that way. True altruism, at least as an experience of one's own motivations, may often be mingled with self-interest or self-regard; but it cannot be wholly illusory, for the simple reason that the need to believe in the purity of one's own motives is itself proof that one's motives truly are, in some very real measure, pure. That is to say, if we must be convinced that we are acting from altruistic impulses, then there really must be a predisposition toward altruism within us, which we have to appease for the sake of our own equanimity. We can need to be deceived that we are selfless in our actions only if we really are selfless in many of our moral intentions; the illusion of selflessness, therefore, would prove the reality of selflessness, at least as a guiding ideal.

I am not questioning the claim, incidentally, that our moral aptitudes have been an aid to the survival of the species. Surely they have. I certainly like to think that there is a great evolutionary benefit in altruism, if only because it suits my metaphysical convictions to do so: I wish to believe that altruism is somehow essentially consonant with being as such, and that moral aptitudes are beneficial to a species precisely because they correspond to the ultimate truth of things and open us to the metaphysical structure of reality. On the other hand, I also know that an absence of altruism has its evolutionary advantages as well (our species has not yet proved anywhere near so perdurable as that debonair stranger to all pity, the insouciant crocodile). Life preserves itself—and is adventitiously preserved—in any number of ways. The interesting question is not whether morality is part of the story of evolution, but instead how it is that a moral sense can have appeared within nature to begin with. Its very structure, even when one takes account of all the practical particularities that attach to any particular ethical act, consists in an indissoluble intentional relation between subjective consciousness and the absolute. Where does such a sense come from? To what reality does it correspond? How does natural selection recognize and preserve so strange a configuration of behavioral forces? How can a purely physical system of causes produce an intentional orientation of desire that is intrinsically directed toward a transcendent end lying entirely beyond nature? And how is it that organisms "programmed" for survival occasionally show themselves capable of extravagant acts of self-abnegating generosity or kindness or love that clearly can have no ulterior purpose within this world (for them or for their genes)? Perhaps one can come up with a naturalistic tale that makes all of that seem perfectly plausible (though it will always be *only* a tale). Even so, if natural selection has given rise to species with this fantastic capacity, it means that it has produced organisms able to act in perfect defiance of evolutionary imperatives, in obedience to a final cause that cannot be comprised within the closed economy of material processes and personal interests. This is quite curious— even perhaps miraculous. It should cause even the most dogmatic of materialists to pause and consider whether it indicates a dimension of reality that materialism fails to account for.

In any event, one may choose to accord a kind of causal supremacy to genes in the story of evolution if one likes, and even to something called "selfishness" if one feels it necessary, but in doing so one obscures the fuller causal complexity and richness of life. From a materialist perspective, the simplest narrative here may be the most desirable; but it may also be the one that explains the least. The mystery remains: the transcendent good, which is invisible to the forces of natural selection, has made a dwelling for itself within the consciousness of rational animals. A capacity has appeared within nature that, in its very form, is supernatural: it cannot be accounted for entirely in terms of the economy of advantageous cooperation because it continually and exorbitantly exceeds any sane calculation of evolutionary benefits. Yet, in the effectual order of evolution, it is precisely this irrepressible excessiveness that, operating as a higher cause, inscribes its logic upon the largely inert substrate of genetic materials, and guides the evolution of rational nature toward an openness to ends that cannot be enclosed within mere physical processes. This, after all, is the way of telling the story that situates intentional and formative causalities where they truly belong, rather than at the mindless level of molecules. If there is such a thing as "kin selection," for instance—the supposedly "selfish" evolutionary tendency of an organism to act in ways favorable to the posterity of its nearest genetic relations— even that is only a process contingent upon a broader, more fundamental, and essentially generous propensity within certain organisms. It is clearly not really the case that genes have intentionally constructed "survival vehicles" for themselves, or cunningly contrived precise behavioral mechanisms that will cause certain members of a species to sacrifice themselves for certain others, in order that particular genetic codes might be preserved. Language of that sort simply inverts cause and consequence. Rather, what has *really* happened in the course of evolutionary history—that is, not metaphorically, not mythologically, not pictorially, not in the fanciful terms of "programs" and genetic "rationales," but really—is that certain gene pools have flourished because true altruism has come into existence, at levels of life (organisms, ecologies, communities, cultures) that genetic codes cannot directly determine. Even where there is some genetic propinquity between benefactors and beneficiaries, the intentional impulse that decides which genes will be passed on to another generation is one whose motives are ontologically selfless. A species that has the capacity for love has a genetic heritage *because* it loves; it does not love because, at the macromolecular level, there exists some "program" for survival, or some "gene for" love. This is not even a debatable issue. Certain genetic codes, which are a kind of "legible" bequest from past generations, survive not because they are in some mystical sense "selfish" but precisely because the complex organisms to which they belong are not. Rather than genes fashioning vehicles for their survival, life has fashioned a special genetic legacy for itself, in the very stable form of genetic potentialities, which emerges from a capacity to exceed the narrow requisites of private survival. As a species, we have been shaped evolutionarily, in large part at least, by transcendental ecstasies whose orientation exceeds the whole of nature. Instead of speaking vacuously of genetic selfishness, then, it would be immeasurably more accurate to say that compassion, generosity, love, and conscience have a unique claim on life. They are the formal— or even spiritual—causes that, by their ever greater impracticality and exorbitance, fashion a being capable of cooperation (which happily proves beneficial to the species), but also capable of a kind of charity that cannot be contained within the reciprocal economy of *mere* cooperation. Since their intentional end is not survival but an abstract and absolute reality, any evolutionary benefit they impart must be regarded as a secondary, subordinate, and fortunate consequence of their activity.

v

At any rate, any sane consideration of the sheer insatiability that the moral appetite in rational beings can exhibit should awaken one to something magnificently strange about these transcendental orientations of the mind. Whatever benefits the moral sense may or may not confer upon a species or an individual, it remains the case that the frame of natural reality as we know it is at once hospitable to it and yet also wholly unable to satisfy the desires that rise out of it. And, whatever occasions for moral community the material order may provide, ultimately the moral impulses that shape and enliven such community are irrepressibly and indivertibly concerned with an immaterial object so absolute in its demands that it can move the will toward utter self-renunciation in service to others. There is something altogether profligate in this passion for the good, something that resists any facile attempt to capture it within the bounds of material or genetic economy. At its most prodigal and abandoned, it can even become that most scandalous violation of the principles of sound evolutionary prudence, holiness—the charity of the saintly soul. "What is a merciful heart?" asks Isaac of Nineveh (d. c. AD 700): "A heart aflame for all of creation, for men, birds, beasts, demons, and every created thing; the very thought or sight of them causes the merciful man's eyes to overflow with tears. The heart of such a man is humbled by the powerful and fervent mercy that has captured it and by the immense compassion it feels, and it cannot endure to see or hear of any suffering or any grief anywhere within creation." The saint, says Swami Ramdas (1884–1963), is one whose heart burns for the sufferings of others, whose hands labor for the relief of others, and who therefore acts from God's heart and with God's hands. The most exalted unity with God is attained, Krishna tells Arjuna in the *Bhagavad-Gita,* by one whose bliss and sorrow are found in the bliss and sorrow of others. Like a mother imperiling her own life in order to care for her child, says the *Sutta Nipata,* one should cultivate boundless compassion for all beings. One's love for one's fellow creatures should be so great, Ramanuja believed, that one will gladly accept damnation for oneself in order to show others the way to salvation. According to Shantideva (eighth century), the true bodhisattva vows to forgo entry into nirvana, age upon age, and even to pass through the torments of the many Buddhist hells, in order to work ceaselessly for the liberation of others.[6]

One could compile an almost endless anthology of citations of that sort, of course. Religious expressions of the desire for goodness are often fairly uninhibited in their rhetorical forcibleness; given that it is a preoccupation with an absolute value, moral yearning naturally tends to find its voice most fully, and with the purest intonations, in a devotional setting. Again, I would not claim that one must be in some explicit sense a "religious" person in order to feel this consuming need to see and serve the good by serving others; but I am afraid I must still assert that to act out of that need is, willingly or unwillingly, to act in relation to God. This is merely a matter of a correct definition of terms. According to the classical metaphysics of divine transcendence and simplicity, it must be recalled, God is not just some ethical individual out there somewhere, a finite subjectivity answerable to some set of moral laws outside himself, but is rather the fullness of being, in whom all powers and perfections are infinitely realized. He is not simply someone who is good, but goodness itself, the ontological reality of that absolute object that moral desire seeks. Or, better, what we call goodness is, in its essence, God in his aspect as the original source and ultimate fulfillment of all love, drawing all things to one another by drawing them to himself. Thus, our rational appetite for being is also a longing for the good, and our longing for the good is an aboriginal longing for God. Moral desire, in its extravagant indifference to the limits of physical reality, seeks its consummation in the bliss of the divine.

This is why, as I mentioned far above, the famous dilemma from Plato's *Euthyphro* is not much of a problem for any of the great theistic traditions. The central question posed in that dialogue (to rehearse it again) is whether the commands of the gods are good because they are the gods' commands, or whether they are the gods' commands because they are good. In the minds of some, this supposedly constitutes an insoluble difficulty for theism of any kind: in the former case goodness would be only an arbitrary product of the divine will, while in the latter the divine would be subordinate to some higher reality; and neither option should seem particularly attractive to pious souls. It is indeed an interesting question for any polytheist culture that conceives of its gods as finite personalities, contained within and dependent upon nature; it is probably a good question to ask of a deist as well, or of any other believer in a cosmic demiurge; but, applied to classical theism, it is simply a meaningless query, predicated upon a crude anthropomorphism. It is no more interesting than asking whether light shines because it is light or whether instead it is light because it shines. One should recall that the entire point of Plato's inquiry in the *Euthyphro* was to show that there must be some eternal principle— which he would call the Form of the Good—beyond the realm of either material nature or limited and willful deities. This is all part of an ancient metaphysical project going back at least as far as Xenophanes, which is the common heritage of philosophy and rational theology alike: the attempt to distinguish the transcendent from the immanent, the changeless from the mutable, the ultimate source from its contingent derivations. For none of the great theistic traditions is "God" the name of a god, some emotionally changeable entity who has to deliberate upon his actions, either in respect of standards independent of himself or in respect of some arbitrary psychological impulse within himself. "God" is the name, rather, of that eternal and transcendent principle upon which the gods (if there are such beings) are dependent for their existence and for their share in all the transcendental perfections of being. For all the great monotheisms, God is himself the Good, or the Form of the Good, and his freedom consists in his limitless power to express his nature (goodness) unhindered by the obstacles or limitations suffered by finite beings. He is "the love that moves the sun and all the other stars," as Dante phrases it, at once the underlying unity and the final end of all things. And the absolute nature of that love is reflected in the unconditional quality of the transcendental or ecstatic desire it excites in rational natures. As Bernard of Clairvaux (1090–1153) says, "Love is sufficient in itself, gives pleasure through itself and because of itself. It is its own merit, its own reward. Love looks for no cause outside itself, no effect beyond itself. . . . I love because I love, I love so that I may love. Love is something great insofar as it returns constantly to its fountainhead and flows back to its source, from which it ever draws the water that continually replenishes it. . . . For when God loves, he desires only to be loved in turn. His love's only purpose is to be loved, as he knows that all who love him are made happy by their love of him."[7]

VI

It is this autotelic sufficiency—this quality of being an absolute end in itself—that is the distinguishing mark of all transcendental properties. For this reason, it may be that in some sense the most exemplary of the transcendentals is beauty. No other is more obviously characterized by an almost perfect absence of utility, or possesses a power to compel that so clearly offers no gratification or profit beyond itself. The apprehension of beauty is something simple and immediate; it is wholly elusive of definition—it never makes sense to say, "This is beautiful because . . ."—and yet it is inescapable in its force. One knows it, one experiences it, but no concept is adequate to it. That same horizon of the absolute that excites the mind's desire for truth and the will's desire for the good is also the splendor or luminosity or radiance of being, in which we delight for the sake of delight alone. Beauty is gloriously useless; it has no purpose but itself.

Not everyone agrees, needless to say. In Western scholastic tradition, for instance, Thomists were often reluctant to identify the beautiful as one of the transcendentals at all (principally because they had a remarkably narrow and impoverished concept of what beauty is). A great deal of modern aesthetic theory tends to avoid talk of beauty altogether (for much the same reason). There are even a few texts of Darwinian aesthetics out there, which regrettably attempt to reduce our sense of beauty to a function of sexual selection or to the neurobiology of pleasure or to the modular brain's recollections of the sorts of landscapes preferred by our phylogenic forebears. Yet, in the end, the experience of beauty is ubiquitous; it is inseparable from that essential orientation toward the absolute that weds rational consciousness to being. And at some level it is clearly an experience of delight—though often a sober delight—without any conceivable ulterior purpose. What we find beautiful delights us because we find it beautiful. Even when the occasion of the experience of beauty is at the same time an object of "interested" desire—an artifact of great monetary worth, a person one finds erotically attractive—one can always in principle distinguish (if not in practice separate) one's recognition of beauty from one's other motives. What one cannot do, however, is reduce one's rational appetite for the beautiful to something more mundane or practical, at least not without a large unexplained remainder.

This should not be a particularly controversial claim. The very nature of aesthetic enjoyment resists conversion into any kind of calculable economy of personal or special benefits. We cannot even isolate beauty as an object among other objects, or even as a clearly definable property; it transcends every finite description. There have, admittedly, been attempts in various times and places to establish the "rules" that determine whether something is beautiful, but never with very respectable results. Thomistic tradition, to take a particularly unfortunate example, enumerates three proper constituents of beautiful things: integrity, right proportionality, and brilliancy. That is, firstly, a thing's beauty is determined to the degree that it is complete, not lacking in any essential feature, and in no way disfigured by privation or distortion; a missing eye or damaged lip detracts from the beauty of a face, a crack deforms the surface of a lovely vase, an off-key note diminishes a bel canto aria. Secondly, all the parts of a beautiful object must be in pleasing proportion to one another, nothing should be either excessive or insufficient, all parts must be arranged harmoniously and in attractive balance. And, thirdly, the beautiful thing must shine, must be radiant, in a quite concretely physical way; it must be clear, distinct, splendid, lustrous, brightly colored.

All of this is practically worthless, as scarcely need be said. It confuses the beautiful with the pretty, the delightful with the merely obliging, enchantment with diversion. Yes, we take pleasure in color, integrity, harmony, radiance, and so on; and yet, as anyone who troubles to consult his or her experience of the world knows, we also frequently find ourselves stirred and moved and delighted by objects whose visible appearances or tones or other qualities violate all of these canons of aesthetic value, and that somehow "shine" with a fuller beauty as a result. Conversely, many objects that possess all these ideal features often bore us, or even appall us, with their banality. At times, the obscure enchants us and the lucid leaves us untouched; plangent dissonances can awaken our imaginations far more delightfully than simple harmonies that quickly become insipid; a face almost wholly devoid of conventionally pleasing features can seem unutterably beautiful to us in its very disproportion, while the most exquisite profile can do no more than charm us. The tenebrous canvases of Rembrandt are beautiful, while the shrill daubs of Thomas Kinkade, with all their sugary glitter, are repellant. Whatever the beautiful is, it is not simply harmony or symmetry or consonance or ordonnance or brightness, all of which can become anodyne or vacuous of themselves; the beautiful can be encountered—sometimes shatteringly—precisely where all of these things are deficient or largely absent. Beauty is something other than the visible or audible or conceptual agreement of parts, and the experience of beauty can never be wholly reduced to any set of material constituents. It is something mysterious, prodigal, often unanticipated, even capricious. We can find ourselves suddenly amazed by some strange and indefinable glory in a barren field, an urban ruin, the splendid disarray of a storm-wracked forest, and so on.

Even sensual pleasure is inadequate to explain aesthetic experience. We may, for instance, be neurologically predisposed to find certain musical intervals pleasant; but simple consonance soon becomes tiresome by itself, and we often find far deeper aesthetic pleasure in the play of dissonance and resolution, or in certain sublime and unresolved dissonant effects. We can even acquire appreciation for a beauty that at first we did not recognize because our neurobiological capacities inhibited us. We can learn to be enraptured by the austere loveliness of Martinů and bored by the vapid prettiness of American minimalism. The tonic oddity of early Takemitsu can provide us with a completely satisfying aesthetic experience, while one of Dvořák's more uninspired pieces, though technically correct by all the canons of tonality, tension and resolution, and modulation, may strike us as little more than tedious pastiche. And, not to belabor the point, it is simply an indubitable fact of experience that aesthetic appetite is formally distinct from any instrumental purpose we might find in the objects we desire, and that aesthetic satisfaction is formally distinct from purely sensory gratification. The ultimate object of aesthetic desire remains absolute, even as it directs attention and longing toward particular things; it lies forever beyond the totality of beings, and far beyond any reckonable economy of survival or material advantage.

This is why it is, I have to say, that I find Darwinian attempts to explain aesthetics particularly unconvincing. They tend to start, soundly enough, from a recognition of an elementary continuity between the physiological, material basis of our likes, dislikes, pleasures, and aversions, on the one hand, and our judgments of beauty, on the other; but they never succeed in moving beyond these things to account for all the ways in which aesthetic desire exceeds the boundaries of the physiological and material. Even the very best and most enjoyable book written in this vein, Denis Dutton's *The Art Instinct,* which ultimately tries to ground the creation and appreciation of art in the Darwinian logic of sexual selection, is an abject failure as an actual explanation of the variety and magnitude of humanity's aesthetic labors and delectations. One finishes the book with a far greater sense of everything that has been left out than of what has been convincingly accounted for. Dutton inventively suggests ways in which artistic achievement, like every other form of achievement, may have some foundation in our need to display ourselves (to attract mates, for the most part), but he does not even begin convincingly to explain how aesthetic values as such should appear within nature at all (after all, being stirred or excited by broad shoulders, shapely hips, displays of physical prowess, and so forth is not the same thing as being moved or fascinated by a particular alignment of hues, or a haunting refrain, or a happy poetic image). Moreover, he excludes far too much of aesthetic experience from his story because he is at such pains, necessarily, to explain the experience of beauty in terms of the material conditions of affective pleasure. For instance, he points out that the most popular sorts of photographs in calendars are of landscapes that supposedly carry us back to our remote evolutionary beginnings in the savannahs of Africa, or at any rate to the sort of watery and lush landscapes our distant evolutionary progenitors would have sought out. This may be true, but it is an observation irrelevant to our experience of beauty. We may enjoy pictures of certain landscapes that are agreeable to us at a purely physiological level, but what we find beautiful is, as a rule, almost entirely unrelated to material conditions of that kind. The form of a representation often seems to enthrall us far more than the objects represented. A magnificent photograph of an uninhabitable desert can delight us in ways that a competent but uninspired photograph of a sapphire lake amid emerald tussocks and flowered rills cannot. It is that difference—elusive, mysterious, formal rather than concrete—that constitutes the qualitative distinction between physiological and aesthetic pleasure. Our sense of what is appealing to us is surely rooted to a great degree in our animal nature, but the actual motive of aesthetic desire is a striving toward the absolute. It is nothing less than our desire for the whole of being, experienced in the form of disinterested bliss.

When we encounter the beautiful, after all, what is it that compels us? What draws us in, and awakens us to a splendor beyond our particular interests and desires and predilections, in a canvas by Titian or Corot, a Bach violin partita, or simply a particularly well-tended garden? It is not simply this or that aspect of its composition, not simply its neurological effect, not simply its clarity or vividness or suggestive associations, and so on; it is not even just the virtuosity of its execution or the mastery exhibited in its composition. Rather, it is all of these things experienced as sheer fortuity. I may be speaking of something that escapes exact definition here, but it seems clear to me that the special delight experienced in the encounter with beauty is an immediate sense of the utterly unnecessary thereness, so to speak, of a thing, the simple gratuity with which it shows itself, or (better) gives itself. Apart from this, even the most perfectly executed work of art would be only a display of artisanal proficiency or of pure technique, exciting our admiration but not that strange rapture that marks the most intense of aesthetic experiences. What transforms the merely accomplished into the revelatory is this invisible nimbus of utter gratuity. Rather than commanding our attention with the force of necessity, or oppressing us with the triteness of something inevitable, or recommending itself to us by its utility or its purposiveness, the beautiful presents itself to us as an entirely unwarranted, unnecessary, and yet marvelously fitting gift. Beauty—as opposed to mere strikingness, mere brilliancy—is an event, or even (one might say) eventuality as such. It is the movement of a gracious disclosure of something otherwise hidden, which need not reveal itself or give itself. In the experience of the beautiful, and of its pure fortuity, we are granted our most acute, most lucid, and most splendid encounter with the difference of transcendent being from the realm of finite beings. The beautiful affords us our most perfect experience of that existential wonder that is the beginning of all speculative wisdom. This state of amazement, once again, lies always just below the surface of our quotidian consciousness; but beauty stirs us from our habitual forgetfulness of the wonder of being. It grants us a particularly privileged awakening from our "fallenness" into ordinary awareness, reminding us that the fullness of being, which far exceeds any given instance of its disclosure, graciously condescends to show itself, again and again, in the finitude of a transient event. In this experience, we are given a glimpse—again, with a feeling of wonder that restores us momentarily to something like the innocence of childhood—of that inexhaustible source that pours itself out in the gracious needlessness of being.

Beauty is also the startling reminder, even for persons sunk in the superstitions of materialism, that those who see reality in purely mechanistic terms do not see the real world at all, but only its shadow. Standing before a painting by Chardin or Vermeer, one might be able to describe the object in terms of purely physical elements and events but still fail to see the painting for what it is: an object whose visible aspects are charged with a surfeit of meaning and splendor, a mysterious glory that is the ultimate rationale of its existence, a radiant dimension of absolute value at once transcending and showing itself within the limits of material form. In the experience of the beautiful, one is apprised with a unique poignancy of both the ecstatic structure of consciousness and the gratuity of being. Hence the ancient conviction that the love of beauty is, by its nature, a rational yearning for the transcendent. The experience of sensible beauty provokes in the soul the need to seek supersensible beauty, says Plato; it is, in the words of Plotinus, a "delicious perturbation" that awakens an eros for the divine within us. All things are a mirror of the beauty of God, says the great Sufi poet Mahmud Shabestari (1288–1340); and to be seized with the desire for that beauty, says Gregory of Nyssa, is to long to be transformed within oneself into an ever more perspicuous mirror of its splendor. Kabir (1440–1518) says that it is divine beauty that shines out from all things, and that all delight in beauty is adoration of God. For Thomas Traherne (c. 1636–1674), one of the sanest men who ever lived, to see the world with the eyes of innocence, and so to see it pervaded by a numinous glory, is to see things as they truly are, and to recognize creation as the mirror of God's infinite beauty.

It would be best to avoid rhapsody here, I suppose. Suffice it to say, as soberly as possible, that the desire for the beautiful is not—and cannot be—a desire *merely* for the pleasurable or the profitable. The beautiful is unquestionably a transcendental orientation of the mind and the will, because the desire it evokes can never be exhausted by any finite object; it is an ultimate value that allows one to make judgments of relative value, and that weds consciousness to the whole of being as boundlessly desirable. Whether or not there actually is such a thing as an eternal beauty beyond the realm of the senses, the effect within us of beauty's transcendence is quite undeniably real. It informs all of rational consciousness as an ideal horizon, toward which the mind is habitually drawn and apart from which the mind would not be open to the world in the way that it is. And that, in itself, is enough to render the physicalist narrative of causality profoundly dubious.

VII

None of these observations amounts, I admit, to a decent treatise on epistemology, ethics, or aesthetics; they are all far too cursory and elliptical. What interests me here, though, and what is most relevant to my topic, is the formal structure of transcendental desire and its presence within rational consciousness. The ways in which that desire is mediated by the shifting forces of material, psychological, and cultural circumstances are endlessly variable, and not always for the best: the search for truth can lead to folly or derangement or arid dogmatism, ethical longings can lead to monstrous deformations of the spirit of a person or a people, the quest for beauty can lose its way in barren defiles of kitsch or preciosity or decadence. Yet our yearning for the utmost value persists amid all our wanderings, no matter how misguided they may become. And when the true absolute shows itself to us, however evanescently or obscurely, it seizes us and demands the surrender of our wills and self-interests. The mere phenomenon of this inner, habitual intentional relation of consciousness to absolute ends casts a particularly clear light upon what the word "God" means in the great theistic traditions. God is the source and ground of being and the wellspring of all consciousness, but also therefore the final cause of all creation, the end toward which all beings are moved, the power of infinite being that summons all things into existence from nothingness and into union with itself; and God manifests himself as such in the ecstasies of rational nature toward the absolute. One has to understand this much if one hopes to grasp the logical content of the concept of God as creator and source of all: not, that is, as a finite entity who can be classed alongside or over against the finite entities that belong to nature, not as a demiurge or god or intelligent designer, not as one more being among all the other beings in the universe, but as that fullness of being in which all things live and move and have their contingent being, and as that highest perfection of being toward which all things are drawn. As the book of Sirach says, "He is the All." And, in the transcendentals upon which rational consciousness subsists, we are addressed not by any limited interest or exhaustible object, but by an absolute source of authority, no less extensive than the whole of being, demanding our attention, and offering us the only true fulfillment possible for rational beings: the super-natural end that makes natural ends conceivable and desirable for us. God is thus experienced as that bliss in which our natures have their consummation because that bliss is already, in God, the perfect consummation of the divine unity of being and consciousness: infinite being knows itself in infinite consciousness and therefore infinitely rejoices.

In this sense, faith in God is not something that can ever be wholly and coherently rejected, even if one refuses all adherence to creeds and devotions. The desires evoked by the transcendental horizon of rational consciousness are not merely occasional agitations of the will but constant dynamisms of the mind; they underlie the whole movement of thought toward the world. But for these formally excessive and ecstatic longings, which seek their satisfaction in an end beyond nature, we would know nothing of nature, could not care for it, could not delight in it. To be rational beings, capable of experiencing reality as an intelligible realm of truth, moral responsibility, and disinterested joy, is to be open at every moment before the supernatural. For classical theism, the transcendental perfections of being are simply different names for—different ways of apprehending—being itself, which is God, and are thus convertible with one another in the simplicity of the divine. In the prism of finite existence, that unity becomes a plurality of distinct aspects of reality, and we only occasionally have any sense of their ultimate unity—when, for instance, we are able to grasp a mathematical truth in part because of its elegance, or when an act of compassion strikes us with its beauty, or when our will to act morally in a certain situation allows us to see the true nature of that situation more clearly, or when we sense that the will to know the truth is also an ethical vocation of the mind (and so on). For the most part, however, we have little immediate awareness of how the transcendentals coincide with one another. Even so, any movement of the mind or will toward truth, goodness, beauty, or any other transcendental end is an adherence of the soul to God. It is a finite participation in the highest truth of existence. As Shankara says, the fullness of being, lacking nothing, is also boundless consciousness, and as such is boundless joy.[8]

This may seem a strange way to bring my meditations on the meaning of the word "God" to an end. I believe, however, that it is a natural terminus for any attempt to identify those aspects of our experience of reality that open up upon the question of God. If nothing else, I think that my approach is largely in keeping with the understanding of God found in the great theistic and metaphysical traditions of East and West, and that it does not require the supplement of any particular theology or any specific creed. Quite apart from what may or may not have been revealed by God in the course of history, the common tendency in all of these traditions to seek out the one source and end of all things directs thinking again and again toward those dimensions of reality that mysteriously escape any simple empirical inventory of what exists. In the being of all things we encounter the primal "supernatural" reality, the premise of all things that cannot be explained by or contained among those things, the ultimate truth that is logically prior to and therefore logically transcendent of nature. In our consciousness of being we are immediately aware of a reality that—in its intentionality, unity, and abstract aptitudes—cannot be given a cogent mechanical explanation, that is more indubitable than any other reality, and that therefore is logically prior to and logically transcendent of mere physical causality; and ultimately we find that being and consciousness may not in fact be truly separable. And in the transcendental structure of consciousness we are confronted by the presence of the absolute within even the most ordinary acts of mind and will, and we find that the extraordinary joys of which rational intellect is capable (whose shadow side are equally extraordinary sorrows) far exceed what nature can adumbrate or warrant; here too we are placed before a reality that is logically prior to and transcendent of the intelligible configurations of nature. And in finding an indissoluble interconnectedness in all three of these realities taken together, we come upon the supreme mystery of all experience. Whether God is indeed to be found in these dimensions of experience, that is where he has traditionally been sought, as the unconditioned and transcendent reality who sustains all things in being, the one in whom all that nature cannot contain but upon which nature depends has its simple and infinite actuality. Any argument for or against the reality of God not so understood—any debate over an intelligent designer, or a supreme being within space and time who merely supervises history and legislates morals, or a demiurge whose operations could possibly be rivals of the physical causes describable by scientific cosmology—may prove a diverting amble along certain byways of seventeenth-century deism or eighteenth-century "natural history," but it most definitely has nothing whatsoever to do with the God worshipped in the great theistic religions, or described in their philosophical traditions, or reasoned toward by their deepest logical reflections upon the contingency of the world.

In the end, however, one might justly wonder whether the God who enters human consciousness through the apparently "super-

natural" dimensions of our experience of nature can ever be anything other than a logical construction, to which we turn in order
to mollify our painful longing for ultimate answers that a finite
mind cannot truly discover. If there is such a thing as reason, to
advert again to the vicious circle I invoked many pages ago, then
it points toward a transcendent God; but, if there is no such God,
then reason itself is only an illusion, a useful one perhaps, but no
more than useful. At the last, then, the only way to know whether
the God who comes into thought when we attempt to understand
reality as a whole, and to understand also our knowledge and love
of that reality, is consciously and conscientiously to pursue the
transcendental ecstasies that open the world to us to their ultimate
end: to seek, that is, a vision of and union with God.

PART THREE

The Reality of God

Having fully awakened from his dream, the dreamer—or former dreamer—might momentarily reflect upon the ingenious intricacy of the distortions by which his sleeping mind had transformed the world around him into another world altogether. He may know that dreams seem coherent only from within, and that the limits that enclose them always lie very nearby, bounded by impenetrable mists. It is only because a dreamer has temporarily lost the desire to turn his eyes toward more distant horizons that he believes he inhabits a reality perfectly complete in itself, in need of no further explanation. He does not see that this secondary world rests upon no foundations, has no larger story, and persists as an apparent unity only so long as he has forgotten how to question its curious omissions and contradictions. Even so, now that the man has arisen he still cannot help but marvel at the artistry with which his dreaming mind wove one reality, however evanescent, from the disparate elements of another: a bell in a tower, a windblown valley, reeds stirring along the banks of a stream, all conjured up from a wind chime ringing beyond an open window, a momentary breeze, a susurration of leaves below the sill. How remarkable that, when the critical intellect has fallen dormant, the imagination is still capable of such feats of invention. And how exquisite the many ways in which the fabric of the dream preserved the shape of the real world within its deepest patterns, and even imitated the cogency of waking consciousness: the reality of things was present all along, but only under the guise of another reality altogether. This is something, though, that one can appreciate only in the light of morning, once one has emerged from dreams. For, while those who have awakened know what it is to sleep, those who are still asleep do not remember what it is to be awake.

CHAPTER SIX

Illusion and Reality

I

I suppose it has been a fairly central (if not always ostenta-
tiously prominent) theme of this book that we should not mistake
our ways of seeing the world for the world as it truly is. To which
I might also add: we should not mistake every pronouncement
made in an authoritative tone of voice for an established truth.
Regarding the ultimate nature of reality, at least, neither the general consensus of a culture nor the special consensus of a creden-
tialed class should be trusted too readily, especially if it cannot
justify itself except by reference to its own unexamined presuppositions. So much of what we imagine to be the testimony of
reason or the clear and unequivocal evidence of our senses is really
only an interpretive reflex, determined by mental habits impressed
in us by an intellectual and cultural history. Even our notion of
what might constitute a "rational" or "realistic" view of things is
largely a product not of a dispassionate attention to facts, but of
an ideological legacy. To some extent, something of the sort is true
of most of our larger convictions about the world. If we examine

the premises underlying our beliefs and reasoning honestly and indefatigably enough, we will find that our deepest principles often consist in nothing more—but nothing less—than a certain way of seeing things, an original inclination of the mind toward reality from a certain perspective. And philosophy is of little use here in helping us to sort out the valid preconceptions from the invalid, as every form of philosophical thought is itself dependent upon a set of irreducible and unprovable assumptions. This is a sobering and uncomfortable thought, but also a very useful reminder of the limits of argument, and of the degree to which our most cherished certitudes are inseparable from our own private experiences.

I find it helpful, at any rate, to keep this in mind when trying to make sense of the current debates regarding belief in God. I have to admit that I find it impossible to take atheism very seriously as an intellectual position. As an emotional commitment or a moral passion—a rejection of barren or odious dogmatisms, an inability to believe in a good or provident power behind a world in which there is so much suffering, defiance of "Whatever brute and blackguard made the world," and so forth—atheism seems to me an entirely plausible attitude toward the predicaments of finite existence; but, as a metaphysical picture of reality, it strikes me as a rank superstition. I cannot imagine how it is possible coherently to believe that the material order is anything but an ontologically contingent reality, which necessarily depends upon an absolute and transcendent source of existence. To me, the argument for the reality of God from the contingency of all composite and mutable things seems unarguably true, with an almost analytic obviousness; and all philosophical attempts to get around that argument (and I am fairly sure I am familiar with all of them) seem to me to lack anything like its power and lucidity. And the same is true in only slightly lesser degree of the argument from the unity, intentionality, rationality, and conceptual aptitudes of the mind, or the argument from the transcendental structure of rational consciousness. Even so, I must ruefully admit, I would be deceiving myself if I did not acknowledge that my judgments follow in large part from a kind of primal stance toward reality, a way of seeing things that involves certain presuppositions regarding, among other things, the trustworthiness of reason. Ultimately, though, I know that, if the materialist position is correct, there can be no real rational certainty regarding ontological questions, or regarding anything at all; so the very assumption that what seems logically correct to me must in fact be true already presumes part of the conclusion I wish to draw.

There, however, my generosity of spirit on the matter is exhausted. True enough, all of us derive our pictures of the world from certain fixed principles that we take as self-evident but can neither prove nor disprove, either empirically or dialectically. If, however, there is any legitimacy at all to the elementary categories of logic or to the discriminatory powers of the intellect (and I think we have to believe there is), we can certainly say which perspectives on reality possess greater or lesser *relative* logical strength and internal consistency. So it is more than fair to point out that philosophical naturalism is among the most irrational and arbitrary visions of reality imaginable. This much is clear simply from the arguments typically made in its favor, all of which tend to be nothing more than catechetical assertions. Consider, for instance, the very popular but also purely doctrinaire claim that the principle of "the causal closure of the physical" precludes all possibility of supernatural agency in the world: an entirely tautological formula, warranted by neither reason nor science. It is indisputably true, admittedly, that any closed physical system that might happen to exist is by definition both physical and closed, but there is no compelling reason to think that our reality is such a system. And, anyway, a "closed" physical system still could not be the source of its own existence, and so would be truly closed only at the mechanical level, not the ontological; its existence would still have to be explained in "supernatural" terms. By the same token, claims that incorporeal realities could not affect material processes, or that any notion of disembodied consciousness (such as God's) is incoherent, or that the physical order is demonstrably devoid of final causality, and so on, are all just so many empty assertions masquerading as substantive arguments. As for the asseveration that naturalist thought has proved its cogency in the success of the modern sciences, this is simply a confusion of issues. Between the triumphs of the inductive, empirical, and theoretical sciences of the modern age (on the one hand) and the metaphysical premises of naturalist thinking (on the other), any association is entirely a matter of historical accident and nothing more. Empiricism in the sciences is a method; naturalism in philosophy is a metaphysics; and the latter neither follows from nor underlies the former.

The most egregious of naturalism's deficiencies, however, is the impossibility of isolating its supposed foundation—that strange abstraction, self-sufficient nature—as a genuinely independent reality, of which we have some cognizance or in which we have some good cause to believe. We may be tempted to imagine that a materialist approach to reality is the soundest default position we have, because supposedly it can be grounded in empirical experience: of the material order, after all, we assume we have an immediate knowledge, while of any more transcendental reality we can form only conjectures or fantasies; and what is nature except matter in motion? But this is wrong, both in fact and in principle. For one thing, we do not actually have an immediate knowledge of the material order in itself but know only its phenomenal aspects, by which our minds organize our sensory experiences. Even "matter" is only a general concept and must be imposed upon the data of the senses in order for us to interpret them as experiences of any particular *kind* of reality (that is, material rather than, say, mental). More to the point, any logical connection we might imagine to exist between empirical experience of the material order and the ideology of scientific naturalism is entirely illusory. Between our sensory impressions and the abstract concept of a causally closed and autonomous order called "nature" there is no necessary correlation whatsoever. Such a concept may determine how we think about our sensory impressions, but those impressions cannot in turn provide any evidence in favor of that concept. Neither can anything else. We have no immediate experience of pure nature as such, nor any coherent notion of what such a thing might be. The object has never *appeared*. No such *phenomenon* has ever been observed or experienced or cogently imagined. Once again: We cannot encounter the world without encountering at the same time the being of the world, which is a mystery that can never be dispelled by any physical explanation of reality, inasmuch as it is a mystery logically prior to and in excess of the physical order. We cannot encounter the world, furthermore, except in the luminous medium of intentional and unified consciousness, which defies every reduction to purely physiological causes, but which also clearly corresponds to an essential intelligibility in being itself. We cannot encounter the world, finally, except through our conscious and intentional orientation toward the absolute, in pursuit of a final bliss that beckons to us from within those transcendental desires that constitute the very structure of rational thought, and that open all of reality to us precisely by bearing us on toward ends that lie beyond the totality of physical things. The whole of nature is something prepared for us, composed for us, given to us, delivered into our care by a "supernatural" dispensation. All this being so, one might plausibly say that God—the infinite wellspring of being, consciousness, and bliss that is the source, order, and end of all reality—is evident everywhere, inescapably present to us, while autonomous "nature" is something that has never, even for a moment, come into view. Pure nature is an unnatural concept.

It is also, one should recall, a concept whose shape has altered over time, in accord with intellectual fashions. Over roughly the last four centuries, Western culture has become accustomed to viewing nature as a collection of organic and inorganic machines and mechanical processes: mindless matter fortuitously or cunningly arranged into elaborate devices, immense or minuscule, elegant or atrocious. This has always been an unfortunate choice of metaphors. Mechanistic imagery may have served some sort of paradigmatic purpose in the epoch of Newtonian physics, or may have aided early modern "natural philosophers" in formulating a model of empirical research free of teleological suppositions; but physics has moved on since then, and organisms are not machines. Living systems grow, unfold, change, regenerate, and *act* in ways that machines do not and can only occasionally be made to mimic; and organisms that possess any degree of conscious awareness are endowed with powers that transcend any merely mechanical function. Really, the mechanical philosophy never had any but a practical and dispensable part to play in the formation of modern scientific method. Modern science is concerned with isolating facts about the physical order and organizing them by way of certain theories, and then with testing theories against observable facts, and so must be by its nature narrow, rigorously exact, tentatively inferential, and endlessly corrigible. All that mechanistic models of nature ever contributed to this tradition was an imaginative picture of the kind of boundaries that ought to be drawn around the proper areas of scientific inquiry. The inductive ideal was an interrogation of nature limited to a specific set of physical interactions and a specific kind of simple causality, isolated for study by the exclusion of all "metaphysical" or "religious" questions regarding purpose, intention, meaning, value, subjectivity, existence, and so on—the exclusion, that is to say, of consciousness and all its products.

When, however, the mechanistic metaphor began to acquire a metaphysical status of its own, it had to begin striving to eliminate its rivals. As a mere adjunct to a method, the mechanical philosophy really should have been nothing more than a prescription of intellectual abstinence, a prohibition upon asking the wrong sorts of questions; transformed into a metaphysics, however, it became a denial of the meaningfulness of any queries beyond the scope of the empirical sciences. Mysteries that might require another style of investigation altogether—phenomenology, spiritual contemplation, artistic creation, formal and modal logic, simple subjective experience, or what have you—were thus to be treated as false problems, or confusions, or inscrutable trivialities. This created something of a difficulty. Since the mechanical philosophy was an approach to nature that excluded all terms peculiar to consciousness, it had no way of fitting the experience of consciousness back into its inventories of the physical order. Hence, the metaphysical ambitions of scientific naturalism inevitably required that everything that in the past had been regarded as belonging inalienably to the mental or spiritual realm would have to come to be seen as, if not simply illusory, at least entirely reducible to the sorts of mindless processes the sciences are competent to discern. In this way, the limits of scientific inquiry—as a result, I suppose, of the irrepressible will to power that corrupts most human enterprises—had come to be equated with the limits of reality.

But the history (and pathology) of the "scientistic" creed has been recounted many times before and needs no elaboration here. It is enough simply to note how painfully absurd the consequences of such thinking have often proved. At a moment in intellectual history when there are a good number of theorists not only willing, but eager, to deny the reality of unified, intentional consciousness—an absolute certainty upon which all other certainties depend—it is depressingly clear that behind the putative rationalism of scientific naturalism there lurks an ideological passion as immune to the dictates of reason as the wildest transports of devotional ecstasy could ever be.

II

Sometimes, when reflecting on the current state of popular debates over belief in God, I think of Aubrey Moore (1848–1890), the Anglican theologian, Oxford tutor, and occasional botanist who eagerly championed Darwinism in his theological writings, in great part because he believed it might contribute to a general recovery of a properly Christian understanding of God and creation. As a scholar of ancient and mediaeval Christian thought, Moore cordially detested the modern, essentially deistic picture of reality—derived from the most unfortunate philosophical and religious developments of the previous three centuries—which portrayed God as merely some supreme being presiding over a cosmos that he had constructed from inert elements outside himself. In Darwin's thought, however, he believed he had found a far nobler conception of the creative potentialities inherent in nature, one worthy of a God who is both the transcendent actuality and the indwelling Logos of all things, in whom all things live and move and have their being. It was a vision of life's mystery that he hoped might help to lead the way beyond the mechanical metaphors and silly anthropomorphisms inherited from a metaphysically degenerate age.

History, however, is destiny. Moore's reasoning was sound enough, but what actually happened was that, for the most part, Darwinism was simply assumed into the mechanical narrative. Rather than inaugurating some penitential return of Christian culture to a metaphysically more sophisticated concept of creation, it was chiefly interpreted (by believers and unbelievers alike) as simply a new explanation of how the machinery of living organisms had been assembled, with natural selection cast in the role previously occupied by an "Intelligent Designer." This was unavoidable. A scientific theory may radically alter our understanding of certain physical processes or laws, but only rarely will it have the power to affect our deepest imaginative and intellectual habits. This is why, as I observed far above, much of what passes for debate between theist and atheist factions today is really only a disagreement between differing perspectives within a single post-Christian and effectively atheist understanding of the universe. Nature for most of us now is merely an immense machine, either produced by a demiurge (a cosmic magician) or somehow just existing of itself, as an independent contingency (a magical cosmos). In place of the classical philosophical problems that traditionally opened out upon the question of God—the mystery of being, higher forms of causality, the intelligibility of the world, the nature of consciousness, and so on—we now concern ourselves almost exclusively with the problems of the physical origin or structural complexity of nature, and are largely unaware of the difference.

The conceptual poverty of the disputes frequently defies exaggeration. On one side, it has become perfectly respectable for a philosophically illiterate physicist to proclaim that "science shows that God does not exist," an assertion rather on the order of Yuri Gagarin remarking (as, happily, he never really did) that he had not seen God while in orbit. On the other side, it has become respectable to argue that one can find evidence of an Intelligent Designer of the world by isolating discrete instances of apparent causal discontinuity (or ineptitude) in the fabric of nature, which require the postulate of an external guiding hand to explain away the gap in natural causality. In either case, "God" has become the name of some special physical force or causal principle located somewhere out there among all the other forces and principles found in the universe: not the Logos filling and forming all things, not the infinity of being and consciousness in which all things necessarily subsist, but a thing among other things, an item among all the other items encompassed within nature. The only question at issue, then, becomes whether this alleged causal force or principle really is a component of physical reality, and the only way of adjudicating the matter is to look for evidence of "divine" intervention in nature's technological structure. That, however, is not a question relevant to the reality of the transcendent God, and for this reason it has never been treated as such in the philosophical traditions of classical theism. It is rather as if a dispute over the question of Tolstoy's existence were to be prosecuted by various factions trying to find him among the characters in *Anna Karenina,* and arguing about which chapters might contain evidence of his agency (all the while contemptuously ignoring anyone making the *preposterous* or *meaningless* assertion that Tolstoy does not exist at all as a discrete object or agent within the world of the novel, not even at the very beginning of the plot, and yet is wholly present in its every part as the source and rationale of its existence). If there is some demiurge out there, delicately constructing camera eyes or piecing together rotary flagella, he or she is a contingent being, part of the physical order, just another natural phenomenon, but not the source of all being, not the transcendent creator and rational ground of reality, and so not God. By the same token, if there is no such demiurge, that too is a matter of utter indifference for the question of God. How, after all, could the existence or nonexistence of some particular finite being among other beings provide an ultimate answer to the mystery of existence as such?

Perhaps, however, it is a mistake to presume good will here. It may be the case that not every party in these debates is especially willing to acknowledge the qualitative difference between ontological and cosmological questions. A devout physicalist is likely to find it not merely convenient but absolutely necessary to believe that the mystery of existence is really just a question about the physical history of the universe, and specifically about how the universe may have arisen at a particular moment, as a transition from a simpler to a more complex state within a physical system. At least, it often seems pointless to try to convince such persons that none of the great religions or metaphysical traditions—absolutely *none* of them—thinks of the "creation of the universe" simply in terms of a cosmogonic process, and that the question of creation has never simply concerned some event that may have happened "back then," at the beginning of time, or some change between distinct physical states, or any kind of *change* at all (since change occurs only within things that already exist), but has always concerned the eternal relation between logical possibility and logical necessity, the contingent and the absolute, the conditioned and the unconditioned. And I suspect this is not simply because they are incapable of understanding the distinction (though many are) but also because they have no desire to do so. The question of being is not one that physics can shed any light upon at all, and so the physicalist has no choice but persistently—even sedulously— to fail to grasp its point. To allow the full force of the question to break through his or her intellectual defenses would be, all at once, to abandon the physicalist creed.

Here, however, I suppose one has to exercise a degree of sympathetic tact. Materialism is a conviction based not upon evidence or logic but upon what Carl Sagan (speaking of another kind of faith) called a "deep-seated need to believe." Considered purely as a rational philosophy, it has little to recommend it; but as an emo-

tional sedative, what Czeslaw Milosz liked to call the opiate of unbelief, it offers a refuge from so many elaborate perplexities, so
many arduous spiritual exertions, so many trying intellectual and
moral problems, so many exhausting expressions of hope or fear,
charity or remorse. In this sense, it should be classified as one of
those religions of consolation whose purpose is not to engage the
mind or will with the mysteries of being but merely to provide a
palliative for existential grievances and private disappointments.
Popular atheism is not a philosophy but a therapy. Perhaps, then,
it should not be condemned for its philosophical deficiencies, or
even treated as an intellectual posture of any kind, but recognized
as a form of simple devotion, all the more endearing for its mix-
ture of tender awkwardness and charming pomposity. Even the
stridency, bigotry, childishness, and ignorance with which the current atheist vogue typically expresses itself should perhaps be ex-
cused as no more than an effervescence of primitive fervor on the
part of those who, finding themselves poised upon a precipice
overlooking the abyss of ultimate absurdity, have made a madly
valiant leap of faith. That said, any religion of consolation that
evangelically strives to supplant other creeds, as popular atheism
now does, has a certain burden of moral proof to bear: it must
show that the opiates it offers are at least as powerful as those it
would replace. To proclaim triumphally that there is no God, no
eternal gaze that beholds our cruelties and betrayals, no final beatitude for the soul after death, may seem bold and admirable to
a comfortable bourgeois academic who rarely if ever has to descend into the misery of those whose lives are at best a state of
constant anxiety or at worst the indelible memory of the death of
a child. For a man safely sheltered from life's harder edges, a gentle

soporific may suffice to ease whatever fleeting moments of distress or resentment afflict him. For those genuinely acquainted with grief, however—despair, poverty, calamity, disease, oppression, or bereavement—but who have no ivory tower to which to retreat, no material advantages to distract them from their suffering, and no hope for anything better in this world, something far stronger may be needed. If there is no God, then the universe (astonishing accident that it is) is a brute event of boundless magnificence and abysmal anguish, which only illusion and myth may have the power to make tolerable. Only extraordinary callousness or fatuous sanctimony could make one insensible to this. Moreover, if there is no God, truth is not an ultimate good—there is no such thing as an ultimate good—and the more merciful course might well be not to preach unbelief but to tell "noble lies" and fabricate "pious frauds" and conjure up ever more enchanting illusions for the solace of those in torment.

No need to argue over the point, however. Religions of consolation belong principally to the realm of psychology rather than that of theology or contemplative faith. At that level, all personal creeds—whether theist or atheist—stand beyond any judgments of truth or falsehood, morality or immorality, rationality or irrationality. One cannot quarrel with sentiment, or with private cures for private complaints. It probably makes no better sense to contest popular atheism on logical grounds than it does to take a principled stand against the saccharine pieties of greeting cards with "religious" themes. In either case, what is at issue is neither belief nor unbelief (at least not in any intellectually important sense) but only the pardonable platitudes of those trying to cope with their own disaffections and regrets. What makes today's popular atheism so depressing is neither its conceptual boorishness nor its self-righteousness but simply its cultural inevitability. It is the final, predictable, and unsurprisingly vulgar expression of an ideological tradition that has, after many centuries, become so pervasive and habitual that most of us have no idea how to doubt its premises, or how to avert its consequences. This is a fairly sad state of affairs, moreover, because those consequences have at times proved quite terrible.

III

Every age has its special evils. Human beings are (among many other things, of course) cruel, rapacious, jealous, violent, self-interested, and egomaniacal, and they can contrive to make nearly anything—any set of alleged values, any vision of the good, any collection of abstract principles—an occasion for oppression, murder, plunder, or simple malice. In the modern age, however, many of the worst political, juridical, and social evils have arisen from our cultural predisposition to regard organic life as a kind of machinery, and to treat human nature as a kind of technology—biological, genetic, psychological, social, political, economic. This is only to be expected. If one looks at human beings as essentially machines, then one will regard any perceived flaws in their operations as malfunctions in need of correction. There can, at any rate, be no rationally compelling moral objection to undertaking repairs. In fact, the machine may need to be redesigned altogether if it is to function as we think it ought. The desire to heal a body or a soul can lead to horrendous abuses, obviously, especially when exploited by powerful institutions (religious or secular) to enlarge their control of others; but it is also, ideally, a desire that can be confined to sane ethical limits by a certain salutary dread: a tremulous reluctance to offend against the sanctity and integrity of nature, a fear of trespassing upon some inviolable precinct of the soul that belongs to God or the gods. This is not true of the desire to fix a machine. In the realm of technology, there is neither sanctity nor mystery but only proper or improper function.

Hence certain distinctively modern contributions to the history of human cruelty: "scientific" racism, Social Darwinism, the eugenics movement, criminological theories about inherited degeneracy, "curative" lobotomies, mandatory sterilizations, and so on—and, in the fullness of time, the racial ideology of the Third Reich (which regarded human nature as a biological technology to be perfected) and the collectivist ideology of the communist totalitarianisms (which regarded human nature as a social and economic technology to be reconstructed). No condition is more exhilaratingly liberating for all the most viciously despotic aspects of human character than an incapacity for astonishment or reverent incertitude before the mysteries of being; and mechanistic thinking is, to a very great extent, a training in just such an incapacity. This is why it is silly to assert (as I have heard two of the famous New Atheists do of late) that the atheism of many of those responsible for the worst atrocities of the twentieth century was something entirely incidental to their crimes, or that there is no logical connection between the cultural decline of religious belief at the end of the nineteenth century and the political and social horrors of the first half of the twentieth. Yes, certainly, a mere absence of belief in God, in the abstract, does not dictate any particular politics or moral philosophy; but, in the concrete realm of history, even essentially innocent ideas can have malign consequences. Atheism is a not merely an attitude toward an isolated proposition regarding some particular fact or other, like whether fairies exist or whether the velocity of neutrinos is consistent with the speed of light, but is instead a conceptual picture of the whole of reality, with inevitable philosophical implications. As such, it opens up a vast array of ideological, practical, and cultural possibilities that other ways of seeing reality would preclude. It is no aspersion upon all those cheerful, goodhearted, kindly atheists out there, who long for a just and compassionate social order and who would never so much as speak harshly to a puppy, to note the great "religious" theme running through the ghastly chronicles of twentieth-century barbarism. In the absence of any belief in a transcendent purpose in life or in an eternal standard of moral truth, the great task that opens up before many imaginations is that of creating some ultimate meaning out of the imperfect—but perhaps corrigible—materials of human nature. Rather than living for a kingdom not of this world, found only in eternity, and rather than surrendering to the absurdity of our accidental universe, we must now apply ourselves to the "heroic" labor of creating the future, wresting a higher and better human reality out of the refractory materials of a defective species, even if that should require completely reconstructing the machine (genetically, racially, socially, politically, economically, psychologically . . .).

In any event, that should all be too obvious to need pointing out. And I am not making any allegations regarding something uniquely perfidious in naturalist thinking. Like most metaphysical creeds, materialism can be translated into a huge variety of cultural and social expressions, many of them quite benign. One ought not to *blame* materialism for the greatest evils committed under its aegis, any more than one ought to blame, say, Christianity for the Crusaders' sack of Jerusalem or for Torquemada's malevolence (and who would be so wretchedly simplistic as to do that?). The belief that we are ultimately only biological machines, erected upon a chemical basis according to inabrogable physical law, does not necessarily lead to the conclusion that we should seek to engineer a master race or a perfect society. That said, considering the matter in reverse order, looking from conclusions to premises, the fact remains that the grand political projects of destruction and reconstruction that imbrued such vast regions of Europe and Asia in human blood in the last century presupposed a very particular concept of nature and humanity, and a very particular range of imaginable futures. Again, every ideology opens its own special space of possibilities. And it is most definitely an ideology that is at issue here. We ought to remember that the mechanical philosophy arose not just as a new prescription for the sciences, unrelated to any of the more general cultural movements of its time, but also in association with a larger Western project of human mastery over the world: the great endeavor to subject nature to impediments and constraints (to use the language of Bacon) or even to "rack" or "torture" nature in order to force her to yield up her secrets (to use the more savage language of Leibniz). The belief that nature is essentially machinery is a license not only to investigate its organic processes but to disassemble, adjust, and use it as we see best. The early modern period was, after all, the great age of conquest: of territory, of "less advanced" peoples or races, even of nature itself; it was the age of nationalism, political absolutism, colonialism, the new imperialism, and incipient capitalism, a period in which it seemed possible, for the first time ever, that human power might one day extend to the farthest reaches of terrestrial reality.

Not even the sciences could escape the force of this new, intoxicatingly audacious cultural aspiration. As I noted above, the alliance between inductive or empirical method and the new mechanical metaphysics was a matter principally of historical accident, not of logical necessity. Once that alliance had been struck, however, it was inevitable that the quiet voice of empirical prudence would have to give way to stentorian proclamations of the limitless scope of the sciences, and of the emptiness of any questions the sciences cannot answer. The discourse of power is, of its nature, bombastic, pontifical, and domineering. And, in one of its uniquely modern inflections, the discourse of power involves the claim that all truth is quantitative in form, something measurable, calculable, and potentially within the reach of human control (if not practical, at least theoretical). Martin Heidegger (1889–1976)—a morally problematic figure, admittedly, but not to be dismissed—was largely correct in thinking that the modern West excels at evading the mystery of being precisely because its governing myth is one of practical mastery. Ours is, he thought, the age of technology, in which ontological questions have been vigorously expelled from cultural consideration, replaced by questions of mere mechanistic force; for us, nature is now something "enframed" and defined by a particular disposition of the will, the drive toward dominion that reduces the world to a morally neutral "standing reserve" of resources entirely subject to our manipulation, exploitation, and ambition. Anything that does not fit within the frame of that picture is simply invisible to us. When the world is seen this way, even organic life—even where consciousness is present—must come to be regarded as just another kind of technology. This vision of things can accommodate the prospect of large areas of ignorance yet to be vanquished (every empire longs to discover new worlds to conquer), but no realm of ultimate mystery. Late modernity is thus a condition of willful spiritual deafness. Enframed, racked, reduced to machinery, nature cannot speak unless spoken to, and then her answers must be only yes, no, or obedient silence. She cannot address us in her own voice. And we certainly cannot hear whatever voice might attempt to speak to us through her.

For what it is worth, though, the age of the great totalitarianisms seems to be over; the most extreme and traumatic expressions of the late modern will to power may perhaps have exhausted themselves. Now that the most violent storms of recent history have largely abated, the more chronic, pervasive, and ordinary expression of our technological mastery of nature turns out to be simply the interminable spectacle of production and consumption, the dialectic of ubiquitous banality by which the insatiable economic culture of the late modern West is shaped and sustained. And this, I think, is how one must finally understand the popular atheist vogue that has opened so lucrative a niche market in recent years: it is an expression of what a Marxist might call the "ideological superstructure" of consumerism. Rather than something daring, provocative, and revolutionary, it is really the rather insipid residue of the long history of capitalist modernity, and its chief impulse—as well as its chief moral deficiency—is bourgeois respectability. Late modern society is principally concerned with purchasing things, in ever greater abundance and variety, and so has to strive to fabricate an ever greater number of desires to gratify, and to abolish as many limits and prohibitions upon desire as it can. Such a society is already implicitly atheist and so must slowly but relentlessly apply itself to the dissolution of transcendent values. It cannot allow ultimate goods to distract us from proximate goods. Our sacred writ is advertising, our piety is shopping, our highest devotion is private choice. God and the soul too often hinder the purely acquisitive longings upon which the market depends, and confront us with values that stand in stark rivalry to the one truly substantial value at the center of our social universe: the price tag. So it really was only a matter of time before atheism slipped out of the enclosed gardens of academe and down from the vertiginous eyries of high cosmopolitan fashion and began expressing itself in crassly vulgar form. It was equally inevitable that, rather than boldly challenging the orthodoxies of its age, it would prove to be just one more anodyne item on sale in the shops, and would be enthusiastically fêted by a vapid media culture not especially averse to the idea that there are no ultimate values, but only final prices. In a sense, the triviality of the movement is its chief virtue. It is a diverting alternative to thinking deeply. It is a narcotic. In our time, to strike a lapidary phrase, irreligion is the opiate of the bourgeoisie, the sigh of the oppressed ego, the heart of a world filled with tantalizing toys.

IV

In any event, no matter how we describe the historical forces that have given us our late modern picture of the world, we have arrived at a cultural situation strangely removed from that immediate sense of the mysterious surfeit of being over beings—that wonder at the ineradicable difference between the "that it is" and the "what it is" of the world—that opens thought to the true question of the transcendent God. The mind unlearned in reverence, says Bonaventure (1221–1274), is in danger of becoming so captivated by the spectacle of beings as to be altogether forgetful of being in itself; and our mechanistic approach to the world is nothing but ontological obliviousness translated into a living tradition. We have spent centuries laboriously learning how not to see the simplest and most immediate of truths about reality, which every child grasps without possessing the concepts necessary to name it. It may be that we can make proper sense of talk about God (as opposed to talk about the demiurgic god of modern belief and unbelief) only to the degree that we free ourselves from that legacy. And the best way to escape the comfortable familiarity of an inherited picture of reality is to try to return to something more original, more immediate: to retreat from one's habitual interpretations of one's experiences of the world and back to those experiences themselves, as unencumbered as possible by preconceptions and prejudices. Admittedly, there is no such thing as *pure* immediacy of experience, entirely devoid of any act of interpretation; but we can certainly attempt to liberate our thinking from all those accretions of cultural and personal history that, except in a few fugitive moments, prevent us from remembering the world, so to speak—from recalling what is uncanniest and therefore most illuminating in our primordial wakefulness to the mystery of being. God, according to all the great spiritual traditions, cannot be comprehended by the finite mind but can nevertheless be known in an intimate encounter with his presence—one that requires considerable discipline of the mind and will to achieve, but one also implicit in all ordinary experience (if only one is attentive enough to notice).

Many of us today, of course, tend to be suspicious or disdainful of appeals to personal experience. This too is part of the intellectual patrimony of modernity. Nor is it an entirely unfortunate condition: a certain degree of canny skepticism in regard to claims made on the basis of private feelings or ineffable intuitions or episodic insights is a healthy thing. But our ideological tradition takes us far beyond mere sane discretion in such matters, and makes us prone to a rather extreme form of the "verificationist" fallacy, the exquisitely self-contradictory conviction that no belief can be trusted until it has been proved true by scientific methods. Today, there are seemingly rational persons who claim that our belief in the reality of our own intentional consciousness must be validated by methods appropriate to mechanical processes, mindless objects, and "third person" descriptions. The absurdity of this becomes altogether poignant when one considers that our trust in the power of scientific method is itself grounded in our subjective sense of the continuity of conscious experience and in our subjective judgment of the validity of our reasoning. Even the decision to seek objective confirmation of our beliefs is a subjective choice arising from a private apprehension. At some very basic level, our "third person" knowledge always depends upon a "first person" insight. In a larger sense, moreover, most of the things we actually know to be true are susceptible of no empirical proof whatsoever, but can only be borne witness to, in a stubbornly first person voice. We know events and personalities and sentiments better and more abundantly than we know physical principles or laws; our understanding of the world consists in memories, direct encounters, accumulated experiences, the phenomenal qualities of things, shifting moods, interpretations formed and reformed continually throughout the course of a life, our own tastes and aversions, the sense of identity each of us separately possesses, and innumerable other forms of essentially personal knowledge. Certainly private consciousness can be deceived, confused, diminished, or deranged; if we are wise, we submit our judgments to the judgments of others, offer our testimony expecting to be challenged by those who have very different tales to tell, learn to distinguish opinion from insight and impulse from reflection, rely upon the wisdom of others, cultivate an aptitude for doubt, and so on. Nevertheless, there remains in each of us an unshakable ground of resolute subjective certainty, which forms the necessary basis of all rational belief. The world that appears *in* consciousness is the only world of which we have anything like immediate assurance. This being so, it would be positively insane to relinquish our confidence in, say, our sense of our own free will, or in the privacy of our qualitative experiences, or in the unity of consciousness, or even in the transcendental reality of goodness or beauty, and so on, simply because this materialist orthodoxy or that pseudoscientific theory urges us to do so. We are not condemned to absolute subjectivity, but our direct experience of reality has to possess an altogether primary authority for us, which may need to be qualified by further experience but which can never be wholly superseded.

I think one has to take a fairly radical line here, to be honest. I am not talking principally about extraordinary experiences, of the sort that might challenge most persons' expectations of what is possible or impossible; but neither would I want to exclude such experiences from the realm of rational belief. It may be wise to be as caustically skeptical as one can in regard to stories about miraculous events, for instance, but not on the emptily dogmatic grounds that such things simply cannot occur. According to David Hume's famous argument for rejecting all reports of the miraculous, miracles are by definition violations of those laws of nature to which the experience of all persons at all times gives universal attestation, without exception; hence, the weight of evidence is preponderantly against any claim that those laws have been violated in some single instance, and logic dictates that all such claims be regarded as products of ignorance, credulity, pious fraudulence, or wishful thinking. Actually, it is a rather feeble and circular argument in a great many ways, and it amounts to little more than an assertion that what is exceptional is incredible because it is not ordinary, and that ostensible miracles are to be disbelieved on the grounds that they would be miraculous. Still, Hume is correct on the quite obvious and uncontroversial point that reports of miracles are, on the whole, implausible and usually ought not to be accepted uncritically. Even so, if one were to hear such a report from the lips of a witness with whom one has had a long personal acquaintance, and whose probity, intelligence, scrupulousness, perspicacity, and perhaps holiness one believes indubitable, then it would be entirely irrational to reject that report simply because one imagines that one knows that the event in question is intrinsically impossible. One cannot observe a law of nature, much less a law that could govern how nature and supernature are related to one another; one can observe only regularities and irregularities, the common and the uncommon; and among the criteria by which one would judge what to believe or disbelieve one would have to include one's experience of the regular and common traits of the person claiming to have witnessed an irregular and uncommon event. Again, one must rely on one's own experience, because there is no purely objective arbiter of credibility in these (or any) matters. And this is even more true, perhaps to an almost absolute degree, in cases where one is not merely challenged to believe another's report of a seemingly impossible event, but confronted by one's own experience of such an event. If one believes one has, on an occasion or two, in circumstances that make deception or delusion more or less impossible, witnessed an event for which the "laws" of nature cannot account (and I suppose I should draw the veil of authorial discretion here and decline to say whether I have ever found myself in this situation), it would not be reason that would dictate that one refuse to believe one's experiences and choose instead to embrace the dogmas of a naturalist metaphysics. Logic would demand belief in the miraculous, at least provisionally; only blind faith in the impalpable and unprovable abstractions of materialism would demand disbelief instead.

My concern here, however, is not with miracles, though the issue is extremely interesting in the abstract (after all, one confirmed miracle would be sufficient to disprove naturalism altogether, whereas all the regularities of natural events throughout all time, taken together, are not enough to prove it). I might just as well confine my observations to the experience of private prayer, and note that, if one feels a firm conviction that one has entered into real communion with the presence of God when praying, those who dismiss such convictions as emotional delusions have no rational arguments on their side. Knowledge of any reality is to be sought out in terms appropriate to the kind of reality it is. The empirical and theoretical sciences grant us the means of understanding vast regions of the physical order, but only in terms of physical processes; they tell us nothing about the innumerable other dimensions of reality—starting with the most fundamental dimension of all, existence as such—that constitute our knowledge of, judgments about, and orientations toward the world. In most essential spheres of inquiry, the sciences are not only subordinate, but also infinitely inferior, to the arts, to spiritual practices, to metaphysical speculations, to logical exercises, to moral reasoning, and perhaps to informed guesses. This remains true even when empirical research can disclose physical concomitants of the realities at issue. About a decade ago, for example, frissons of excitement coursed through certain journalistic quarters when Michael Persinger and Faye Healey claimed to have proved, with the aid of an outlandish contraption that came to be known as the "God Helmet," that religious experiences could be induced by a weak electromagnetic stimulation of the brain's temperoparietal regions. Surely this meant, many concluded, that all such experiences were nothing more than fantasies arising from neurological agitations. As it happened, a team of researchers at Uppsala University later completely discredited Persinger's and Healey's studies, but it would hardly have mattered had some synaptic throne of God really been discovered in the brain. No one truly doubts that states of consciousness are associated with events in the cerebral cortex. There are certainly neurological activities attendant upon religious or mystical experiences—how could there not be?—but in no way does that imply that such experiences are *nothing but* neurological activities. Certain brain events attend the experience of seeing a butterfly or of hearing a violin as well, but that ought not lead us to conclude that butterflies and violins are only psychological fictions.

That religious experience can be induced in part by one's physical state is scarcely any great secret. It is precisely because mental states rest upon a physiological foundation that all the established contemplative traditions insist that one must undertake physical disciplines, many of them quite ascetic in nature, if one is to detach one's mind from the distractions of daily existence and penetrate the surface of normal perception, to see what may be found in the hidden depths of things.

It is good to keep this in mind if one really wants to discuss the search for God, or simply the issue of whether there is a God to be sought. Any search, if it is to be successful, must be conducted in a manner fitted to the reality one is looking for. I happen to think that reason alone is sufficient to compel assent to some sort of formal theism, at least insofar as reason is to be trusted; but that still leads only to the logical postulate of God, which may carry with it a certain arid certitude, but which is in no sense an actual knowledge of God. However great the force of a rational conviction may be, it is not yet an experience of the truth to which that conviction points. If one is really to seek "proof" one way or the other regarding the reality of God, one must recall that what one is seeking is a particular experience, one wholly unlike an encounter with some mere finite object of cognition or some particular thing that might be found among other things. One is seeking an ever deeper communion with a reality that at once exceeds and underlies all other experiences. If one could sort through all the physical objects and events constituting the universe, one might come across any number of gods (you never know), but one will never find God. And yet one is placed in the presence of God in every moment, and can find him even in the depth of the mind's own act of seeking. As the source, ground, and end of being and consciousness, God can be known *as God* only insofar as the mind rises from beings to being, and withdraws from the objects of consciousness toward the wellsprings of consciousness itself, and learns to see nature not as a closed system of material forces but in light of those ultimate ends that open the mind and being each to the other. All the great faiths recognize numerous vehicles of grace, various proper dispositions of the soul before God, differing degrees of spiritual advancement, and so forth; but all clearly teach that there is no approach to the knowledge of God that does not involve turning the mind and the will toward the perception of God in all things and of all things in God. This is the path of prayer—contemplative prayer, that is, as distinct from simple prayers of supplication and thanksgiving—which is a specific discipline of thought, desire, and action, one that frees the mind from habitual prejudices and appetites, and allows it to dwell in the gratuity and glory of all things. As an old monk on Mount Athos once told me, contemplative prayer is the art of seeing reality as it truly is; and, if one has not yet acquired the ability to see God in all things, one should not imagine that one will be able to see God in himself.

V

Contemplative prayer can be, I should point out, an extremely simple thing. It often consists in little more than cultivating certain habits of thought, certain ways of seeing reality, certain acts of openness to a grace that one cannot presume but that has already been granted, in some very substantial measure, in the mere givenness of existence. It is, before all else, the practice of allowing that existential wonder that usually comes to us only in evanescent instants to become instead a constant inclination of the mind and will, a stable condition of the soul rather than a passing mood. There are also, however, more advanced stages of contemplation, which require one to enter into the depths of the self, into one's own "heart," and here the final state that one seeks is nothing less than a union in love and knowledge with God. Among those who are especially suspicious of religious ecstasies or enthusiasms, the word "mysticism" can often conjure up odd images of emotional frenzies, or "prophetic" hallucinations, or occult divinations, or something of the sort. If one consults the vast literature produced by the world's mystical traditions, however, though one may come across the occasional visionary or clairvoyant (an exceedingly rare and marginal phenomenon), the feature one finds to be most conspicuously common in the contemplative experience of the divine is clarity. For the most part, the spiritual life is one of sobriety, calm, lucidity, and joy. The life of contemplative prayer invariably includes episodes of both profound dereliction and exorbitant ecstasy; as the mind gradually rises out of the constant flow of distraction, preoccupation, self-concern, and conflicting emotion that constitutes ordinary consciousness, one can swing between extremes of sorrow and joy, between (to use the Sufi terms) the crushing forsakenness of *qabd* and the expansive delight of *bast*. But these are neither acute emotional disturbances nor fits of derangement but merely passing states of the soul, moments of moral and temperamental clarity, necessary phases in the refinement of one's experience of reality into a habitual transparency of the mind and will before the "rational light" that fills all things.

Nearly all traditions seem to agree, in fact, that even the raptures one experiences in first breaking free from the limits of normal consciousness are transient, and must be transcended if one is to achieve the immeasurably fuller and more permanent delight of mystical union with God. To a very great extent contemplative prayer involves the discipline of overcoming, at once, both frantic despair and empty euphoria, as well as a long training in the kind of discernment that allows one to distinguish between true spiritual experience and mere paroxysms of sentiment. This is the art of what Sufi tradition calls *muraqaba,* attentive care and meditative "watchfulness"; it requires the sort of scrupulous examination of one's own mental and emotional states described with such precision by Evagrius Ponticus (345–399), Maximus the Confessor, and countless other writers. In Christian tradition, the mystical ascent to God has often been described as a passage (with many advances, retreats, saltations, and reversions) through distinct phases of purgation, illumination, and union: a process by which the contemplative is stripped of selfish attachments and finite emotional supports, then filled with happiness and insight and luminous confidence in God's indwelling presence, and then borne entirely beyond the circumscriptions of the self to dwell in God. Other traditions also speak of the different stages of spiritual progress in analogous, if differently inflected, terms. In every tradition, however, there seems to be clear agreement that one can reach the proper end of the spiritual life only through an ardent persistence in devotion, which outlasts whatever ecstatic elations and shattering despondencies may arise and melt away again. For the Christian contemplative, even the delights of spiritual illumination must be superseded by the beatitude of mystical union, the transfiguring experience of *theosis,* or "divinization," in which one is made a vessel of the divine nature. For the Vedantist, the bliss of spiritual peace, achieved through intense devotion and meditation, is still not the bliss of *turiya,* release in the pure consciousness of the divine. For the Sufi, the ecstasy of *fanaa fillah,* dissolution or annihilation in God, must terminate in *fanaa al-fanaa,* an "annihilation of annihilation" in the supreme happiness of *baqaa billah,* the state of abiding constantly in God.

It is not my intention, however, to produce a treatise on contemplative prayer. The literature of mysticism is abundant and comprehensive and, in many instances, ravishingly beautiful, and I surely have nothing of consequence to add to it; and I am not qualified to write in the guise of a spiritual guide for others. My principal purpose here is to point out again, yet more insistently, that one cannot meaningfully consider, much less investigate, the reality of God except in a manner appropriate to the kind of reality God has traditionally been understood to be. Contemplative discipline, while not by any means the only proper approach to the mystery of God, is peculiarly suited to (for want of a better word) an "empirical" exploration of that mystery. If God is the unity of infinite being and infinite consciousness, and the reason for the reciprocal transparency of finite being and finite consciousness each to the other, and the ground of all existence and all knowledge, then the journey toward him must also ultimately be a journey toward the deepest source of the self. As Symeon the New Theologian was fond of observing, he who is beyond the heavens is found in the depths of the heart; there is nowhere to find him, William Law (1686–1761) was wont to say, but where he resides in you; for Ramakrishna (1836–1886), it was a constant refrain that one seeks for God only in seeking what is hidden in one's heart; for God, as a Sufi of my acquaintance tirelessly reminds his students, is both the most outward of realities (*al-Zahir*) and the most inward (*al-Batin*). The contemplative seeks to be drawn ever more deeply into the circle of divine being, consciousness, and bliss, the circle of God knowing and delighting in the infinity of his own essence. The practice of contemplative prayer, therefore, is among the highest expressions of rationality possible, a science of consciousness and of its relation to the being of all things, requiring the most intense devotion of mind and will to a clear perception of being and consciousness in their unity.

It was more or less for this reason that the great scholar of mysticism Evelyn Underhill, in her somewhat mordant moments, seemed to regard materialist thinking as a form of barbarism, which so coarsens the intellect as to make it incapable of the high rational labor of contemplative prayer. Certainly the literature of every advanced spiritual tradition bears witness to rigorous regimes of scrutiny and reflection and mental discipline, in light of which the facile convictions of the materialist can appear positively childish, even somewhat "primitive." We late moderns can be especially prone to mistake our technological mastery over nature for a sign of some larger mastery over reality, some profounder and wider grasp of the principles of things, which allows us to regard the very different intellectual concerns and traditions of earlier ages or of less "advanced" peoples as quaintly charming or attractively exotic or deplorably primitive or unintelligibly alien, but certainly not as expressions of a wisdom or knowledge superior to our own. But there really is no such thing as general human progress; there is no uniform history of enlightenment, no great comprehensive epic of human emergence from intellectual darkness into the light of reason. There are, rather, only local advances and local retreats, shifts of cultural emphasis and alterations of shared values, gains in one area of human endeavor counterpoised by losses in another. It may well be, in fact, that it is precisely the predominance of our technological approach to reality that renders us pathetically retrograde in other, equally (or more) important realms of inquiry. We excel in so many astonishing ways at the manipulation of the material order—medicines and weapons, mass communication and mass murder, digital creativity and ecological ruination, scientific exploration and the fabrication of ever more elaborate forms of imbecile distraction—and yet in the realms of "spiritual" achievement—the arts, philosophy, contemplative practices—ours is an unprecedentedly impoverished age. (What, after all, is civilization except a fruitful dialectic between material economy and spiritual exorbitance, physical limitation and metaphysical aspiration?) We have progressed so far that we have succeeded in tearing the atom apart; but to reach that point we may also have had to regress in our moral vision of the physical world to a level barely above the insentient. The mechanical picture of reality, which is the metaphysical frame within which we pursue our conquest of nature, is one that forecloses, arbitrarily and peremptorily, a great number of questions that a truly rational culture should leave open. And that, after all, is the basic pathology of fundamentalism. For all we know, the tribal shaman who seeks visions of the Dreamtime or of the realm of the Six Grandfathers is, in certain crucial respects, immeasurably more sophisticated than the credulous modern Westerner who imagines that technology is wisdom, or that a compendium of physical facts is the equivalent of a key to reality in its every dimension.

In any event, even if one's concept of rationality or of what constitutes a science is too constricted to recognize the contemplative path for what it is, the essential point remains: no matter what one's private beliefs may be, any attempt to confirm or disprove the reality of God can be meaningfully undertaken only in a way appropriate to what God is purported to be. If one imagines that God is some discrete object visible to physics or some finite aspect of nature, rather than the transcendent actuality of all things and all knowing, the logically inevitable Absolute upon which the contingent depends, then one simply has misunderstood what the content of the concept of God truly is, and has nothing to contribute to the debate. It is unlikely, however, that such a person really cares to know what the true content of the concept is, or on what rational and experiential bases the concept rests. In my experience, those who make the most theatrical display of demanding "proof" of God are also those least willing to undertake the specific kinds of mental and spiritual discipline that all the great religious traditions say are required to find God. If one is left unsatisfied by the logical arguments for belief in God, and instead insists upon some "experimental" or "empirical" demonstration, then one ought to be willing to attempt the sort of investigations necessary to achieve any sort of real certainty regarding a reality that is nothing less than the infinite coincidence of absolute being, consciousness, and bliss. In short, one must pray: not fitfully, not simply in the manner of a suppliant seeking aid or of a penitent seeking absolution but also according to the disciplines of infused contemplation, with real constancy of will and a patient openness to grace, suffering states of both dereliction and ecstasy with the equanimity of faith, hoping but not presuming, so as to find whether the spiritual journey, when followed in earnest, can disclose its own truthfulness and conduct one into communion with a dimension of reality beyond the ontological indigence of the physical. No one is obliged to make such an effort; but, unless one does, any demands one might make for evidence of the reality of God can safely be dismissed as disingenuous, and any arguments against belief in God that one might have the temerity to make to others can safely be ignored as vacuous.

VI

At the beginning of this book, I suggested that atheism may really be only a failure to see something very obvious; and that is more or less where I wish to end as well. It has also, however, been a persistent theme in these pages that ours is a culture largely formed by an ideological unwillingness to see what is there to be seen. The reason the very concept of God has become at once so impoverished, so thoroughly mythical, and ultimately so incredible for so many modern persons is not because of all the interesting things we have learned over the past few centuries, but because of all the vital things we have forgotten. Above all, somehow, we have as a culture forgotten being: the self-evident mystery of existence that only deep confusion could cause one to mistake for the sort of mystery that admits of a physical or natural or material solution. Perhaps that is attributable not only to how we have been taught to think, but how we have been taught to live. Late modernity is, after all, a remarkably shrill and glaring reality, a dazzling chaos of the beguilingly trivial and terrifyingly atrocious, a world of ubiquitous mass media and constant interruption, a ceaseless storm of artificial sensations and appetites, an interminable spectacle whose only unifying theme is the imperative to acquire and spend. It is scarcely surprising, in such a world, amid so many distractions, and so many distractions from distraction, that we should have little time to reflect upon the mystery that manifests itself not as a thing among other things, but as the silent event of being itself. Human beings have never before lived lives so remote from nature, or been more insensible to the enigma it embodies. For late modern peoples, God has become ever more a myth, but so in a sense has the world; and there probably is no way of living in real communion with one but not the other.

The greatest metaphysical allegory of Western tradition, to which all our philosophies explicitly or implicitly respond, is Plato's allegory of the cave in *The Republic,* which tells us that the world most of us inhabit is really only an illusion, and that the true world lies beyond what our ordinary vision can perceive. We are, so the story goes, like captives bound in the darkness of a cave, forced to face a wall where flickering shadows are cast by a large fire and by a variety of solid objects behind us and hidden from our view. Knowing no other reality, we mistake those shadows—as well as occasional echoes from movements at our backs—for the only reality there is. Even if we were released from our chains and forced to turn our eyes to the realities hitherto concealed from us, our immediate response would be to turn back again from the dazzling light of the flames, and continue to gaze toward the shadows, as the only realities we can easily understand. And if we were to be forcibly dragged out of the darkness into the full light of day beyond the cave's mouth, we would angrily resist, and then would be struck blind by the radiance of the sunlit world. In time, though, our vision would adjust, and we would become able to see the things of the outer world clearly, and would ultimately be able to look upward to the sun itself, which we would now recognize as the source and steward of nature's order, and the ultimate source of all vision. And if we were then to return to the obscurity of the cave, those who still reside in the darkness might well regard us as deluded fools and lunatics for trying to convince them that they have mistaken shifting shadows for the fullness of reality. It is a powerful story, and one that no truly reasonable person can cursorily dismiss as only a pretty fable. I happen to believe it contains a profound truth that one can appreciate even if one cannot easily accept Plato's metaphysical picture of a transcendent reality beyond the immanent: one can grant, that is, that there is at least a kind of hierarchy of understanding, and that the mere possession of information is not yet knowledge, and that knowledge is not yet wisdom, and that therefore whatever one thinks one understands might in fact be only the shadow of some greater truth.

The image of the ascent to that truth, however, should not obscure the reality (which Plato acknowledges in many other places) that knowledge of the transcendent is not something gained simply by a flight from the realm of the senses. It begins in one's ordinary experiences of the world. What provokes us to seek the highest truth—what wakens in us that eros for the divine of which mystics speak—is the immediacy with which the transcendent shows itself within the immanent. Our wonder at the mystery of being, however fleeting and elusive it often proves, is a partial encounter with a divine reality. As I said above, wisdom is the recovery of innocence at the end of experience. It may be the Wordsworthian Romantic in me, but I do believe that all of us, as persons and as cultures, enjoy an initial state of innocent responsiveness to the mystery of being, a spiritual dawn unburdened by presuppositions and interests, when we are aware of a truth we can express (if at all) only by way of a few imaginative gestures—stories or myths or simply guileless cries of fear and delight. We stand amazed before the gratuity of being and the luminosity of consciousness and the transcendental splendor that seems to shine in and through all things, before indurated habits of thought and will can distance us from the radiant simplicity of that experience. We see the mystery, are addressed by it, given a vocation to raise our thoughts beyond the apparent world to the source of its possibility. In time, though, we begin to seek power over reality and so become less willing to submit our minds to its power over us. Curiosity withers, ambition flourishes. We turn from the mystery of being to the availability of things, from the mystery of consciousness to the accessible objects of cognition, from the mystery of bliss to the imperatives of appetite and self-interest. We gain what we can take by relinquishing what we can only receive as a gift, and obtain power by forgetting that dimension of reality we cannot dominate but can approach only when we surrender ourselves to it. And late Western culture may well be the social order that has ventured furthest away from being in its quest to master beings.

The path to true wisdom, then, is a path of return, by which we might find our way back to the knowledge of God in our first apprehension of the inseparable mysteries of being, consciousness, and bliss. Our return to that primordial astonishment, moreover, must be one in which we bring along all we learned in departing from it, including the conceptual language needed to translate wonder into knowledge. We shall then be able clearly to see how the contingency of finite existence directs our thoughts toward an unconditional and absolute reality, and how the intentional unity and rationality of the mind opens up to an ultimate unity of intelligibility and intelligence in all things, and how the ecstatic movement of the mind and will toward transcendental perfections is a natural awareness of an ideal dimension that comprehends and suffuses the whole of existence. More simply, we shall arrive at a way of seeing that sees God in all things, a joy that encounters God in the encounter with all reality; we shall find that all of reality is already embraced in the supernatural, that God is present in everything because everything abides in God, and that God is known in all experience because it is the knowledge of God that makes all other experience possible. That, at least, is the end we should seek. For the most part, though, we pass our lives amid shadows and light, illusions and revelations, uncertain of what to believe or where to turn our gaze. Those who have entirely lost the ability to see the transcendent reality that shows itself in all things, and who refuse to seek it out or even to believe the search a meaningful one, have confined themselves for now within an illusory world, and wander in a labyrinth of dreams. Those others, however, who are still able to see the truth that shines in and through and beyond the world of ordinary experience, and who know that nature is in its every aspect the gift of the supernatural, and who understand that God is that absolute reality in whom, in every moment, they live and move and have their being—they are awake.

Notes

Chapter One. "God" Is Not a Proper Name

1. See Victor Stenger, *God: The Failed Hypothesis: How Science Shows That God Does Not Exist* (New York: Prometheus, 2008); Richard Dawkins, *The God Delusion* (New York: Houghton Mifflin Harcourt, 2006). A lovely contrast to Stenger's book, also written by an accomplished physicist, but one with a considerably greater range of philosophical and theological erudition, is Stephen M. Barr's *Modern Physics and Ancient Faith* (Notre Dame: University of Notre Dame Press, 2003). As for Dawkins's argument, it is that any creator of the cosmos would have to be a very complex being indeed, and since complexity is produced by evolution the existence of such a being is vanishingly unlikely. This argument, needless to say, parodies itself. To begin with, there is the rather confused notion that a *mechanically* complex reality can be *created* only by something even more *mechanically* complex; this does not even follow from the logic of mechanical causation, since a structurally simpler object can be the efficient cause of an object structurally more complex than itself. But, since mechanisms cannot *create* anything in the proper sense, because creation is the donation of existence to what has no existence in itself, mechanical complexity is of no relevance here at all. In fact, all advanced theistic traditions insist that God is metaphysically simple, as will be discussed below: he is not composed of parts or processes, is not finite, and so on, and it is for this very reason that he is capable of being the source of the complex structure of finite things. In any event, Dawkins need not, given his premises, have rested content with the assertion that the god he is talking about is merely an improbable being. Such a god would in fact be quite impossible, inasmuch as he would be both a product of nature and the cre-

ator of nature, which means he would have had to create himself. This is a notoriously difficult feat to pull off.

2. See Origen, *On First Principles* (*De Principiis*) IV.ii.1; Basil of Caesarea, *On the Six Days* (*Homiliae in Hexaemeron*) I.vi; Gregory of Nyssa, *Commentary on the Song of Songs* (*In Canticum Canticorum*), prologue; idem, *On the Six Days* (*In Hexaemeron*); Augustine, *On Genesis Read Literally* (*De Genesi ad litteram*) V.xxiii; idem, *On the Trinity* (*De Trinitate*) III.ix.

3. Swami Prabhavananda, with Frederick Manchester, *The Spiritual Heritage of India* (Garden City, N.Y.: Doubleday, 1963), p. 6. See, for instance, the *Mundaka Upanishad* II.1.7 and the *Bhagavad Gita* XI.21–22.

4. *Adi Granth,* 1039.

5. Thomas's shipwright analogy appears in his *Sententiae super Physicam,* II.xiv.268.

6. For a sympathetic and mild-mannered presentation of the arguments from the statistical improbabilities in the structure of the universe by a distinguished mathematician, one who is fairly careful about the scope of the claims he makes, see John C. Lennox, *God's Undertaker: Has Science Buried God?* (Oxford: Lion Hudson, 2009). Regarding Hawking's (absent) demiurge, see Stephen Hawking and Leonard Mlodinow, *The Grand Design* (New York: Bantam, 2010).

7. See, for example, the *Taittiriya Upanishad* II.1.3.

8. See Gregory of Nyssa, *On the Soul and Resurrection* (*De Anima et Resurrectione*); Augustine, *On the Trinity* VI.x.11–2. See Reza Shah-Kazemi, *Paths to Transcendence: According to Shankara, Ibn Arabi, and Meister Eckhart* (Bloomington, Ind.: World Wisdom, 2006), p. 92.

Chapter Two. Pictures of the World

1. For an elegantly clear treatment of the arbitrary presumption of materialism by many modern philosophers, particularly in regard to the philosophy of mind, see Laurence Bonjour, "Against Materialism," in Robert C. Koons and George Bealer, eds., *The Waning of Materialism* (Oxford: Oxford University Press, 2010), pp. 3–23.

2. Aristotle, *Physics* VIII.10, 276b; cf. idem, *De Caelo* I.9, 279a. The perhaps most winsome and accessible description of the ancient and mediaeval vision of the cosmos is to be found in C. S. Lewis, *The Discarded Image* (Cambridge: Cambridge University Press, 1964).

3. Few of the fervent materialists in the sciences are conscious of or willing to acknowledge the sheer willfulness of their commitment to the materialist vision of reality; but honorable mention should be made of Richard C. Lewontin, the distinguished gene-theorist and evolutionary biologist, who in his review of a book by Carl Sagan in the *New York Review of Books* ("Billions and Billions of Demons," 9 January 1997) allowed himself a moment of delightfully unabashed candor on the matter: "It is not that the methods and institutions of science somehow compel us to accept a material explanation of the phenomenal world but, on the contrary, that we are forced by an a priori adherence to material causes to create an apparatus of investigation and a set of concepts that produce material explanations, no matter how counterintuitive, no matter how mystifying to the uninitiated. Moreover, that materialism is absolute, for we cannot allow a divine foot in the door."

4. Simpson's remark is cited approvingly by Richard Dawkins, in *The Selfish Gene*, 30th anniversary ed. (Oxford: Oxford University Press, 2006), p. 1. See Peter Atkins, "The Limitless Power of Science," in John Cornwell, ed., *Nature's Imagination: The Frontiers of Scientific Vision* (Oxford: Oxford University Press, 1995), p. 125.

Chapter Three. Being (*Sat*)

1. Richard Taylor, *Metaphysics,* 4th ed. (Englewood Cliffs, N.J.: Prentice Hall, 1992), pp. 100–103.

2. *Mundaka Upanishad* I.i.

3. E. L. Mascal, *He Who Is: A Study in Traditional Theism* (London: Longmans, Green, 1943), p. 9; S. Radhakrishnan, *Indian Philosophy,* rev. ed. (Oxford: Oxford University Press, 1929), vol. 1, pp. 174–175.

4. Actually, the third way is often read incorrectly. As stated, it asserts that if nothing existed except contingent things, which come into and pass out of existence, then at one time nothing could have existed, and so—since nothing comes from nothing—nothing could exist now. Some accuse Thomas here of making the logically invalid assumption that, just because all things *individually* might not exist at one time or another, there must have been a point in the past when all things *collectively* did not exist. That, however, is not what he is saying. His argument's conditional premise is very precise: *If* all things were temporal in nature, and *since* (as has been shown in the first two ways) an infinite regress of *ontological* causes is impossible, *then* anything

that exists would be traceable back to a first purely contingent cause, which means a reality that would have had to arise from nothingness without any prior cause at all, which is clearly impossible. This would mean that all things would ultimately be reducible back to an original state of nonexistence. Simply said, such a universe could never have come to be because, again, a finite regress of contingent causes is equivalent to nonexistence.

5. A meticulous explication of this argument from contingency in terms of the necessary conditions of existence can be found in Robert J. Spitzer, *New Proofs for the Existence of God: Contributions of Contemporary Physics and Philosophy* (Grand Rapids: Eerdmans, 2010), pp. 110–143.

6. Radhakrishnan, *Indian Philosophy,* vol. 2, p. 542.

7. A more egregious example of this sort of confusion might be the argument made by Anthony Kenny (an agnostic) against Thomas Aquinas's ontology, and especially against Thomas's claim that God's essence and existence are one and the same. Most of Kenny's case is reducible to an imposition of Fregean logic on Thomas's language, the results of which are quite predictable. If "existence" is taken to mean simply the instantiation of some concept, then to say God's essence and existence are the same would mean that the answer to the question "What is God?" would simply be "There is one." This is not an interesting insight, however, and certainly does not amount to a meaningful critique of Thomas's ontology. The illicit merging of two entirely different philosophical vocabularies will always produce nonsense (especially, I might add, if priority is ceded to the conceptually more impoverished of the two). See Kenny, *Aquinas on Being* (Oxford: Oxford University Press, 2005).

8. Moses Maimonides, *The Guide for the Perplexed* I.52–59; Spitzer, *New Proofs for the Existence of God,* pp. 110–143.

9. A good treatment of simplicity as a metaphysical description of God's essence, as distinct from the question of God's spiritual acts of will and knowledge, from a (let us say) creatively Thomistic perspective, is W. Norris Clarke, "A New Look at the Immutability of God," in idem, *Explorations in Metaphysics: Being, God, Person* (Notre Dame: University of Notre Dame Press, 1994), pp. 183–210.

10. See Augustine, Sermon 52 and *Confessions* III.6.2; Maximus the Confessor, *Ambigua;* Moses Maimonides, *The Guide for the Perplexed* I.58; the *Isha Upanishad* V; cf. the *Mundaka Upanishad* II.2.7.

11. The most popular way of making this case is an argument—advanced by Peter van Inwagen (a Christian, incidentally) and a few other philosophers—concerning an immense "conjunctive" proposition. Suppose, so the argument

goes, one were to place all the contingent truths of the whole universe into a single set; this set could be taken as one very large proposition, conjoining all these contingent truths in one immense descriptive sentence; if there must then be some explanation for the truth of this proposition, as the Principle of Sufficient Reason seems to say, that explanation cannot be a contingent truth, because then it would have to be included in the set and so would explain itself (which is impossible); but then, if it is a necessary truth, all its effects must be necessary too, and so the set of contingent truths disappears and we must assume that everything that is happens to be necessary (which seems clearly untrue). Thus no sufficient reason can be found for this immense conjunctive proposition, and so the principle is false. This argument —which is really little more than a defective version of the argument against the possibility of a set of all sets (there cannot be a contingent set of all contingent things)—is problematic in several ways, most of which are not important here. The simplest problem lies in its failure to distinguish the logic of causality from the logic of propositional truth, as I have already hinted. A set, after all, is not a substance but only a purely notional abstraction, which merely delimits a certain collection of similar things in an altogether neutral way. It is indeed perfectly true that a substance cannot be the cause of some other substance upon which it is dependent; an object dependent upon the universe could not also be the cause of the universe without causing itself, which is of course impossible. But the relation between a set and its contents is not one of causal dependency, and so it simply is not true that the explanation for a set of facts cannot be included among the items of that set. If on the stroke of noon I make a decision about my life that obliges me to make a dozen more decisions before an hour elapses, all in accord with my first decision, there now exists a set of the thirteen contingent decisions I made during lunch, the *sufficient* reason for which is the first decision in that series. Why I made that first decision is another question altogether, admittedly; but all sufficient explanations can always be traced back indefinitely to logically prior reasons, until one arrives at the first cause of all things. This consideration, however, only makes one wonder whether the immense conjunctive proposition at issue really requires any external explanation at all for why it is true. What is it, after all, but an inconceivably large catalogue of truths whose explanations are already contained within the huge causal description that constitutes it ("Janet slapped Henry because Henry got fresh because Henry was raised badly because his father was habitually debauched because . . .")? If though, after all the causal connections in this vast farraginous proposition have been accounted for, the real issue turns out simply to be why it is that this universe as a whole exists, and whether its first cause is a necessary one, and whether then everything that follows from it must be necessary too, then I submit that this has little bearing on the Principle of Sufficient Reason. If by "first cause" one means, say, God in himself, the "first substance," then clearly he can be necessary in the logical sense (uncaused, simple, infinite, and so on) and still produce free but contingent creatures (things dependent on him). If by "first cause" one means instead God's presumed decision to create the universe, one may debate the metaphysics of divine and created freedom and of creation from nothingness all one likes; one can even debate whether there might be such a thing as a necessary cause that, of its nature, necessitates indeterminate results, or a contingent truth that explains itself without remainder; one can argue about half a hundred other related issues as well, without reaching a conclusive answer; but none of that provides adequate warrant for doubting that all truths are *in principle* explicable in some way or other.

Chapter Four. Consciousness (*Chit*)

1. *Taittiriya Upanishad* II.2–5; III.2–6; see also *Paingala Upanishad* II.7.
2. The "argument of reason" against materialism or naturalism has been made by a number of thinkers, and far more comprehensively and precisely than I have done here. Two extremely interesting formulations of and variations upon the argument can be found in Alvin Plantinga, *Warrant and Proper Function* (New York: Oxford University Press, 1993), pp. 216–237, and William Hasker, *The Emergent Self* (Ithaca, N.Y.: Cornell University Press, 1999), pp. 58–80. For an example of an atheist willing to grasp the nettle, however, and fling reason to the winds, see Alex Rosenberg, *The Atheist's Guide to Reality: Enjoying Life Without Illusions* (New York: W. W. Norton, 2011).
3. The compass argument appears in Fred Dretske, "If You Can't Make One, You Don't Know How It Works" in idem, *Perception, Knowledge and Belief: Selected Essays* (Cambridge: Cambridge University Press, 2000), pp. 208–226.
4. The triangle-or-trilateral example appears in J. J. C. Smart and J. J. Haldane, *Atheism and Theism*, 2nd ed. (Oxford: Blackwell, 2003), esp. pp. 106–107. Haldane's discussions of the mind's abstract and intentional powers is at once exceedingly concise and admirably broad in its implications, while also being very clear. A good introduction to and treatment of the topic of inten-

tionality—both more comprehensive and more lucid than I have offered here—can be found in Edward Feser, *Philosophy of Mind* (Oxford: Oneworld, 2005), pp. 171–210.

5. An extremely lucid discussion of the "binding problem" (as it is often called) can be found in Hasker, *Emergent Self,* pp. 122–146.

6. Smart's discussion of consciousness as proprioception, such as it is, is found in Smart and Haldane, *Atheism and Theism,* pp. 157–158.

7. See John R. Searle, *The Rediscovery of the Mind* (Cambridge, Mass.: MIT Press, 1992), pp. 197–226. See also idem, *The Mystery of Consciousness* (New York: New York Review Books, 1997), pp. 95–131, which includes both Searle's review of Daniel Dennett's *Consciousness Explained* and Dennett's own letters to the editor in response. Searle's critiques of the computational model of the mind clearly roused Dennett's ire, but neither Dennett nor anyone else has really succeeded in deflecting their force. Searle's greatest complaint is against the odd dualism that seems to pervade the computational model: the notion that the brain is just a sort of digital computer and the mind just a kind of software that happens to be run on the brain but that, as a functional system, could in principle be run on some other sort of machine as well. This, for him, leaves the problem of consciousness impossible to solve because, on the one hand, computation would still be irreducible to preconscious causes while, on the other, the physical reality of the brain would not be able to tell us anything about consciousness as such (being only one possible computer capable of running the "program" of mind). Searle, being himself metaphysically committed to naturalism, believes consciousness is self-evidently real but that it must be explicable in terms of the specific neurobiology of the brain, as a biological function no more dualistically separable from that neurobiology than respiration or digestion is separable from the cells and organs of the body. He is not saying that consciousness in the abstract is possible only for certain sorts of biological substances, however (an artificial machine might become conscious, only it would not be conscious by virtue of merely computational functions); he is saying only that our consciousness is clearly the product of our biology: it is a raw physiological function. In a sense, this is a much more purely materialist position than Dennett's. While it seems obvious to me (and to most disinterested observers of the debate) that Searle is superior to Dennett as a logician, still the notion that neurobiology will explain consciousness is as implausible as any other attempt to reduce the mental to purely material causes. The argument between Searle and Dennett has been vigorous and, from Dennett's

side, childishly vicious, and I suspect this is because the two disputants are defending opposite poles of the same paradox, each attempting to deny that the other pole is really there. Searle acknowledges that consciousness is real and recognizes that it cannot be explained in computational terms, and so wants to ground it directly in physiology. Dennett recognizes that consciousness is irreconcilable with a properly mechanistic (or non-teleological) view of matter, physiological or otherwise, and so wants to deny its reality by way of a computational model of the brain. Their disagreement, then, is a poignant dramatization of a contradiction inherent in materialism itself.

8. Lonergan's argument is laid out in the nineteenth chapter of his magnum opus *Insight: A Study of Human Understanding,* 5th ed. (Toronto: University of Toronto Press, 1997), pp. 657–708. To understand it perfectly, however, probably involves reading the entire volume (and a very long book it is). A somewhat clearer variation on the argument appears in Spitzer, *New Proofs for the Existence of God,* pp. 144–176.

9. *Shvetashvatara Upanishad* VI.2.

Chapter Five. Bliss (*Ananda*)

1. *Chandogya Upanishad* III.xiv.2–4; Augustine, *Confessions* I.i.1.

2. See Michel Morange, *The Misunderstood Gene* (Cambridge, Mass.: Harvard University Press, 2001), and idem, *Life Explained* (New Haven: Yale University Press, 2009).

3. Richard Dawkins, *The Selfish Gene,* 30th anniversary ed. (Oxford: Oxford University Press, 2006), pp. 19–20; Denis Noble, *The Music of Life* (Oxford: Oxford University Press, 2006), pp. 12–13. It is a curious fact that Noble is more generous in excusing Dawkins's metaphorical excesses than is Dawkins himself. For the thirtieth anniversary edition of his book, Dawkins provides a lengthy footnote (pp. 270–271) justifying his use of the term "lumbering robots," arguing that in today's "golden age of electronics . . . robots are no longer rigidly inflexible morons but are capable of learning, intelligence, and creativity," and he excoriates those "who think that robots are by definition more 'deterministic' than human beings." This is utter pseudoscientific twaddle, and the worst kind of magical thinking. In fact, the robots of old were not morons, for the simple reason that they had no intelligence at all, and so were neither stupid nor brilliant nor anything in between; and today's robots are every bit as entirely devoid of any capacity for "learning, intelli-

gence, or creativity." Nor will any computational robot ever be fabricated that possesses such traits. Certain programmers have, through *their* intelligence and creativity, written cybernetic programs that allow external forces to affect and alter the functioning of the automata that run those programs. But (to repeat myself) computation has no intrinsic physical existence and cannot generate consciousness, and without consciousness intelligence and creativity do not exist. No computer has ever thought or created or used language or learned or even computed. None ever will. And the notion that human beings are no less deterministic than robots is execrable nonsense, not so much because it is an assault upon human dignity as because it is an assault upon elementary logic. A robot functions according to inflexible computational algorithms; any apparent plasticity within its functions is determined by those algorithms. Human beings, by contrast, possess intentional consciousness, which is not an algorithm of any kind. To confuse the two is a feat of consummate intellectual incoherence.

4. Morange, *Misunderstood Gene,* p. 159. Morange goes on to remark that "this fact undermines genetic determinism . . . so much that the word 'determinism' is no longer appropriate to describe gene function."

5. Robert Wright, "Science and Original Sin," *Time,* 28 October 1996. Marilynne Robinson calls attention to this very same article in her extremely perceptive essay "Darwinism," in Robinson, *The Death of Adam: Essays on Modern Thought* (New York: Picador, 1998), pp. 28–75.

6. Isaac of Nineveh, *Ascetical Homilies* LXXXI (translation mine); see Swami Ramdas's poem "Such Is a Saint"; *Bhagavad-Gita* VI. 32; *Sutta Nipata* 148; Shantideva, *Bodhicaryavatara:* see, for example, III.10–21. In the case of Ramanuja, I am thinking specifically of a famous incident in which, as a young monk, he visited the saintly contemplative Gosthi-purna, who (more or less, it seems, as a kind of moral test) taught him the mantra "Om namo Narayanaya," but with the admonition that he must never share it with anyone else: for, though it would bring salvation to those who heard it, it would bring damnation to anyone who divulged it to the uninitiated. Ramanuja promptly assembled a crowd around him in a temple and spoke the mantra aloud, telling Gosthi-purna afterward (to the latter's delight) that, if his damnation could bring salvation to so many, then he desired damnation for himself above all other things. Whether the tale is apocryphal or not, it is a splendid illustration of Ramanuja's teachings on selfless love for others.

7. Bernard of Clairvaux, Sermon LXXXIII.4–6 (translation mine).

8. Shankara, *Brahma Sutras Bhashya* I-I.i.12; II-III.3.11–13.

Bibliographical Postscript

For me, one very considerable advantage of having written a book intended only to describe the logic of the traditional understanding of God, rather than to defend every premise thereof as exhaustively as possible, is that I have been able with a clear conscience to proceed in a largely synoptic fashion, merely touching on many themes that by all rights deserve entire books to themselves. After all, my ambition in these pages has been only to show how certain classical religious and metaphysical understandings of God are grounded in the phenomenology of our experience of reality, in the hope of clarifying what the great theistic traditions truly claim regarding the divine nature. For this very reason I have not been motivated by any great desire for innovation. I might claim some originality for my particular synthesis of certain materials and ideas, or for a few of my critical assertions, or for a few distinctively personal inflections in my argument; but for the most part I have invoked philosophical principles along the way that have already enjoyed centuries—even millennia—of advocacy and comprehensive exposition by very formidable thinkers. So it seems sufficient to me to offer here a few suggestions for further reading, for those genuinely interested in these matters (though, of course, I can provide only a microscopic sampling of a vast literature).

Many of the clearest general treatments of traditional Christian metaphysics available in English, not surprisingly, have been produced by scholars of Thomas Aquinas's thought. For a lucid course of Christian metaphysical studies, for instance, I would recommend W. Norris Clarke, S.J., *The One and the Many: A Contemporary Thomistic Metaphysics* (Notre Dame, 2001), supplemented by the various essays collected in the same author's *Explorations in Metaphysics: Being—God—Person* (Notre Dame, 1994). For an even clearer (and somewhat more traditional) treatment of the same ideas, I would recommend two books by the Anglican theologian E. L. Mascall, both of which have unfortunately been out of print since the 1970s, but used copies of which are easy to find: *He Who Is: A Study in Traditional Theism* (Longman, Green, 1943) and its sequel *Existence and Analogy* (Longman, Green, 1949). There are some readers who, due to some peculiarity of temperament or the tragic privations of a misspent youth, prefer their metaphysics to come wrapped in the language of analytic philosophy; for them, happily, there exists Barry Miller's impressive trilogy: *From Existence to God: A Contemporary Philosophical Argument* (Routledge, 1992), *A Most Unlikely God: A Philosophical Inquiry into the Nature of God* (University of Notre Dame Press, 1996), and *The Fullness of Being: A New Paradigm for Existence* (University of Notre Dame Press, 2002). For still more ambitious readers, with an appetite for contemporary attempts at creative philosophical retrievals and reinterpretations of the Christian metaphysical tradition, a few recent titles occur to me: Oliva Blanchette's *Philosophy of Being: A Reconstructive Essay in Metaphysics* (Catholic University of America Press, 2003); Lorenz Bruno Puntel's *Structure and Being: A Theoretical Framework for a Systematic Philosophy* (Pennsylvania State University Press, 2000) and *Being and God: A Systematic Approach in Confrontation with Martin Heidegger, Emmanuel Levinas, and Jean-Luc Marion* (Northwestern University Press, 2011); and William Desmond's ecstatically original trilogy, *Being and the Between* (State University of New York Press, 1995), *Ethics and the Between* (State University of New York Press, 2001), and *God and the Between* (Blackwell, 2008). I would also recommend various volumes by Stephen R. L. Clark, a philosopher to whose style of thought I am perhaps inordinately partial: *From Athens to Jerusalem: The Love of Wisdom and the Love of God* (Clarendon, 1984), *The Mysteries of Religion: An Introduction to Philosophy Through Religion* (Basil Blackwell, 1986), and *God, Religion, and Reality* (SPCK, 1998). And, for an especially creative and careful attempt to produce newer arguments for the classical approach to God as the source of all being and intelligibility, see Robert J. Spitzer, *New Proofs for the Existence of God: Contributions of Contemporary Physics and Philosophy* (Eerdmans, 2010).

There are fewer exhaustive treatments of the history of traditional Jewish metaphysics in English than there ought to be. The first volume of *The Cambridge History of Jewish Philosophy: From Antiquity Through the Seventeenth Century* (Cambridge University Press, 2008), edited by Steven Nadler and T. M. Rudavsky, is quite good (and quite expensive). *The Jewish Philosophy Reader* (Routledge, 2000), edited by Daniel H. Frank, Oliver Leaman, and Charles H. Manekin, is an excellent anthology, though it accomplishes only what an anthology can. Frank and Leaman are also the editors of *The Cambridge Companion to Medieval Jewish Philosophy* (Cambridge University Press, 2003), a very fine collection of essays, and Manekin is also the editor of *Medieval Jewish Philosophical Writings* (Cambridge University Press, 2008), a very good if all too brief selection of texts.

For an introduction to Islamic metaphysics, remarkably comprehensive for so moderately sized a volume, one should read Seyyed Hossein Nasr's *Islamic Philosophy from Its Origin to the Present: Philosophy in the Land of Prophecy* (State University of New York Press, 2006). One might also consult Majid Fakhry's *A History of Islamic Philosophy*, 3rd ed. (Columbia University Press, 2004). Oliver Leaman's *Islamic Philosophy: An Introduction,* 2nd ed. (Polity, 2009) is another good survey of the topic. And there are many illuminating essays to be found in *The Cambridge Companion to Arabic Philosophy* (Cambridge University Press, 2005), edited by Peter Adamson and Richard C. Taylor.

The long and varied history of Hindu metaphysics and religion has been recounted in many books, either in whole or in part, and really there is such an embarrassment of bibliographical riches here that it is difficult to choose one or two exemplary texts. That said, I still think it is very hard to find a better survey—either for scholarly range or expository felicity—than Sarvepalli Radhakrishnan's classic *Indian Philosophy,* 2nd ed., 2 vols. (Oxford University Press, 1929). Radhakrishnan is also editor, along with Charles A. Moore, of *A Sourcebook in Indian Philosophy* (Princeton University Press, 1957), which is about as judicious a selection of texts as one could desire. And, providing yet further evidence of my predilection for books on Indian religion that were still influential when I was very young, I cannot resist recommending the somewhat "evangelical" treatment of Hindu thought (from a distinctly neo-Vedantic perspective) written by Swami Prabhavananda with the assistance of Frederick Manchester, *The Spiritual Heritage of India* (Doubleday Anchor, 1963). For a largely topical rather than philosophically sectarian survey of Indian metaphysical tradition, there is much to be said for J. N. Mohanty's brief but illuminating *Classical Indian Philosophy: An Introductory Text* (Rowman and Littlefield, 2000). It is of course all but impossible to understand the development of Hindu metaphysics and religion, at least in the main, without some familiarity with the Upanishads; among currently available English translations of the major texts, I think I would recommend Patrick Olivelle's *Upaniṣads* (Oxford University Press, 2008), if only for its general accuracy and clear diction. For those with a special interest in the mediaeval Vedantic systems, it is worth reading, on the one hand, *The Vedānta Sutras of Bādarāyana* with Shankara's commentary, of which the complete English translation by George Thibaut appeared in two of the volumes of the old Sacred Books of the East series (1890, 1896) and then was reprinted by Dover Press in 1962, still in two volumes; and, on the other, the Sutras with the commentary of Ramanuja, also translated by Thibaut and published in the Sacred Books of the East (1904). And, chiefly on account of my own deep interest in and affection for the thought of Ramanuja, I would also recommend Julius J. Lipner's *The Face of Truth: A Study of Meaning and Metaphysics in the Vedāntic Theology of Rāmānuja* (State University of New York Press, 1986).

For a religious tradition of such beauty and nobility, Sikhism has received curiously inadequate treatment in English. There are many books on the history of Sikhism and a number of brief introductions to its spiritual practices and teachings, but very few treatments in depth. Among general introductory texts, W. Owen Cole's *Understanding Sikhism* (Dunedin, 2004) is quite trustworthy. For a good concise historical treatment, often delightfully opinionated in tone, see Patwant Singh, *The Sikhs* (Doubleday, 1999).

On the "question of consciousness" and the philosophy of mind (a field that generates a great deal of print but not, alas, a great deal of cogent theory), I would certainly urge interested readers to make their way through a collection of essays edited by Robert C. Koons and George Bealer entitled *The Waning of Materialism* (Oxford University Press, 2010), which contains an impressive variety of arguments against the reduction of consciousness to purely physical processes (though not all of the alternatives proposed strike me as plausible). William Hasker's *The Emergent Self* (Cornell University Press, 1999) is a frequently devastating critique of the materialist account of mind; and I say this even though I do not believe that Hasker's own solution to the mind-body problem—which he calls "emergent dualism"—can possibly be correct. Similarly, I can recommend Edward Feser's *Philosophy of Mind* (One World, 2005) as an excellent introduction to the discipline, requiring no specialized knowledge from its readers, but cannot wholly endorse his ultimate preference for the Aristotelian-Thomistic hylomorphic account of the relation of soul and body (to which I am sympathetic but which I regard as ultimately inadequate). And while I am recommending books with which I am not in perfect agreement, I might mention that the books of the great brain scientist (and confirmed dualist, of a fairly Cartesian variety) Sir John C. Eccles are well worth reading, if only because they tend to be so infuriating to doctrinaire materialists of the sort who believe that neurobiology will one day discover the physiological springs of consciousness; a good volume with which to begin might be *Evolution of the Brain: Creation of the Self* (Routledge, 1989). For a particularly thorough and robust defense of consciousness as a reality formally distinct from mere brain processes, see Edward F. Kelly, Emily Williams Kelly, et al., *Irreducible Mind: Toward a Psychology for the 21st Century* (Rowman and Littlefield, 2007). I also highly recommend the seventh chapter of Stephen R. L. Clark's *From Athens to Jerusalem* (see above), "Could Consciousness Evolve?" In Thomas Nagel's recent *Mind and Cosmos: Why the Materialist Neo-Darwinian Conception of Nature Is Almost Certainly False* (Oxford University Press, 2012) one encounters the fascinating phenomenon of an intellectually honest atheist who recognizes the logical deficiencies of the mechanistic materialist account of (in particular) consciousness, and who finds himself irresistibly drawn toward a picture of nature to which teleology (the final causality that the mechanical philosophy exorcised from the physical realm) has been restored. The book has been reviewed poorly by a number of critics who have, without exception, failed to understand its central arguments (which are very clearly stated, to be honest), and as far as I can tell it has been well received only by theists. And it is hard not to feel that Nagel is able to maintain his own atheism consistently only because the picture of God with which he is familiar is that of a deistic demiurge who constructs a cosmos out of otherwise mindless elements external to himself; thus he sees cosmic teleology as somehow an alternative to the idea of divine creation rather than (as it is) an essential feature of any classical picture of God's relation to the world. For those interested in questions regarding the status of mind in light of quantum physics, and specifically whether the consciousness of an observing mind must stand somehow outside the probability wave of the physical events it observes, I suppose I might recommend Henry P. Stapp, *Mindful Universe: Quantum Mechanics and the Participating Observer,* 2nd ed. (Springer-Verlag, 2011); it is an issue I raise nowhere in this book, but it is quite fascinating.

For a more general treatment of the true relationship between modern science and traditional metaphysics, and of the distinction between their proper spheres of inquiry, I earnestly recommend Stephen M. Barr's *Modern Physics and Ancient Faith* (Notre Dame University Press, 2003); unlike so many physicists (Victor Stenger, Lawrence Krauss, and so on) who have attempted (blunderingly) to write about such matters as the metaphysics of creation ex nihilo and the contingency of the physical universe upon God, Barr actually understands the philosophical ideas with which he engages. Equally admirable is Conor Cunningham's splendid and sprawling *Darwin's Pious Idea: Why the Ultra-Darwinists and Creationists Both Get It Wrong* (Eerdmans, 2010), which contains a great deal of material relevant to topics raised in chapter five of this book. Cunningham's book is also a splendid riposte to Richard Dawkins, simply in providing an example of how a genuine scholar goes about arguing across disciplinary lines; whereas Dawkins has repeatedly flung himself into philosophical disputes whose most elementary principles he has never managed to learn, Cunningham devoted considerable time and effort to the study of modern molecular and evolutionary biology before presuming to enter these debates, and as a result produced a book that does far more than merely embarrass its author (though also, admittedly, a book unlikely to become a bestseller). While we are at it, incidentally, for approaches to evolutionary biology and genetic inheritance somewhat richer and more sophisticated than those provided by the metaphor of genetic selfishness, see Denis Noble, *The Music of Life: Biology Beyond Genes* (Oxford University Press, 2006) as well as two books by Michael Morange: *The Misunderstood Gene* (Harvard University Press, 2001) and *Life Explained* (Yale University Press, 2008). No more recent account of the rise of modern science and of the metaphysical revolution that accompanied it has surpassed—or for that matter equaled—E. A. Burtt's classic *The Metaphysical Foundations of Modern Science,* 2nd ed. (Kegan Paul, 1932), currently available from Dover Books.

For larger surveys of the rise of modernity, from a variety of perpectives, I also recommend Michael J. Buckley's *At the Origins of Modern Atheism* (Yale University Press, 1990), Michael Allen Gillespie's *The Theological Origins of Modernity* (University of Chicago Press, 2009), Stephen Toulmin's *Cosmopolis: The Hidden Agenda of Modernity* (University of Chicago Press, 1990), Louis Dupré's *The Enlightenment and the Intellectual Foundations of Modern Culture* (Yale University Press, 2004), and Charles Taylor's *A Secular Age* (Belknap Harvard, 2007).

On the matter of the relative authority and credibility of personal religious experience, the interested reader should probably consult William P. Alston's *Perceiving God: The Epistemology of Religious Experience* (Cornell University Press, 1993). I would also recommend chapter twelve of Stephen R. L. Clark's *The Mysteries of Religion* (see above).

Ours is something of a golden age for the publication of the primary texts of the world's great contemplative traditions. When Aldous Huxley wrote *The Perennial Philosophy: An Interpretation of the Great Mystics, East and West* (Harper, 1945)—a seminal anthology of the mystical literature of both the East and the West, as well as an extraordinarily interesting analysis of contemplative tradition —the number of texts at his disposal was remarkably small, at least by current standards. It is still something of an indispensable text in the field, despite a few small eccentricities; but were Huxley writing it today he would have a vastly larger reservoir of good translations of the world's mystical literature upon which to draw. For instance—and this is my chief recommendation for further reading—

Paulist Press has been issuing volumes in its Classics of Western Spirituality series for decades now, and so far has produced over a hundred volumes of Christian, Jewish, Muslim, and Native American texts in English critical editions, whose scholarly apparatus are never either inadequate or excessive, all obtainable at exceedingly reasonable prices. No comparable series of Eastern texts exists in English, unfortunately, but those too are more widely and readily available than was the case not long ago. For a sound popular introduction to Indian contemplative tradition one might read Arvind Sharma's concise *A Guide to Hindu Spirituality* (World Wisdom, 2006). Readers interested in Sufi tradition should read Seyyed Hossein Nasr's *The Garden of Truth: The Vision and Promise of Sufism, Islam's Mystical Tradition* (Harper One, 2007). Nasr is also editor of *Islamic Spirituality: Foundations* (Crossroad, 1991) and *Islamic Spirituality: Manifestations* (Crossroad, 1997), which are as comprehensive an introduction to their topic as can be found in English. Some particularly good anthologies of Christian spiritual writings would be Olivier Clément's *The Roots of Christian Mysticism: Texts from the Patristic Era with Commentary* (New City, 1996), Harvey D. Egan's *An Anthology of Christian Mysticism,* 2nd ed. (Liturgical Press, 1991), and James S. Cutsinger's *Not of This World: A Treasury of Christian Mysticism* (World Wisdom, 2003). There are a number of general anthologies of mystical literature out there, among which I am rather partial to F. C. Happold's *Mysticism: A Study and an Anthology* (Penguin, 1963). For anthologies of a more devotional cast, those compiled by the remarkable Eknath Easwaran are all quite good, especially *God Makes the Rivers to Flow: Sacred Literature of the World* (Nilgiri, 1982).

And, for any atheist readers of this book who are earnestly committed to their unbelief, I hope it will not seem presumptuous of me if I make this earnest plea. If you truly wish to reject entirely all belief in God, and to do so with real intellectual integrity and consistency, have enough respect for your own powers of reason to read atheist philosophers of genuine stature and ability. If you have cluttered your shelves or (God forbid) your mind with the arguments of the New Atheists or similarly slapdash polemicists, then you have done yourself a profound disservice. The books these writers produce and the arguments they advance, without exception, fall below even the most minimal standards of intelligent and informed debate. This is true even in the case of the academically certified philosophers in their ranks; you may find it possible to take some pleasure in, say, the dainty poisoned pastries confected by A. C. Grayling or the laboriously wheezing engines of confusion constructed by Daniel Dennett, but it is a pleasure purchased at the price of mental indolence. For recent atheist texts that require a genuine engagement of the thinking mind, I would recommend, before any other, J. L Mackie's *The Miracle of Theism: Arguments for and Against the Existence of God* (Oxford University Press, 1982); and I would also suggest reading his *Ethics: Inventing Right and Wrong* (Viking, 1977) for a wonderfully candid approach to moral questions in the absence of any belief in God. Perhaps the second-best book in this line would be Jordan Howard Sobel's *Logic and Theism: Arguments for and Against Belief in God* (Cambridge University Press, 2003). And, perhaps a rank or two below both of these but still very thoughtful, stands Graham Oppy's *Arguing About Gods* (Cambridge University Press, 2009). I admit that I believe that all of the arguments in these books can be defeated by the better arguments to be found on the side of belief in God, but not without a real effort of thought; and, while all of these books contain certain misconceptions regarding traditional metaphysical claims, none of them is a exercise in casual ignorance in the way that all the recent texts in popular atheism are. If nothing else, these texts invite one to think, rather than merely to think one is thinking, and so allow for genuine debate, of the kind in which it is possible for truth actually to appear as the governing ideal to which all parties are answerable. Since I believe, as I have argued above, that "truth" is one of the names of God, I cannot help but admire anyone willing to enter into such debates honestly for his or her piety.

Finally, however, when all arguments have subsided and one must decide what it is one truly believes regarding God—or, at least, how one understands one's experience of the world in relation to the question of God—there are very few books that can properly prepare one for the contemplative task of making that decision. So, for my last recommendation, principally as an expression of my own sensibility, I think I should like to suggest Thomas Traherne's *Centuries*, which I regard as one of the most compelling and beautiful descriptions of seeing reality as it truly is, in both its immanent and transcendent dimensions. I might on another day have chosen another book, I confess; but I doubt I could choose a better one.

Index

Augustine: and concept of God, 10,
43, 141, 142, 229; on eternal
principle of God's *Logos*, 26; on
repose in God, 248

Bacon, Francis, 56, 64, 310
Bahá'í, 30
Barr, Stephen M., 333n1
Basil of Caesarea, 26
Beauty: attempts at defining of,
278–82; experience of, 282–85;
as mirror of God's beauty,
284–85; as transcendental
ideal, 242, 243–44, 245, 246,
277–85, 286, 287, 288
Being (*sat*): beauty of, 151; and
bliss, 248; and consciousness,
227–36, 239, 243, 249, 288–89;
contingency of, 93, 94, 99–100,
101, 102, 104–6, 107, 109,
111–12, 114, 127, 134, 143,
144, 145, 146–49, 150, 244,
254, 335–36n4; distinction
between essence and existence,
92, 100, 105, 110, 128, 132–34,
136, 314, 336n7; and ethics,
254, 255; God as being itself, 30,
31, 36, 39, 42–45, 58, 62, 83,
107–8, 109, 122–34, 143, 237,
248, 249, 254, 274, 286, 287,
314, 324, 327; God as metaphysically simple, 128, 134–42;
God as source of, 95, 105, 106,
107–13, 114, 139, 228, 235,
286, 289, 298, 302, 321; God's
being as necessary, 109–10, 113,
114–22, 134; goodness of being,

242, 243, 254, 255; and grace,
321–22; and impermanence,
91–92, 93; interdependencies of,
92–93; and metaphysical theory,
95–96, 99–101, 129–31, 134,
149; mystery of, 87–94, 110,
127, 152, 212, 227, 249, 303–4,
305, 308, 311, 314, 328–31; and
naturalism, 95–96, 98–99; and
nonbeing, 34, 92, 95, 97, 98,
101, 109, 110, 124, 127, 145,
147, 148, 303, 336n4; and ontological causes, 55, 89, 90, 91, 92,
97, 115, 143, 335–36n4; particular beings, 108–9, 118, 120–21,
130–31; and physical realities,
63, 96–99, 100, 105, 112, 145,
147; and power, 131–33, 135,
136, 141, 235–36; and question
of God, 94–96, 99, 288, 302,
314; as transcendental ideal,
242–43; as transparent to mind,
153; unity of, 152, 227, 235,
287, 324, 325
Belief/unbelief debates: as argument
between religion and science, 77,
300–301, 302; and concept of
God, 28, 32, 33–35, 314; and
culture, 20; and ethics, 255–57;
lack of public debate, 23; and
logic, 16–17, 327; in modern
period, 61; and naturalism,
17–18, 23, 32; and reason, 19,
34, 45, 290, 294; and transcendent ideals, 250; and understanding, 14–16. *See also* Reality of
God